AND

hin

A **NEW**

Tree of Life

FOR Planetary Ascension

Other Publications by
David K. Miller

A NEW Tree of Life

FOR Planetary Ascension

David K. Miller AND
Mordechai Yashin

LIGHT Technology
PUBLISHING

For more information about special discounts for bulk purchases, please contact Light Technology Publishing Special Sales at 1-800-450-0985 or publishing@LightTechnology.net

ISBN-13: 978-1-62233-012-6
Published and printed in the United States of America by:

PO Box 3540
Flagstaff, AZ 86003
800-450-0985
www.lighttechnology.com

Contents

Foreword

This is the second book David Miller has written about the Kabbalah. His first book, *Kaballah and the Ascension*, introduced basic concepts in the Kabbalah and linked them to the ascended masters and the process of ascension. In this second book, David has teamed up with Torah scholar and Kabbalist expert Mordechai Yashin, who resides in Jerusalem, Israel. This book is based on unique lectures and classes David and Mordechai gave over an eight-month period between 2012 and 2013. These lectures on Jewish and Hebraic lessons were held in an open discussion group and offer a truly unique perspective into the Kabbalistic Tree of Life and how it has been expanded.

This book functions as a manual explaining the Kabbalistic Tree of Life and the Arcturian Planetary Tree of Life, which is an expansion of the concepts contained in the Kabbalistic tree. The idea behind the Arcturian Planetary Tree of Life is to demonstrate through a paradigm shift how planetary energies can be used to rebalance our planet. The basic assumption is that Earth is currently unbalanced due to a variety of factors, including environmental contamination, global warming, and usage and extinctions of forests and ocean life on a mass basis.

The authors believe that to understand this expanded concept, readers first must have a basic grasp of the Kabbalistic Tree of Life. The Kabbalistic Tree of Life comes from Jewish mystical thought and is based on several sources. One important idea contained within it is the expression of the names and energies of the Godhead; there are ten different expressions, characteristics, or emanations of the divine nature. A second important aspect of the Kabbalistic Tree of Life is found as an expression of the Hebrew alphabet. The tree is based on ten different spheres that are called *Sephirot* in Hebrew. The connecting lines between each of these spheres are known as pathways. The pathways are expressions of how to demonstrate and manifest the connecting spheres on Earth.

In the Kabbalistic Tree of Life, each pathway has been assigned a Hebrew letter; there are twenty-two letters in the Hebrew alphabet, and there are twenty-two pathways. In summary, the Kabbalistic Tree of Life is based on ten spheres and twenty-two pathways connecting those spheres. A further explanation uses the sacred geometric configuration of three triangles and three pillars.

The true Planetary Tree of Life is an expression of these basic Kabbalistic concepts with an additional new paradigm based on channelings by David Miller. As a channel, David receives Arcturian energies from fifth-dimensional beings of higher light. Edgar Cayce originally described these specific beings as the Arcturians. They come from a higher dimension and are telepathically communicating healing messages on how to bring this planet back into a new system of order for higher thinking. The Arcturians explained that the Kabbalistic Tree of Life is also galactic and that there are secrets contained in it that we can adapt to create new healing methods for planetary survival.

The Arcturian Planetary Tree of Life has minor additions not contained in the original Kabbalistic Tree of Life. Two spheres have been added that represent the new connection made between the third and fifth dimensions. In part, the Arcturian Planetary Tree of Life demonstrates a new fifth-dimensional awareness. Additionally, it designates specific locations on Earth that are representative of each of its spheres. Thus these spheres are coordinated with twelve individual places on Earth that have been designated by the Arcturians to contain fifth-dimensional etheric crystals. In this presentation, the Arcturian Tree of Life also has specific fifth-dimensional guides and teachers who have been assigned to represent and present teachings from each of these spheres. In the older, more traditional Tree of Life, Jewish patriarchs are usually assigned to the spheres instead.

It must be pointed out that David has been working with the Arcturians to further upgrade the Planetary Tree of Life. This upgrade includes one totally new sphere that relates to the ascension and to the fifth dimension. This new sphere will be described in detail to explain how to use the new energy. Besides great pictorial descriptions of the Hebrew letters, a detailed Kabbalistic map and paradigm of the Tree of Life are also included. Many parts of these lectures are very technical in nature. For example, the meaning and structures of the Hebrew alphabet are explained, as well as the names of God in Hebrew. However, no prior knowledge of the Hebrew language is needed, because the words and Hebrew alphabet are presented in great clarity, and an extensive discussion of the Hebrew letters and how they are linked to each sphere of the Kabbalah is offered. In addition, key Hebrew expressions and important Kabbalistic words are clarified in detail, and charts of the letters are given throughout the book. Readers will not only learn a great deal about the workings of the Tree of Life but will also gain more intimate knowledge of how it relates to the Hebrew alphabet and the special Hebrew words that are used to describe the spheres.

As a reader, you do not need prior knowledge of the Kabbalah; but rather it is assumed you have an interest in learning more about the specific and detailed nature of the Jewish Kabbalah and how the Kabbalistic Tree of Life relates to the Arcturian Tree of Life. This book explains that relationship. An informative appendix is included to help readers understand and grasp the many different concepts in both Hebrew and in English that are referred to in the text.

Because this book is based on lectures, the conversational nature of the presentation is retained so that the flavor of the energies between Mordechai and David is presented in an informal but informative dialogue. Some of the lectures contain short channelings from David, and a series of channeled lectures on the Tree of Life is offered in the beginning of the book to help prepare readers for the more advanced and technical discussion in the later parts of the book.

The authors do not claim that this book will present a comprehensive explanation of the Tree of Life or the Kabbalah. These are deep and expansive subjects, and a comprehensive study of them is beyond the scope of this book. However, the goal of this manual is to offer a unique and technical explanation of some very important concepts of the Kabbalistic Tree of Life as they relate specifically to planetary healing.

Please be aware that the entire Tree of Life, all the spheres, and even all the letters of the alphabet are not completely covered in this volume.

Linda Abell, Editor
San Antonio, Texas

Acknowledgments and Comments

from David Miller

I wish to thank David Arbizu and Magda Ferrer at the Associacion Grupo Unicornio in Spain (www.grupounicornios.com) for their help in transcribing these lessons for the book.

I wish to also thank Linda Abell, my personal editor, for her invaluable assistance.

Finally, I wish to thank my wife. Gudrun R. Miller, for her unending support and assistance.

from Mordechai Yashin

First, I would love to acknowledge my wife, Shira, for her unending patience with me — for transcribing my difficult verbiage in lectures, for the other three books that have not been printed yet, and for being there for all that was needed in the past ten years.

I would like to thank David and Gudrun Miller for the opportunity to put this knowledge of Kabbalah into this book and onto audio, and for their desire to foster, direct, and support the Group of Forty organization into what it has become since its onset more than twenty-five years ago. Their relentless, untiring work and travels are not only paying off in the third dimension with the expansion of the planetary cities of light but are also providing spiritual garments for all members of the organization.

I would like to seriously acknowledge my teacher of gematria, Rav Yitzchak Ginsburgh of Israel, for the half-dozen of his books I've read — especially the book titled *The Alef-Bet*, which I use as a simple outline for the Hebrew letters and their gematria, which I take to a galactic/cosmic level.

I would like to thank Rabbi Aryeh Kaplan, who passed away before I even knew what Kabbalah was. May he rest in peace.

I would like to acknowledge Rabbi Joel Bakst, who has offered a beautiful intellectual "pineal" perspective to meditation in the acknowledgment of the Western Wall and the Foundation Stone.

Next, I would like to acknowledge the sages who offered this hidden knowledge: Adam, Chanoch (Enoch), King Solomon, Rabbi Akiva, Rabbi Shimon bar Yochai, the *Ari Hakadosh* (Rabbi Isaac Luria), Rabbi Chaim Luzzatto, the Gaon of Vilna (known as Rabbi Eliyahu Kramer, who discovered or channeled Kramer's principle of mathematics), the *Baal Shem Tov*, and Rabbi Shneur Zalman of Liadi.

Last, but not least, I would like to thank the environment that fostered my knowledge of Kabbalah, which was provided by Rabbi Phillip Berg and his wife, Karen, from the Kabbalah Centre and all their teachers who lectured for the sake of spreading the Kabbalah.

This is a wonderful experience. David and I plan to take our experience and all the awakening starseeds all the way up the ladders of ascension into the stargate and beyond. Blessings to all.

✳   ✳   ✳

Mordechai learned much of the information included in this section from Rabbi Yitzchak Ginsburgh's book *The Alef-Bet: Jewish Thought Revealed through the Hebrew Letters*. During the lectures, he read from that text and then elaborated on the key concepts with his own explanations. See the bibliography for the specific pages referred to in each class.

Introduction:
a Summary of
the Tree of Life

JULIANO AND THE ARCTURIANS

Shalom, Shalom, Shalom. Greetings. I am **Juliano**. We are the Arcturians. It is no secret that this planet is at a tipping point. It is clear that this planetary crisis is intense. There is a point that has been called "the point of no return." What is it?

The point of no return means that an accumulation of circumstances can tip the balance so that there will be a series of changes you have called "the Earth changes." The Earth changes are events that have been described as catastrophic. These events can include violent volcanic eruptions, firestorms, tornados, hurricanes, and other dramatic events.

Why is Earth at this point? And what can you, as planetary healers, do to help rectify or correct the situation?

The Planetary Tree of Life, as we are working with it from the Arcturian perspective, attempts to give you an overall presentation of how planetary energy works. I'm talking about energy within the planet and within you personally.

Interaction and Balance

Everything can be defined in the universe as interaction. There is nothing in the universe that really stands alone; the only exceptions would be the Great Void and the Creator. When I say "the Creator," I have to explain to you that the Creator energy force is a multidimensional multipresence in a multiuniverse. The essence of the Creator is not affected by what happens in the creation. This is a paradox, because the Creator is also involved in every aspect of creation.

The Void is an intermediary place between the creation and the Creator in which there is nothing. And when I use the word "nothing," I mean that there is nothing — or no thing — in existence in the Void.

The pathway to enlightenment, the pathway to achieving the highest state of consciousness, usually entails the experience of traveling through the Void. There are many descriptions about that. However, in general, the entire universe and all of the planets, solar systems, galaxies, and stars are interacting with each other outside of the Void.

The Tree of Life, as it was presented originally, is a paradigm that was given to explain the nature of the interactions of the universe. I want to emphasize that the Tree of Life is a galactic energy — a galactic gift. Originally it was brought down through the energies of the rabbis and the Jewish mystics. However, the real essence of the Tree of Life and the energies that it describes is a description for the way the universe works and the planet operates. Overall, the main idea of the Planetary Tree of Life is to look at how energies are in balance.

We have modified and applied the Tree of Life for the planet. One reason why we are working with this energy is because there are keys for how to heal the planet in the principles in the Tree of Life. The other reason is the spiritual light quotient (SLQ), which is based on the necessity for raising the spiritual light energy of people and of the planet.

The Tree of Life is a spiritual energy. It is an interactive energy, and studying it helps to raise your SLQ. Teaching and explaining it to other people will help raise their SLQs as well.

When I talk about this planet being in a crisis, I'm referring to the fact that if things continue the way they are going at these lower spiritual energies, the tipping point will be reached, and a series of catastrophic events will occur. There are particularly dangerous and crisis-oriented points, or periods, in this planetary situation. There are several of what I refer to as "trigger points" that are very explosive. For example, weather patterns will become extremely hot in the summer. There are going to be extreme weather patterns, extreme political situations, extreme economic situations, and other Earth changes.

When you look at the balance that is occurring, you understand that a lot of the energies are coming from the concept of imbalance. I want to take two aspects of the Tree of Life in this lecture and discuss them with you in detail so that you can understand how they apply to the whole planet.

Rebooting the Planet

The first situation I want to discuss is called the sphere of judgment. The sphere of judgment, overseen by Archangel Michael (as well as

Sanat Kumara, assigned there by Juliano for planetary healing), has to do with the results of imbalance. It has to do with the concept of discipline, the concept of punishment, and the concept that if you are going too far out of balance, Earth will respond with harshness. A simple example of this is how, if you cleared the forest of trees, there would not be a sustainable way to deal with rainwater, flooding, and landslides.

This has happened in many parts of the planet already, such as in the Philippines and in rainforest areas, and of course in the United States. The planet can respond harshly to an intrusion on its balance. When you are working with the planet, there are certain energies that you have to take into consideration. If not, there can be harsh judgment and harsh discipline against the people and against the planet in general.

The planet is capable of doing a total clearing. We call this clearing, in your computer terminology, a reboot. The planet is capable of a total clearing of energy, as was shown in the days of Noah and the Great Flood. Obviously, you, I, and the ascended masters do not wish to see this reboot happen again — this total clearing.

Raising Earth's Spiritual Light Quotient

Other circumstances that can be discussed in terms of this imbalance are meridians and the energy pathways on Earth. These energy pathways can become blocked. Some people have built dams at rivers to block the flow of the life force energy for the planet. Some may wonder, "What difference does it make whether the energy is flowing through the river or if there is a dam that is blocking it? After all, it is only water." But Earth has energy fields and meridian lines, and Earth also has acupressure and acupuncture points — just as you have.

These points can become blocked. These points are especially sensitive and can effect volcanic eruptions, in particular, because there are great flows that are occurring underneath the earth. For example, if you look on the surface, you might not think that volcanic eruptions are affected by the meridian lines where rivers flow.

Remember, I said that the basic law of the universe is that everything interacts together. Somehow this is a difficult concept for people on this planet to understand. Many people do understand this; many native peoples understand. Incidentally, I also want to bring in the sphere of understanding when I'm discussing judgment.

Some are incarnating, like you, to assist in planetary healing. Some are coming to learn and to understand certain things about the planet.

I am particularly referring to many of the Atlanteans who are reincarnating now on Earth. One reason they are here is to learn and understand how a planet operates and that there are certain events that can knock the planet totally off balance. An example is nuclear energy use or nuclear accidents.

On Atlantis, one issue that occurred was that they were using dynamic energy and forces they did not totally understand. There was a period of energy implementation that was unpredictable, and they did not consider all possibilities. Therefore, they were unable to even prepare for all possible occurrences.

A similar example was shown at the Fukushima Power Plant accident in which the people in Japan did not take the time to predict what would happen if there were to be a major earthquake with a magnitude of more than 9. There were no studies, and there was no preparation done in the unlikely event that a category 9 earthquake would occur. This is a good example of people not considering all the possibilities. Another example is people who think this way about a tsunami: "Well, that is an unlikely possibility. It has a low probability of occurring, so there is no need to plan for it." And, of course, as they say in your language, the rest is history, because the catastrophe did happen.

What do you need to understand, and what is the lesson from the Tree of Life when we talk about the sphere of understanding? Understanding in planetary healing means that you have to realize that this is a balance on Earth. You have to understand that unpredictable, unlikely events are possible, and you have to prepare for the possibilities — especially when you are using energies and forces you don't totally understand. This is a difficult planetary lesson.

If you look at the Tree of Life and at the opposite of judgment, you will find that the opposite of judgment is loving kindness and compassion. That is an important balance. Remember, it doesn't really make sense to look at one sphere in isolation. You have to look at the spheres in pairs. You have to look at the spheres in triads, and eventually, as you gain a greater understanding, you will see that the planet — like the Tree of Life — is a whole interactive field.

When you achieve understanding at that level, you will be truly developing a very high spiritual frequency, a very high SLQ. Then you can begin to grasp that you have all these other forces that are now acting on the planet. The fact that you can even grasp — that you want to learn, that you want to talk about — this Planetary Tree of Life is an

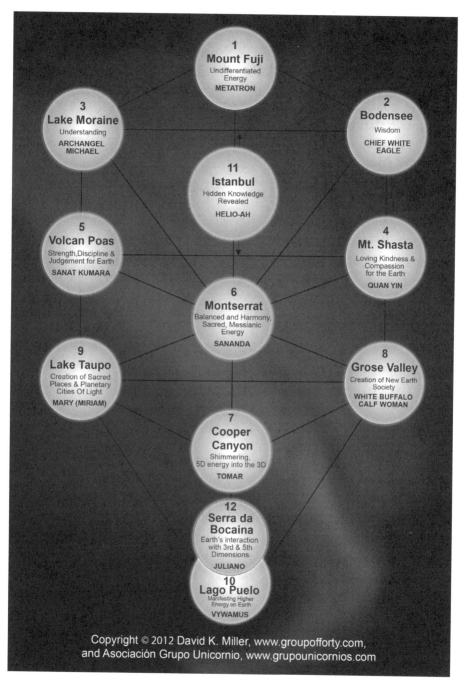

Figure 1. Arcturian Crystal Tree of Life for Planetary Healing

example of the high SLQ you have. It is important that we, together, think of and work with ways to develop plans to raise the SLQ of the whole planet. Some ideas for planetary healing are contained in the Tree of Life because it is saying to you, "If there is imbalance, blockage, and a lack of respect for Earth, then you have to bring the planet back into balance through creating more sacred places." This has been one of the main thrusts of the idea of creating sacred areas, such as the planetary cities of light.

Interpreting Loving Kindness

I return to the idea of loving kindness because it is a beautiful energy. We know that there is great kindness on Earth; there are great healings, a great renewal of energy and light force on Earth. Earth is your mother, as the native people say, and Earth does have a great loving kindness.

You could say that the nuclear power plant accident at Fukushima was not an example of loving kindness. And you would be correct; it was not. It was an example of the energy of justice. It was an example of the energy of harshness in which one of the overall lessons (and I agree that it was a very harsh lesson) is to make Earth aware of the dangers when you are working with energies that are unpredictable in places that also are precarious.

The truth is that, in this case, there was carelessness. It was carelessness in Fukushima because there was a history of major earthquakes in that area of that magnitude of those earthquakes. Perhaps those earthquakes only occur every 500 or 600 years, but that doesn't really excuse the lack of planning.

When we look at the Kabbalistic interpretation of loving kindness on the Tree of Life, we have to explain that there are several different worlds and several different planets like Earth that have been in existence in the galaxy. This is not the first Earth. There are other planets that are similar to Earth that have existed, and in some cases, they still continue to exist in the galaxy.

Searching for Another Earth

Earth astronomers are looking for certain extrasolar, extraplanetary bodies that can support life. When they look in the star systems, they are looking for planets that meet certain circumstances similar to Earth's. For example, the planet can't be too far from a sun or too close.

The planet should have at least one or two moons, because moons are necessary for rotational reasons on the axis of a planet and also are important for balancing the energy between a star and a planet. There should also be other planets in the new solar system. For example, Jupiter plays a vital role in this solar system: It acts as a shield, absorbing asteroid or comet strikes. Asteroids that are coming into this solar system would otherwise be able to reach Earth and cause a planetary annihilation of all life forms. That would be considered a harsh judgment.

But planets such as Jupiter that have such strong magnetic fields can attract asteroids and make those kinds of events unlikely. You saw this with Comet Shoemaker-Levy 9 that crashed into Jupiter several years ago. If Jupiter had not been there, that comet could have easily come into Earth's orbit. And, from the observations, it would have been extremely damaging if that comet crashed into Earth.

Now, you can use the argument that the comet might have been pulled into the orbit of the Sun, as well as the orbit of Earth, and missed Earth. But the point I am making is that it is necessary to have a large planet serving as a shield in case an asteroid is on a path toward Earth.

The Earth astronomers are looking for the circumstances that mimic your solar system, and this should be natural. They will find that there are several other systems that almost totally match your solar system. Even though you could say there is uniqueness in Earth, which there is, there still is a high likelihood that there are other planets that are similar to Earth and that have had advanced life forms.

We study and we travel throughout the galaxy looking and working with these other planets. We have noticed that some of the planets have gone on to the ascension, but some planets have become stuck and have not been able to progress. Additionally, some planets have actually destroyed themselves.

Balance and Loving Kindness

What does this have to do with loving kindness? Well, a planet needs to be in balance, and if there is too much permissiveness, things can get out of control. Following is an example from the Kabbalah perspective about balance, which is more on a personal basis.

There are many terrorists on this planet — people who wish to destroy the existing structure and who want to cause harm to as many people as possible in hopes of achieving certain political agendas. Now, being kind and loving to the terrorists is not going to work because they see loving kindness as a weakness. So the better response often is to deal with them with discipline and harshness. If you are able to capture them, you will have to give them harsh judgments because if you do let them go, they will continue to harm you.

On a planetary basis, loving kindness will not always work. There are numerous nuclear power plants, and there have been at least two major nuclear power plant accidents that most people are aware of: Chernobyl and Fukushima. It would be helpful to deal with the people and the structure that is propagating and misusing this type of energy by not taking proper precautions. Shall you be loving and kind to these people? Would you tell them, "Yes, I understand that you are misusing this energy, and we are going to allow you to continue"? My point is that loving kindness will not stop a destructive force. There have been planets that had an emphasis on loving kindness, and those planets perished as well as their life forms. The planet itself may still be in existence, but the life forms — the higher life forms, life forms that are similar to you — did not continue.

Balancing Judgment

Let's look at the opposite of loving kindness: judgment. There are planets and places in this galaxy that have predominantly been energetically dealt with through judgment.

Imagine, on a personal basis, the mistakes that you have made in this lifetime. Let's just take a simple example, such as driving through a red light. You know that driving through a red light is a very dangerous thing to do — especially in a large city with lots of traffic. Terrible things could happen, such as a deadly accident or crash. Probably everyone who is reading this lecture has gone through a red light. In a world that is predominantly based on judgment and harshness, when you are caught, you are immediately dealt with. Your car is taken away, you are put in jail for five years, and you aren't able to work. That would be a very harsh judgment, but it is a small example of how overly harsh judgments can have negative consequences.

If the world we have observed is overly out of balance and overly emphasizing harsh judgment, then that planet could also be destroyed, as there is no balance. The Creator energy fields and those who are overseeing planets understand that there must be a balance between loving kindness and discipline and harshness.

You are seeing a cosmic drama on Earth. There is a certain energy field that has been set up on Earth at this time to try to work out the energetic relationships that are expressed in the Tree of Life. One of the energetic relationships is the interplay of harshness and judgment versus loving kindness.

There are unique aspects of the energy in Earth. I will be explaining those in a minute, but I want to just finish this section by pointing out that we, in our travels around the galaxy, have seen many other planets dealing with similar cosmic dramas. Some of them have not made a successful transition. The transition that Earth is in right now is a crisis. It is possible that this planet will not make the transition successfully.

The transition would be defined as being able to sustain life, raising the SLQ of the planet, and resolving the crisis. One aspect of the crisis could be de-finished as a conflict of technology versus spiritual awareness and spiritual energy. That crisis has to be resolved, and if it is not, as I said, there will be destruction. That means the harsh energy, the energy of discipline, actually would emerge. A major judgment would occur. In certain periods of a planet, you see the variances where sometimes the harsh energy must be more predominant.

What Is Free Will?

Earth is a freewill zone, and this is one of the unique aspects of the Earth energies. This fact that Earth is a freewill zone has to be taken into consideration when you are looking at this cosmic drama. Earth has unique balances and unique energies. The overseers of this planet have worked with the energies to created the freewill zone here.

The freewill zone means that you are free to think what you want; you have free choice. I know that there are many discussions about what exactly free will is, and many people think everything is predetermined. I'm not prepared to go into a long discussion about that at this point. I just want to say this: The idea of free will I am speaking about is based on the third-dimensional perspective. This means you are on the bottom floor of reality, and on the bottom floor, there is free will. You can say that if we go to the higher perspective, everything is predetermined, and you can make a very strong argument for that. But when you go to that level, you are bringing in other energies that are multidimensional, and then free will as a whole concept doesn't work. The reason why this doesn't work is that free will is a linear idea; it is based on cause and effect and the idea that you have a choice.

So for the purpose of this discussion, we will focus on free will only from the third-dimensional perspective. Earth has, then, the ability to choose. You have that ability. For example, you could come to this workshop or you could not come to the workshop. You have the ability to listen to what I'm saying or not listen to what I'm saying. You could decide to go to sleep during my lectures, or you could sit there and take notes and listen to every word I say. This is the level of free will about which I am speaking. That power or attribute is so desirable; it is so valuable. The reason why it's so valuable is because you are soul beings who are evolving. The way of evolution is such that you can evolve quicker and more effectively when you are living on a freewill planet — in a freewill zone.

The Importance of Earth's Diversity

The idea of choice means that you can integrate and you can evolve at a tremendous rate. This is why so many people want to come to Earth now. In our travels, we have constantly observed that most planets do not have seven billion people on them. This is a rarity, just as I have said. Also, most planets don't have fifty or one hundred different religions. Most planets don't have 150 different languages. I know that there is biodiversity on Earth, and it is extraordinary, but there also is a human diversity, which includes religions, politics, and languages that are totally diverse.

The reason why there is so much diversity here is because of the attractive energy of this planet. Earth, the Blue Jewel, has an attractive energy force that is based on free will. Many people have been attracted to and have wanted to incarnate here. People would want to incarnate here even if they could only be here for a year so that they could have the ability to experience free will.

In our excursions around the galaxy, we have seen planets that have too much harshness. We have seen planets that have too much loving kindness. Then we have seen planets that have integrated and come into a balance. This description of balance is what I want to show when speaking of the Kabbalistic Tree of Life as well as the Planetary Tree of Life. Remember, the Planetary Tree of Life is taking the concepts of the Kabbalistic Tree of Life and using them to understand how the planet works. If you notice that the planet is too lax in compassion, then you can predict with fair accuracy that there will be harshness and judgment.

That is why there are so many predictions now about the end times and about some catastrophic events that are going to happen, because people intuitively know that Earth can respond to pollution and other abuses. They understand, perhaps, that Earth does have a feedback loop system.

Interaction and the Feedback Loop System

The Tree of Life also represents how a feedback loop system functions. In fact, the Tree of Life is the primary example of the feedback loop system because all parts of the sphere are interacting with each other. You can see the energy pathway going in one direction, which is just a symbol of how energy comes down. All of the spheres are interacting. It is truly one of the great truths, insights, and understandings that all energies are interacting with each other. So the energy of Earth is also interacting with all aspects of the planet, including the biodiversity, Inner Earth, and the inner worlds. Most astounding is that Earth is interacting with the solar system and the Sun, with the galaxy and the Central Sun.

These ideas are probably revolutionary. Most people would not comprehend how it is possible, especially when you consider that Earth is so far removed from the center of the galaxy. One estimate of that distance is 27,000–30,000 light-years, and at that distance, how could Earth interact with the center of the galaxy? But the principle is that everything is interacting with everything else. It is a challenge to understand how that is happening and how to apply it for healing.

Spiritual Energy Has No Boundaries

One way to understand this is knowing that spiritual energy is not bound by time or distance. There is a strong spiritual energy from the Central Sun. Its distance is not a factor because you will be able to be and already have been influenced by the spiritual energy coming from the Central Sun, even though it is so far away.

You are still influenced by the spiritual energy of Sananda; even though he lived more than 2,000 years ago, you still are being affected by his spiritual energy. You are still being affected by spiritual energies of many of the ascended masters, and you are still being affected by spiritual energies of Atlantis, which may have existed 12,000–14,000 years ago.

Spiritual energy also transcends time. Remarkably, spiritual energy in the future can affect you. Recently, people have thought about using certain spiritual technologies to access the future and future spiritual energy. There is an exercise to show how you can access future spiritual energies for yourself and for the planet.

I would like to take a pause here to see whether there are any comments or questions about what I have said. If there are, I will try to answer them.

Participant 1: *What are the most propitious actions that we can take to help Earth, and what are the most auspicious times to do that?*

This question has to do with what can we do. The most powerful intervention each of you can do is focus on three things: (1) Work with a planetary city of light to make your city and your area have the highest and most spiritual energy possible, (2) engage in Biorelativity and the exercises of Biorelativity, and (3) work with the energies of the Arcturian temple so that you are able to generate powerful thought forms and thought fields.

The planet responds to thought field energies, and you have the potential to globally interact with other starseeds. It is our belief and our teaching that the necessary number of people to affect the planetary energy field is 1,600. I know that is a small number, but our basic teaching has always been that you would work with the forty Groups of Forty. These groups would be around the planet, and when they are coordinated, their power and energy would be magnified far beyond the small number. There is a magical power in 40 and in forty groups of forty. There is a magical power in 1,600.

Work in particular with the Arcturian temple energy. You can generate thought fields. Thought fields actually are energies. I understand that there is a tremendous polarization going on throughout Earth. When there is a tremendous polarization like this, then that is the time to really work on establishing planetary cities of light and creating sacred spaces. It is the time to work stronger with Biorelativity, and it is beyond just one person. There has to be a system in place.

When we are working on our planet, we work deeply with our Arcturian temple energy. One main focus is that we want to generate the thought field of a strong energy to hold a certain vibration. Polarization and crises also are opportunities. Remember that a crisis is an opportunity for a shift in spiritual vibration. So that would be the main answer on how to deal with polarizations.

Problems with the Financial System

There are aspects of Biorelativity that can be applied to political and economic energies. For example, you can send energy fields to the

European economic crisis because a lot of that crisis is based on anxiety and fear or contraction. Actually, the financial system is based on a false premise. If you look at it logically, how could one small country [Author's Note: referring to Greece and the economic instability there in 2012] unbalance all the financial powers of ten or fifteen other countries? How can one small country — consisting of only ten million people, for example — that already has a shattered economic system unbalance all the rest? The answer is in part because of the psychological energy of panic and fear.

When I say that the economic system is already based on a false premise, I mean that wealth is measured by money. But the true wealth on this planet is in its resources. The true wealth on this planet is its biodiversity. The true wealth on this planet is in its oceans, and much of the life in the oceans is being destroyed at a fantastic rate. Remember, I have said that you are facing — you are experiencing — mass extinctions on this planet. The wealth of this planet lies in its environment, not in its finances.

The whole idea of world finance is based on a psychology that could even be called an illusion. But the existing financial system needs to continue, because there will be much more hardship if the current financial system collapses. I know there is a movement on this planet based on the concept called the National Economic Stabilization and Reform Act (NESARA). In this concept, the people are waiting for the financial system to collapse so that a whole new monetary system can be introduced. Then hopefully all the wealth could be distributed equally through a new system. But NESARA is based on a false premise: If there is a collapse, there will be stability afterward when a new financial system is implemented. If you look through your history (and you don't have to go very far), you will see that a sudden financial collapse often is followed by great instability. Revolution is often followed by more political instability, and eventually, at some point, there is stabilization.

If this financial system collapses, there will be great hardship throughout the world — hardship even worse than what now exists. The current financial system is unfair. It is also related to poor distribution. There are many things we can say about how terrible the financial system has become, but it is similar to what one of your famous leaders [Editor's Note: Winston Churchill] stated: "Democracy is the worst form of government, except all those others that have been tried." I can say that this financial system you are operating under is the worst financial system, except for all the other ones in existence. It would not help this planet to go into economic chaos.

Other questions?

What About Increasing Intensity?

Participant 2: I ask about the Central Sun and the Sun. They are increasing in intensity: Is it good? Is it not good? Should we be enjoying it? Should we be protecting ourselves from this?

The question is, "If the Central Sun and the Sun are increasing in intensity, is this good? Should we enjoy it?" Is that the question?

Participant 2: Yes.

Well, actually, there are several aspects. The first aspect has to do with an alignment. People think of intensity as more energy coming, but overall, you could say that the Sun is not really putting out that much more energy. The variance of the energy of the Sun over 200 years might be immeasurable. It might be half of 1 percent or something, but there are other variances. The more important factor is interaction — the interaction of this Earth with its Sun, of this Sun with the center of the galaxy, and of the alignments.

To understand all of this, you must first have an understanding of all the other factors going on. I would say to you that yes, everything is more intense, but it is more intense because there is more intense interaction and more intense alignment.

Is it good? Should you enjoy it? Well, if you can enjoy it, I would say yes. Is it good? I don't know if I want to say good or bad; it just is. What it is doing is this: The energy is so much more intense because of the alignments, because of the interactions, and it is therefore creating more polarizations.

I don't know if you enjoy polarizations or not. If that is your thing, then you will really be happy here. I say that jokingly, but there is a plus to polarizations. It is true that people who are getting more polarized have opposing views, but it also is true that people who are in the spiritual light and in the spiritual energy are becoming stronger.

Now, somebody may say, "Well, people are losing their spiritual focus, and now they don't believe in the ascension, and they are giving up." You know, that can also happen in this kind of intense energy because people get pulled to the other side. That is why we wanted to work with groups — specifically with groups of forty — because you need to have a coherent cohesiveness in order to hold the spiritual side. You also are affected by the polarization. You can go out and look at the weather, and you can already see that storms are coming. You could quickly despair because of the weather conditions; I'm sure that regardless of whether it is going to continue, the polarized climate is going to make you more worried.

I cannot say you could or should enjoy this intensity. You can use the polarization to your advantage. Use your spiritual tools. Part of our teaching is that you need to use these tools to maintain your spiritual stability, which is going to be difficult in a time of polarization. It is much more fun to live on a planet that is in harmony and balance.

Remember, some ascended guides and teachers say, "I'm glad I'm not on Earth; this is a difficult time to live there." So being on Earth now definitely is a challenge. There are places on Earth where you could live that still are in balance. That's the idea behind the planetary cities of light: They provide places to live in areas that are more in balance. But overall, I can assure you it is much more pleasant to live on a planet that is in harmony and balance. It is much more pleasant to live on a planet that has a high SLQ.

Finally, I want to repeat that it is not that the Sun is emitting that much more intense energy. In fact, this solar cycle you are now in is rather moderate or mild; it hasn't been tremendous. There have been some storms, there have been some coronal mass ejections, and so on, but it hasn't been beyond average.

What is different is that Earth's electromagnetic field is more compromised. The difference is that the ozone layer is being compromised. There are more holes in Earth's aura because of the nuclear radiation experiments and because of time distortions caused by military exercises. That has increased the vulnerability of this planet.

This is a planetary crisis. I don't want to pretend that everything is in balance. I don't think you see everything in balance on this planet, do you? Does this planet seem in balance to you?

Participant 2: No.

At least we agree on that.

The Positive Side of Polarization

This is an extraordinary time on this planet, and from the standpoint of biology, you are living in a time of mass extinction of biodiversity on this planet. Do you agree with that?

Participant 2: Yes.

I have wanted to start with that fact because a lot of people might want to say, "The ascension is a done deal, so we don't need to look at what is happening." This planet also is experiencing a tremendous spiritual opening. In the face of the planetary crisis, in the face of mass extinction, in the face of all of these imbalances, simultaneously, Earth has a beautiful spiritual opening, a beautiful spiritual energy. This spiritual energy and spiritual opening are unprecedented on this planet. That is the positive side of this polarization.

Participant 2: The spiritual part is coming in, which will support everything without denying the fact that these other things are out of balance.

The other things are out of balance, but I want to speak some more about the spiritual energy because that is truly phenomenal. There have never been so many spiritual masters on this planet in the history of this planet. You have never had the total ability to interact and communicate with the whole planet as you do now, even in the time of Atlantis. They didn't have the Internet. There are also a tremendous number of ascended masters who are hearing the calling to come to this planet and work with you. The spiritual energy and powers are so intense now on this planet. We also will refer to the Messianic energies that are being carried over because this planet is right for a Messianic intervention.

Learning from the Mistakes in Atlantis

Participant 3: A lot of what you have said about what we are doing with our tools and that we are here for spirituality indicates changing the attitudes that have been imprinted from Atlantis. We are coming into a feeling that our responsibility, if you will, is to answer the spiritual call. We must focus on bringing a shift in a way that is an integrated flow of work without completely blocking the negativities.

Actually, you are saying it very well, and I think you definitely are on the right track. I just want to point out that not everyone here is learning the lessons that were not learned in Atlantis. There are some people, some scientists and some leaders, who are making the same mistakes. But you are here as a witness to them, and you can see and understand that these mistakes were also made on Atlantis that still are being repeated.

There also are mistakes that have been made on other Earth-like planets. Remember, I have said that there have been other Earth-like planets, and these other Earths also made some mistakes. But, generally, each of you has a unique mission within the soul context. It is not everyone's role to go out and teach about the downfall of Atlantis and the lessons to learn. It is not everyone's mission to speak out and stop nuclear radiation and nuclear power. Everyone has a different piece in this whole process.

Some of you may just want to be here to observe it all because it is quite fascinating, even though it is painful and a lot of suffering is occurring. Some of you have a unique personal role to play, and you have to figure out what that role is. Is it to be a starseed and then a teacher? Is it to be a mediator? Is it to organize a temple? Is it to work as a group leader or to be a teacher and talk about personal transitions?

All this affects your personal psychology too. All this information, all that you are observing, affects your psyche. You could be experiencing different emotions, different moods, including despair and doubt that all will be normal because you are living in an evolutionary transition period. That means that all species have to adapt. The species have to adapt to survive. That adaptation requires a new consciousness.

An Evolutionary Transition

We are at a critical evolutionary crisis in that there are a few things that are needed for survival, and those are based on spiritual consciousness and integrations of spirituality with a new spiritual technology. A new spiritual consciousness has to be implemented, and there needs to be a core group who has that consciousness. Some of you are here just to hold that consciousness.

This evolutionary idea is a key point to understand because, from our perspective, you are right in the middle of an evolutionary transition of the species. Living in that evolutionary crisis is stressful. When we look at the evolutionary crisis, we see the possibility that the species will not survive. It is stressful for all species. Remember, you still possess your animal nature.

I know we are talking about the higher self, but you still have an animal nature. We cannot deny that. The most natural function for an animal is to survive no matter what, and if that survival is threatened, then the animal can act radically. You have seen a lot of radical actions happening on the planet. Even though everything looks peaceful in some places on Earth, your animal nature senses that there is a survival issue for this entire planet.

To put it another way, you are not aware of 90 percent of what's going on in your body right now. You aren't aware of your digestion or what is going on in your intestinal systems or your blood system. All these things are going on right now despite your awareness. That is the way it should be. I'm not saying this is negative, but what I am saying is that your animal nature is continuing, and it is picking up all kinds of things happening on this planet. Your animal nature is very attuned to this planet. Your animal nature is sensing a huge survival issue coming that is already here on this planet. My point is that this is affecting you.

Participant 4: I would like to ask a personal question. I know that the work I'm doing here has a connection to another life, another place, another family, another thing that I'm doing at the same time. I don't understand the connection between what I am doing here and what I'm doing there. I just know that what I'm doing here affects this other life. Is the other life simultaneous?

I just want to say one thing about it and hope it helps you. Even though it is affecting the other life, the most important thing is to just do what you are doing in this life with the greatest focus and the greatest effectiveness. It is good that you are aware of all the other lives and the simultaneous lives, but remember, in terms of survival, multi-awareness of other lifetimes could be a hindrance because it is not a normal thing. There is so much to do here.

There are times and periods when you can go into meditation and be aware of that, and there are times and periods when you can bring the information from that other lifetime into this lifetime to help you with this lifetime. There are times when you can send the information from this lifetime to that other lifetime as well. But the key is that there are times to do that; there are special moments. Some people are working in certain holy times, and then they give themselves the space to allow this kind of freedom to connect with multiple lives. Blessings to you all. I am Juliano.

Channelings on
the Tree of Life

ARCHANGEL MICHAEL, SANADA, CHIEF WHITE EAGLE,
ARCHANGEL METATRON, AND VYWAMUS

Receive Understanding

Shalom, Shalom, Shalom. Greetings. I am **Archangel Michael**. I bless
you and bless your work as planetary healers. Today we are working
with the sphere at Lake Moraine in Canada, which is the third sphere
and represents understanding. The sphere represents the third etheric crystal. Understanding is related to wisdom. Wisdom, however, is
more related to the intuitive grasping and the intuitive process of the
higher knowing.

Understanding has to do with your ability to make sense of this
reality, to put it together in a coherent manner. We are looking now at
making understanding more active on this planet. We are saying that
the world, the world population, and the world leaders must understand what is going on now on the planet. They must understand what
is going on regarding the life forms of the planet. They must understand
that there is a relationship between people's actions and how the planet
is reacting. This energy of understanding is contained and represented
as an energy field now at Lake Moraine in Canada. Lake Moraine has
this beautiful Arcturian etheric crystal that holds the energy of light
for understanding the planet. This is now a great opportunity for the
world to understand what the Blue Jewel is, how a planet operates and
thinks, and how a planet can be influenced by planetary healers.

Visualization: a Golden Ball of Light Filled with Understanding

I, Archangel Michael, connect now with the lightworkers and the
Group of Forty members. Visualize yourself there at this moment in
Lake Moraine, in the Canadian Rocky Mountain area. I ask each of you

to send energy and light as I, Archangel Michael, raise the etheric crystal at Lake Moraine. [Chants.]

Let the holy light from this etheric crystal shine as the crystal is raised out of Lake Moraine, one of the great homes for my energy. Lake Moraine is in beautiful balance in beautiful northern Canada in the northern Rockies. Now we have the great privilege of doing an energetic healing for understanding. The crystal at Lake Moraine is now above the lake, and a huge energy ball of golden light is filled with understanding.

[Chants: *Binah, Binah.*] Understanding.

Let each of you now hearing these words also receive the golden ball of understanding so you can understand why you are here on Earth, so you can understand your soul lessons, so you can understand your soul journey and soul history. Many of you are wondering why this transition is happening on Earth, why there is this polarization, why there is this upheaval. Let the cosmic light of understanding fill each of you with this beautiful golden light of understanding so your vessel can hold the new understanding that is now available with this activation. [Chants.]

Let the great understanding come to this planet at this time with the full moon that will occur. There is a great gathering of the starseeds. Let the wisdom and the understanding be connected. Now a balance for the wisdom of the native people is also rising. Let the wisdom of the natives come to this planet and be accepted. [Chants.]

Let the understanding of the ancient teaching, the ancient teachings of the natives, come now into an awakening for everyone on Earth — especially those leaders who are able to make the changes. Let them understand the energy of understanding that is now flowing out from the etheric crystal at Lake Moraine with the help of your visualization. Let this energy flow.

Now a second sacred great ball of energetic light of understanding is filling all of Lake Moraine. The ball of understanding is going to descend to Lago Puelo in Patagonia, Argentina. Other starseeds in Argentina will receive this great ball of understanding.

In the Tree of Life, Lago Puelo represents the basic foundation, the basic ability to manifest and send the light — the energy from this wisdom and from this understanding — to all the different parts of this Earth. So visualize now a great ball of light coming out from Lake Moraine. The ball is filled with the energy of wisdom. Remember, wisdom is actually an etheric energy — just like we have talked about chi energy, just like we have talked about the life force energy.

Now, you can imagine that understanding is a thought vibration, is an energetic field that brings calmness and the ability to make good choices. The golden ball of light from understanding is filling up now in Lake Moraine at the top of the crystal. On the count of three, we will send this golden ball of understanding to Lago Puelo. One, two, three, now!

The huge ball of golden light is leaving Lake Moraine and is going directly in an arc to Lago Puelo. The crystal at Lago Puelo is now rising above the water, right where the other starseeds are, and the golden ball of light that is filled with understanding descends directly into the crystal at Lago Puelo.

The energy is received, and the crystal has received this powerful connection, connecting understanding with the kingdom of Earth, known in Hebrew as *Malchut*. The third-dimensional reality and wisdom are now connected. The golden light of wisdom is now being distributed throughout this planet to all places where there is polarization, to all places where there is conflict, to all people who are spiritually minded, and to all people who want a new harmony, a new dimensional society of justice — a just society — for you need understanding.

You who are reading this and participating are now able to connect the sphere of understanding with your manifested third-dimensional body on this kingdom of Earth. Feel internally your connection with understanding and manifestation in your life. Hold now in your higher self the ability to integrate understanding into your manifested world.

Let all living beings on this planet be activated with this beautiful light of understanding. Let the galactic understanding come to this planet. Let the galactic understanding of planetary evolution, of planetary development, come to Earth. Let the knowledge, the hidden knowledge, come forward so all on this planet can understand and have the perspective of understanding.

A beautiful connection between Lake Moraine and Lago Puelo is made extremely strong as the lightworkers are holding and anchoring this powerful energy.

Meditation: Release and Receive Understanding

Let us meditate now and see the release of balls of golden light of understanding around the planet and around Lago Puelo. You also can meditate on receiving understanding — the energy of understanding. We will go into silence.

Remember, there is big understanding and small understanding. There is the big mind and the little mind. There is the little understanding mind and the big understanding mind. The big understanding is the cosmic mind — the greater perspective.

I, Archangel Michael, am calling on this greater perspective of understanding to go through the whole planet. Let the greater perspective of understanding come to you for whatever problem, whatever energy, you are trying to resolve. We call this *Binah Hagadol*, the great understanding — the perspective of the galaxy, the perspective of the cosmic light, the perspective of cosmic karma.

Let all beings on this planet who are human come immediately to an understanding in a better doing — especially if they are doing something wrong, especially if they are doing something that creates more disharmony. Let the golden light of understanding fill human consciousness now.

Please repeat this mantra: "Let the golden light of understanding fill all human consciousness now. Let the golden light of understanding fill all consciousness now. Let the golden light of consciousness fill all human understanding now. Let the golden light of consciousness fill you now. Let the golden light of understanding fill your consciousness now." Feel it. Feel the golden light of consciousness in your energy field. What a gift, to have understanding!

In conclusion, I say a special prayer for tranquility and calmness in Tijuana, Mexico, where it was reported that there have been many minor earthquakes. We send you blessings; we send you calmness. Know that the timeline of Earth is releasing energies, and there will be calmness, a return to tranquility there, and the light of our father (Hebrew prayer): *Ehyeh Asher Ehyeh* — I Will Be That I Will Be. I Am That I Am.

I am Archangel Michael, from Lake Moraine connecting to Lago Puelo. Blessings in the light of *Binah*, in the light of understanding. Good day.

Harmony and Wisdom

Shalom, Shalom, Shalom. Greetings. This is **Sananda**. I send you blessings from the center of the Tree of Life, from the beauty of Montserrat, which is the holding place for this etheric crystal known as beauty. Let the harmony and beauty that is the core of the goodness of this dimension emerge directly into your lifetime, into this lifetime.

This is the beauty of the Tree of Life. This is the beauty of *Tiferet*. This is the understanding that you can call on beauty and harmony to fill your life *now*. Isn't this a great gift — to have this power? You have the power to speak; you have the power to pray with great prayer, to pray with great intention.

You can call on the center of this Tree of Life and speak these words: "May the beauty, the wisdom, the understanding, the loving kindness, and the divine judgment, which is for the good — may all of these things emerge now into my life and be merged into a unity." This is what the Tree of Life is showing you: All these spheres can be united, and they are united in *Tiferet*. They are united in Montserrat, Spain. This is the great beauty; this is the great strength — that everything is united.

We also have this beautiful concept of the Holy Spirit. All of you know that the Holy Spirit is also talked about as the Father, Son, and the Holy Ghost. But they are united in the Holy Spirit. The Holy Spirit is the divine light, the divine spirit that comes to this planet, that comes to you from this place of beauty and harmony, where you can call on *Ruach Hakodesh* — the Holy Spirit — to be with you.

I will sing through the channel the words *Ruach Hakodesh*. As you hear the vibrations of these words, speak to yourself and say: "Let the *Ruach Hakodesh* fill my life today."

[Sings: *Ruach Hakodesh.*]

May the Holy Spirit fill you with the harmony and the light of *Tiferet*, the harmony and light that is represented by Montserrat. And may the Holy Spirit also bring you wisdom in this month.

Now, Chief White Eagle will speak to you. Blessings in the Holy Spirit, which is filling each one of you now. This is Sananda. Good day.

[Chants: *Hey ya ho ya hey. Hey ya ho ya hey. Hey ya ho ya hey. Hey ya ho. Hey ya ho.*] Greetings. I'm **Chief White Eagle**. I bless each of you and let you connect with your inner wisdom. This Tree of Life is showing that you contain all of these aspects within you, for God, our Creator, works in you so that you have the divine wisdom. Let the divine wisdom come to you, and let the cosmic understanding of this planet, of this dimension, and of this universe be downloaded now inside of you.

In a sense, this is a return. The Kabbalah is a galactic map, and really, it is not that you are gaining new wisdom but that you are returning to your nature. You are returning to the wisdom.

I, Chief White Eagle, call on Father/Mother Creator of light, of all, for each of you to be filled now with divine wisdom, represented by Bodensee, the second etheric crystal and represented by this chanting: [Chants: *Hey ya ho ya hey*].

Know that the ancient Israelites were also native peoples. Know that they were like the Native Americans: They were in the desert, they were living close to nature, they were looking at the skies, and they were harvesting the beauty in agriculture. Ultimately, we are all native peoples, and all our roots go back to a time when humans were native. This is the unification of the Holy Spirit that Sananda talked about. I am Chief White Eagle. All my words are sacred. *Ho!*

✳   ✳   ✳

The Vibrational Energy of Words and Names

Greetings. I am **Archangel Metatron**. I have many functions and many roles to play in the ascension and in working with the Arcturians at the Arcturian stargate. But I also am offering guidance and teachings on the inner light, on the inner mystical thoughts, and how to raise your vibrational frequency using tones and sounds.

The Kabbalah is a body of knowledge that is passed on from generation to generation, and ultimately, the belief is that Moses first received the Kabbalah information on Mount Sinai. But this knowledge was received even before Moses. The word "Kabbalah" in the Hebrew language means "to receive," and there is a powerful meaning in those words. Part of the idea of receiving is that you have to be receptive, and to be receptive, you must empty yourself in order to have space to receive.

Now, you understand this in your terminology, perhaps, as "emptying the ego." Because if you think that you know everything and then somebody presents you with a higher truth, then there is no room in you to receive that truth. You're already full. It is a paradox that to receive the highest information and knowledge, you have to be empty. So in the Kabbalah, there's a great emphasis on humbleness and a lack of ego. This is necessary for the ability to receive, but the emptiness has to be sincere.

It's not a matter of, "Okay, I'm going to do emptying, but still I will maintain my ego." People are confronted with their egos in many different ways, and it becomes necessary to resolve some of these problems. There are many cases of people who incarnate in order to resolve the problems of ego. Ego is a big issue on this planet now, and part of the problem is made worse because the ego of humankind has led to the domination of — or the desire to dominate — Earth and the desire to be in control.

On the Arcturian Planetary Tree of Life, I've been designated as the holder of the cosmic undifferentiated light, or the first sphere on the top. Perhaps "holder" is not the right word ... maybe as the "explainer" of cosmic light. To understand the cosmic light, I like to use the energy metaphor of electricity because electrical power can be at a high voltage, but you cannot use it unless it is stepped down to a voltage that is appropriate for your home. So if you have 1,000 volts, then that's not any good — even though it's a lot of power — because your home is only able to process 220 or 110 volts.

In many ways, the top of the Planetary Tree of Life and cosmic light represent this power that is indescribable but also needs to be stepped down. There are two ways of looking at this: One way is that we step down the power, and the other way is that you increase your capacity to receive so that you can process a higher light. Part of the teachings of the Kabbalah is to work in both ways. On one hand, we work to bring your vibration up, and on the other hand, we work to bring the light into a form that you can work with and perhaps step down.

Your Link to Adam

There are many stories and plenty of information about Adam — or A'dam, as he is called in Hebrew. It is interesting that A'dam comes from the Hebrew word for "earth" or "ground," *Adamah*. So when you are saying the name Adam, you are also alluding to the earth. It's like saying the name originates from the word "ground," or "he comes from the earth." Now, it doesn't sound the same as Adam to you, but A'dam had the power and the vibrational frequencies to see the highest light and to see the undifferentiated light. It is said that his abilities were so strong that he could see the light across the universe — the unending light. It is also said that all of the genetic codes and seeds for all humanity were contained in Adam's original genome structure. So when you say that we are related, you really are speaking the truth.

It was known among the spirit guides and teachers that there had been interference in the genetic codes over time. The original genetic codes from Adam are still basically intact and in place, but in some people, the purity has been lost. Their codes have been corrupted by downloading through other alien or extraterrestrial sources — sources that were not of the highest intention. But the predominant genetic structure within you is still directly linked to Adam. The genetic codes that you hold also contain the programs for your ascension.

Your Body Knows How to Ascend

You have the ability, the structure, and the inner knowledge to ascend. It is similar when you speak about dying. We know that many of you on the conscious level may not know how to die, yet you go to sleep every night, and in a way, that's a type of "little" dying, because you end the waking reality for a period of time. When you do reach a level of sickness and you become unconscious, your body knows what to do.

Your body has a certain protocol or procedure that it goes through for dying. You don't know what this procedure is unless you've studied it or observed it, yet your body knows how to die. Sometimes modern medical technology interferes with that process.

I'm suggesting to you that dying has similarities to ascension. Your body knows how to ascend. The only difference is that there are certain inner codes that have to be opened, and these inner codes can be opened by a vibrational tone or sound. It is like an awakening; in order to ascend, you have to be vibrating at a certain level. If you cannot vibrate at that level, then you are not able to ascend. In the Kabbalah, we are teaching that the vibrational frequencies and the activational tones that are required are contained in the sacred Hebrew chants. There is a particular chant or sound that can be used for the ascension.

In the *Kabbalah*, it's not just the saying of the chant but also the intention behind it. It's also the emptying and the preparation. Some people could be saying a sacred chant over and over again and not experience an effect. But you, as lightworkers, can hear this chant and have the intention and open up for the ascension, and it will have an effect on you. So we are going to have the channel sing and tone this special chant, which is an activation for unlocking the codes of ascension.

Your job is only to listen and allow the tones and frequencies of the chant to set up and open vibrational frequencies within your inner soul, in your inner mind. Let the words open and unlock the codes of ascension. In many ways, the codes of ascension are already opened for you, but this will bring you into a higher-vibrational activation even more so. This is the activation sound or chant in preparation for unlocking the codes of the ascension:

Kadosh, Kadosh, Kadosh, Adonai Tzevaoth.
Kadosh, Kadosh, Kadosh, Adonai Tzevaoth.
Kadosh, Kadosh, Kadosh, Adonai Tzevaoth.

Try to sing it together with me:
Kadosh, Kadosh, Kadosh, Adonai Tzevaoth.
Kadosh, Kadosh, Kadosh, Adonai Tzevaoth.
Kadosh, Kadosh, Kadosh, Adonai Tzevaoth.

Let the codes of ascension be unlocked inside of you. Let the vibrational frequencies that are necessary for you to experience your ascension now open.
Kadosh, Kadosh, Kadosh, Adonai Tzevaoth.
Holy, Holy, Holy is the Lord of Hosts.
Holy, Holy, Holy is the Lord of Hosts, is the Lord of Hosts.

In Kabbalah, we like to understand the names and sounds of names. There is much discussion and writing about the name of the God known as *Adonai Tzevaoth*, "Lord of Hosts" ("my Lord of Hosts" is a more precise translation). The terms "My Lord" and *Tzevaoth* could be referring to the angelic hosts and comparing them to the corps of an army. So "Lord," or "my Lord," is "my Lord over the army of angelic hosts" — the angelic realm, for example. But *Adonai Tzevaoth* is also a name of God. Each name has a meaning; thus, A'dam means or refers to the earth or ground.

It may not have the same meaning or the same vibration in your native language; if you called somebody, "Hey, Ground, come over here," nobody would like it. There's a vibrational frequency of the Hebrew name Adam or A'dam, so even if you don't know the Hebrew, you can feel, I believe, the vibrational frequency of the Hebrew name.

If you know the name of someone, then you are able to experience that person's vibrational frequency and have closeness with him or her. You've experienced that yourself. For example, if someone you don't know very well or who doesn't know you at all calls you by your first name, then you are going to at least stop and listen and be open to that person.

Getting Closer to the Creator
One goal in the Kabbalistic world is to achieve closeness to the Creator.

Ultimately, when you talk about the mission, you are here on Earth to do, and when you talk about soul development and soul evolution, you can generalize and say that the overall goal of the evolution of the soul is tied directly to experiencing more closeness with the Creator.

The divine will of the Creator is such that you are here on Earth. The will of the Creator is that you are here to do this service and the service for the starseeds, for the ascension, and for the planetary healing. All of these activities are directed toward this closeness. The fact that you know or can experience the name of God is another indicator of your ability to be close to the Creator.

You can achieve a greater closeness with the Creator. The greatest joy in creation, in existence, is being of service to the Creator and doing your mission. There is a special compensation, a special experience, awaiting those who incarnate on the third dimension and do service. There is a special closeness that becomes available. It is interesting that the closeness is only made possible through this third-dimensional experience. You come down into the third dimension and are contracted, so to speak. Contraction is necessary so that you can come into the third dimension. Then you expand and return home.

In the interim, you are doing the will of the Creator. Some of you have asked, "So why do I have to come to the third dimension, especially if I have been in the higher realms before? Why do I have to come here?" This whole process ultimately will lead to a greater closeness to the Creator. It is a great gift to be able to know the name of the Creator and to speak the name of the Creator, because it says that you are able to have closeness to the Creator. That is beautiful.

Now, there are many names in the Kabbalah for the Creator, and *Adonai* is one. *Adonai Tzevaoth* is another. But there's also the name *Elohim*, and we believe that this name is sacred. We will not even speak it; rather, we will first write the name *Elohim* as *Elokeem*, and then pronounce it with the *K* sound instead of the *H* sound. Why? Because we have to honor the name, and we have to say we are pure in vibration to experience the light and the energy of that name. The vibrational frequencies of the name when it is enunciated so directly can put us in a state of consciousness so profound that we must be sure we are pure enough energetically to hold the energy and light of that frequency.

[Tones: *Elokeem, Elokeem.*]

The vibrational frequency activated by that name allows your energy field to go to a higher level, so the name and enunciation of it with intention can bring you into higher energy states.

Jesus's Names

Now let us look at the name of Jesus. Jesus is in the center of the Arcturian Planetary Tree of Life. He is the center, the holder of Messianic light. In Hebrew Kabbalah, his name is *Yeshua*. It can be translated as "he who saves." He can be referred to as "son of David." The Hebrew Kabbalistic enunciation of that name is *Yeshua ben David*. You also may hear his name only as *Yeshua*. The enunciation of his name in this way brings you an energy of closeness to him: *Yeshua ben David, Yeshua ben David*, may the light, the energy, and the love of *Yeshua ben David* fill your heart. *Yeshua ben David*. [Tones.]

Yeshua holds a special place on the Tree of Life because he is in the center and also because he is able to download the higher frequencies with undifferentiated cosmic light into an energy form that can be used and activated. On Earth, however, it is not useful to have a higher spiritual voltage than what your house — your body — can process. So he is able to help step down this light/spiritual voltage. What is this higher spiritual light? This light is a vibrational frequency that's coming from a higher source, and we call it holy light. Holy light, again, is coming from the highest source, and we experience an activation within ourselves when we receive the holy light.

The words for the holy light in the Kabbalah are *Aur Hakadosh*.

[Sings: *Aur Hakadosh, Hakadosh.*]

Baruch Hu is another name for God.

[Sings: *Hakadosh Baruch Hu*, the Holy One. Blessed is he. *Hakadosh, Hakadosh, Aur Hakadosh, Aur Hakadosh.*]

Vibrations and Names

Some of you have had the experience in this lifetime of feeling as though you are willing to change your name. I encourage you to follow that intuition because the desire to change your name may be an indication of a vibrational energy frequency, activation, and shift that is necessary. So your intuition telling you to change your name is good.

Different letters and aspects of a name represent different forces. The energies of the letters represent forces that come together in a name. I also like to point out to people that the original Adam was a hermaphrodite — a being who was both male and female together.

Now, "hermaphrodite" is a strange word in your language, but there are other beings in the galaxy who are hermaphrodites.

Vibrations and names — can you elaborate more on that?

Everything in the universe is a vibration. The existence you have is a unique, individual vibration. It's like a snowflake; no two snowflakes are exactly the same. So your name and the sound of your name have a resonant relationship to your own unique vibration. When we speak of names, we want to say to you that your names are changing over incarnations. You don't have the same name in each incarnation; your name and your vibrational frequency could move to a higher level in different lifetimes. If you change your name, it could go to a higher vibration.

The sound and vibration of a name carry power. It is great in the spiritual world to have the name of God contained in your name. For example, Michael (Mih-ha-el) means "he who is like God." Rafael means "he who heals like God." Those are general interpretations. So your name activates a vibrational relationship to your energy field.

Know that each of you has a unique vibration. Each of you is carrying a unique energy field. It's not a matter of everybody being higher or lower; it's a matter of you fulfilling and expressing your energy in the vibration that you carry and that you are permitted and allowed to express and heal.

Sharing the Message of Unity

This brings me to the concept of unification, which is another key contribution to the Kabbalah. The concept of unification focuses on uniting the discordant parts of this creation, of this world. Anything you do to bring together a unity serves the divine will and helps heal this dimension. So on a great level, the spiritual paradigm of the Sacred Triangle is bringing together and unifying galactic spirituality with native and mystical teachings.

The Sacred Triangle teaches a spiritual unity, and the unities are also in your daily life. Unities are also in your own personal work, in your work for the world. You may be coming and doing work as a healer, helping people unite with their greater selves so they become better healed. Each of you has a unique set of parameters to work with to do this unification and this healing. You have a unique group of people with whom you can work and do healings. This is all part of the vibrational energy you carry and through which people will be attracted to you.

In some cases, you can expand the range of people with whom you work. I can say that the channel, David, expanded his boundaries. We could work with him when he began to travel, even though it was a great stretch for him and he didn't want to travel. But the higher guides prevailed and assured him that he would be safe and well taken care of. It's a great gift of service to expand the number of people you can reach, but we are not saying that each of you has to travel.

In your current life, you have a range of people whom you are able to heal, to whom you're able to bring this message of the unity, or whom you could help to unify. Ultimately, you are reunifying with your higher self. You are unifying with your fifth-dimensional self. So this teaching about unity and unification is also with you. You are unifying your lower third-dimensional self with your higher fifth-dimensional self. Your name is part of the vibrational energy. Your name can indicate a teaching about what you need to do, so you may see a need to change your name in some way.

El Shaddai Chai, the living almighty, omnipotent God, is another powerful name. Or you could say *El Shaddai*, God Almighty — *El Shaddai, El Shaddai*. People have asked, "Why do you need to say it in Hebrew, and what is the right pronunciation?" I refer to the original concept that you heard with the name "ground" and then with A'dam, which carries a vibrational frequency for you.

The name God Almighty has a frequency. Some English words carry a frequency, but some words don't carry the frequency as well as the Hebrew words. Some words in Sanskrit carry a very powerful frequency that you know cannot be replicated in other languages. What sound can come close to "Om," for example? In other languages, there really is nothing quite like the unique sound. Having said that, we can also say *Shalom* carries a strong vibration. We can find the word "Om" in *Shalom*. So there are certain sacred languages on the planet, and Hebrew and Sanskrit are two that are able to carry intense frequencies of light. I am Archangel Metatron. Good day.

❋   ❋   ❋

The Tip of the Iceberg

Shalom, Shalom, Shalom. Greetings. I'm **Vywamus**. I'm a soul psychologist, but I'm also here to work with you on the kingdom, which is manifestation. What you need to understand about this reality, the third dimension, is that it is a manifestation. What does it mean to say it is a manifestation? It is manifesting as a result of the other energies above.

A good analogy would be an iceberg: You see the tip of the iceberg, as they say. If you just look at the top of the ocean, all you see is the tip, and you don't understand that underneath is a whole different world. There is history; there is centuries of ice built up, and there is an unbelievable amount of energy jelled together below.

Now, when you look at the Tree of Life, you should understand that this reality you see is a result of higher spheres that are interacting, that are manifested, and you are now seeing that manifestation. This is both a personal and a planetary tree. That means what you are seeing, how things are manifesting now, is an accumulation of billions of years in the universe. Remember, the universe goes back approximately fourteen billion years to when the big bang happened.

This is one thing. The other thing is when you look at the Tree of Life, you should remember that the spheres do not stand alone. This is an interactive Tree of Life in which each sphere is related to the other spheres. So even though you see *Malchut*, even though you are experiencing the bottom part of the Tree of Life, the kingdom is related to all the other spheres.

This is a profound teaching that is so important for planetary healing, because in planetary healing, you cannot have compassion and kindness and at the same time allow overuse of everything. There has to be some type of restriction. There has to be some type of judgment, and there has to be some type of justice. Everything cannot just go unrestricted. You cannot work on this planet without wisdom. Now, because this planet has gotten so out of balance, Earth needs a Messiah. This planet needs a new harmony and a balance.

So remember, the Tree of Life has one pillar that is positive, one pillar that is negative; one pillar that is feminine, one pillar that is masculine; and then there is a pillar in the center of balance. These are prototypes. These spheres and pillars are teaching you that you will interact with all of them.

Now, on a personal basis, each of you may be most attracted to a certain sphere, so don't necessarily think you have to integrate all the spheres at once. You may be initially attracted to just one sphere right now; you may just be attracted to harmony.

Maybe you are using unity. Maybe you are here to help a Messianic light. Maybe you are here to experience the shimmering and you want to work with that. Maybe you are here to experience the planetary cities of light and the sacredness. Maybe you are here to help with the New Earth's just society and are helping to create that. Maybe you are here to just bliss out in the divine light and to feel what it is like to experience that light in the kingdom — the bottom sphere.

There are many ways of experiencing this Tree of Life. The most helpful message to remember is that there are spheres above, and they are all interacting and reaching high. You can bring down the higher energy to Earth. Bring down those higher lights. Bring down those higher balances. Bring down the higher wisdom, the higher knowledge, and if possible, even try to bring down the undifferentiated light. It is a true blessing. I'm Vywamus. Good day.

The Arcturian Tree of Life for Planetary Healing
with the Hebrew Names and Gematria

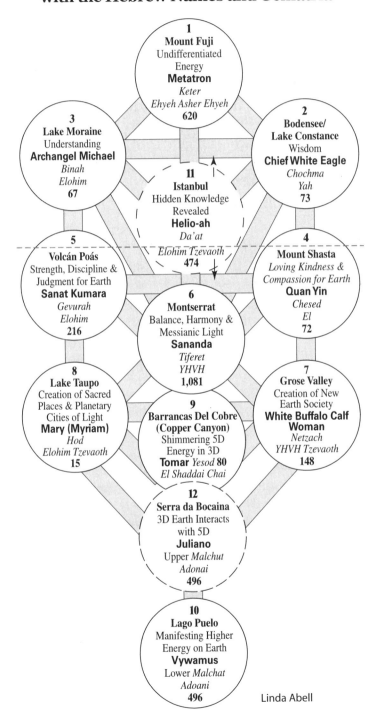

1
Mount Fuji
Undifferentiated Energy
Metatron
Keter
Ehyeh Asher Ehyeh
620

3
Lake Moraine
Understanding
Archangel Michael
Binah
Elohim
67

2
Bodensee/
Lake Constance
Wisdom
Chief White Eagle
Chochma
Yah
73

11
Istanbul
Hidden Knowledge Revealed
Helio-ah
Da'at
Elohim Tzevaoth
474

5
Volcán Poás
Strength, Discipline & Judgment for Earth
Sanat Kumara
Gevurah
Elohim
216

4
Mount Shasta
Loving Kindness & Compassion for Earth
Quan Yin
Chesed
El
72

6
Montserrat
Balance, Harmony & Messianic Light
Sananda
Tiferet
YHVH
1,081

8
Lake Taupo
Creation of Sacred Places & Planetary Cities of Light
Mary (Myriam)
Hod
Elohim Tzevaoth
15

9
Barrancas Del Cobre
(Copper Canyon)
Shimmering 5D Energy in 3D
Tomar *Yesod* **80**
El Shaddai Chai

7
Grose Valley
Creation of New Earth Society
White Buffalo Calf Woman
Netzach
YHVH Tzevaoth
148

12
Serra da Bocaina
3D Earth Interacts with 5D
Juliano
Upper *Malchut*
Adonai
496

10
Lago Puelo
Manifesting Higher Energy on Earth
Vywamus
Lower *Malchat*
Adoani
496

Linda Abell

Tree of Life Key

Note to Readers: The Tree of Life Key and the *Aleph-Bet* chart that follows are provided as visual support for the information delivered in the classes. You may want to refer to these as you read.

Sphere One

Mount Fuji in Japan
This crystal holds the energy of life forces from Lemuria, which have now been unlocked by its arrival. It is an ancient crystal containing great secrets of light and ancient knowledge of the planet. It has a connection with the ancient grandmothers and grandfathers.

Keter (Undifferentiated energy)
This is the *Sephirah* of the crown. Its energy, like ten quintillion volts, is called "undifferentiated light."

Metatron
Tradition associates Metatron with Enoch, who "walked with God" (Genesis 5:22) and who ascended to heaven and was changed from a human being into an angel. His name has been said to mean "the angel of presence," or "the one who occupies the throne next to the divine throne." Another interpretation of his name is based on the Latin word *metator*, which is a guide or measurer. In the world of the Jewish mystic, Metatron holds the rank of archangel. According to the Arcturians, Metatron is associated with the Arcturian stargate and assists souls in their ascension to higher worlds.

Ehyeh Asher Ehyeh
"I Am That I Am" is a misinterpretation of this that is frequently used. There is no present tense of the verb "to be" in Hebrew because the present only lasts a nanosecond, so you can't always put Hebrew into English. "I Will (Shall) Be That I Will (Shall) Be" is the only correct interpretation.

Sphere Two

Lake Constance in the Bodensee in Germany
This crystal provides new information, new codes, new structures, and new dynamics for the Earth's ley lines and allows us access to new information.

Chochma (Wisdom)

Chief White Eagle
An ascended fifth-dimensional Native American guide who is very connected to Jesus and other higher fifth-dimensional beings.

Yah

Sphere Three

Lake Moraine in Canada
This crystal contains the quantum-etheric, energy-activation light that can bypass the normal laws of linear time/space and cause/effect.

Binah (Understanding)

Archangel Michael
His name is actually a question: "Who is like God?" He is perhaps the best known of the archangels and is acknowledged by all three Western sacred traditions. He has been called the prince of light, fighting a war against the sons of darkness. In this role, he is depicted most often as winged with an unsheathed sword, the warrior of God and slayer of the dragon. His role in the ascension is focused on helping us cut the cords of attachment to the Earth plane, which will allow us to move up to higher consciousness. In the Kabbalah, he is regarded as the forerunner of the *Shekinah*, the Divine Mother.

Elohim
This is the level of divinity that manifested creation, which has a sense of plurality and oneness.

Sphere Four

Mount Shasta in California in the United States
The combination of this crystal, the Galactic Kachina, and the imprint of the stargate means that Mount Shasta has become a powerful ascension point. It also gives us an easy connection to our souls, our soul power, and our soul mission.

Chesed (Loving Kindness and Compassion for Earth)
We can use the energy of this sphere for many different purposes, such as treating the next human being with "human dignity." It is also the energy of restriction, the energy we use for things like judgments and different ways of containing things so they don't get out of balance.

Quan Yin
A female member of the spiritual hierarchy. In her previous incarnation, she performed many acts of kindness and compassion and is known as the goddess of mercy.

El

Sphere Five

Volcán Poás in Costa Rica
This crystal is linked to the great attractor force that pushes and pulls the galaxies in different directions. It also helps attract and discharge blocked energy in Earth's energy channels. One example of this is the way it has modified the Ring of Fire to create balance in that area.

Gevurah (Strength, Discipline, and Judgment for Earth)
It also represents greatness and justice.

Sanat Kumara
An ascended master whose main role is to oversee the physical evolution of planet Earth.

Elohim
This is the level of divinity that manifested creation, which has a sense of plurality and oneness.

Sphere Six

Montserrat near Barcelona in Spain
This magnificent place is a holy site. Juliano tells us it is mostly free from wars and polarization. It has a powerful, sacred, and holy energy. This crystal was downloaded to work with holy sacred light and will help the sites of the other crystals become truly sacred energy sites.

Tiferet (Balance, Harmony, and Messianic Light)
The word *Tiferet* means "beauty."

Sananda

Sananda is known to us as the Master Jesus. He is considered one the greatest Jewish Kabbalists of all time. His galactic name, Sananda, represents an evolved and galactic picture of who he is in his entirety. In the Kabbalah, Sananda is known as Joshua ben Miriam of Nazareth, which can be translated as Jesus, son of Mary of Nazareth.

YHVH

One of the many sacred four-letter names of God known as the *Tetragrammaton*. The letters are sacred and should not be pronounced. Instead, one should say *Hashem*, which means "the name."

Sphere Seven

Grose Valley in the Blue Mountains National Park of Australia

The Grose Valley crystal connects with the Rainbow Serpent, which is the feminine goddess energy of Mother Gaia and an area of great significance to the aborigines of Australia.

Netzach (Creation of New Earth Society)

This sphere represents eternal victory/glory. It also represents Moses and his attempt — with divine help — to spread the light to a New Earth society.

White Buffalo Calf Woman

In Lakota Native American folklore, she is the fifth-dimensional spirit being who appeared to bring forth special information about holy ceremonies and accessing higher spirit. She taught the necessity of being in harmony with Earth. Her focus is on the unity of all beings and that all are related. She is representative of the dawning of a new age.

YHVH Tzevaoth

Sphere Eight

Lake Taupo in New Zealand

This crystal is representative of good luck, good fortune, wealth, and prosperity and is a great attracting force of energy for those who work with it. It is also a reaffirmation of the spiritual strength and power of the native peoples on Earth and will help to reawaken them to their mission.

Hod (Creation of Sacred Places and Planetary Cities of Light)

The *Sephirah* of brilliant light and splendor. It is the last bit of left-column energy in the Tree of Life before the funnel of *Yesod*.

Mary (Myriam)

Elohim Tzevaoth

Sphere Nine

Barrancas del Cobre (Copper Canyon) in Mexico
This crystal gives us a new link to Arcturian energy, a link we can use to connect with the planet Alano and the fifth-dimensional master Alano who resides there. This crystal also carries the special energy of shimmering, enabling us to move ourselves or objects into another dimension.

Yesod (Shimmering Fifth-Dimensional Energy in the Third Dimension)
This sphere in the central column funnels all the energy from above it into the world, *Malchut*. It also represents the bonding of shimmering.

Tomar
An Arcturian ascended master whose specialty is using and describing the Arcturian temple energy.

El Shaddai Chai
El Shaddai translates to "God Almighty" and is the garment of Lord Archangel Metatron. It is the energy that protects the doorposts that contain a *Mezuzah*. *Chai* is "life."

Sphere Ten

Lago Puelo in Argentina
Lago Puelo is the home of the first crystal to be brought down to Earth. The crystal holds the primordial energy for the whole planet. It is an energy of initiation and connection.

Lower *Malchut* (Manifesting Higher Energy on Earth)
This sphere is known as the kingdom, which is Earth, where we must burn off karma through service (with good deeds), sharing, and correcting ourselves.

Vywamus
A fifth-dimensional soul psychologist known for his insight into the psychology of Earth problems and resolution of issues related to starseeds incarnated on Earth.

Adonai
The female energy and the galactic/cosmic name that rules the third and fifth dimensions. It means "my Lord."

Sphere Eleven

Istanbul in Turkey
This crystal is the seat of hidden knowledge revealed.

Da'at (Hidden Knowledge Revealed)

Helio-ah
A female Arcturian ascended master and Juliano's twin flame.

Elohim Tzevaoth

Sphere Twelve

Serra da Bocaina
This crystal represents the interaction between the third and fifth dimensions.

Upper *Malchut* (Third-Dimensional Earth Interacts with the Fifth Dimension)

Juliano
The main Arcturian guide and ascended master working to help activate Earth and the Arcturian starseeds toward the ascension.

Adonai
The female energy and the galactic/cosmic name that rules the third and fifth dimensions. It means "my Lord."

The *Aleph-Bet* and Number Values

Order	Hebrew Letter	Spelling	English Letter	Value
1st letter:	א	(Aleph)	A	1/111
2nd letter:	ב	(Bet)	B	2/412
3rd letter:	ג	(Gimmel)	G	3/73
4th letter:	ד	(Dalet)	D	4/434
5th letter:	ה	(Hey)	H	5/6
6th letter:	ו	(Vav)	V	6/22
7th letter:	ז	(Zayin)	Z	7/67
8th letter:	ח	(Chet)	Ch	8/418
9th letter:	ט	(Tet)	T	9/419
10th letter:	י	(Yud)	Y	10/20
11th letter:	כ	(Kaph)	K	20/100
12th letter:	ל	(Lamed)	L	30/74
13th letter:	מ	(Mem)	M	40/80
14th letter:	נ	(Nun)	N	50/106

The *Aleph-Bet* and Number Values

Order	Hebrew Letter	Spelling	English Letter	Value
15th letter:	ס	(Samekh)	S	60/120
16th letter:	ע	(Ayin)	(silent)	70/130
17th letter:	פ	(Pey)	P	80/85
18th letter:	צ.	(Tzadi)	Z	90/104
19th letter:	ק	(Kuf)	Q	100/186
20th letter:	ר	(Resh)	R	200/510
21st letter:	ש	(Shin)	Sh	300/360
22nd letter:	ת	(Tav)	T	400/406
1st final letter:	ך	(Kaph-Sophit)		500
2nd final letter:	ם	(Mem-Sophit)		600
3rd final letter:	ן	(Nun-Sophit)		700
4th final letter:	ף	(Pey-Sophit)		800
5th final letter	ץ:	(Tzadi-Sophit)		900

Introducing Hebrew Terminology and Numbers to the Tree of Life

CLASS 1

MORDECHAI, DAVID, AND JULIANO

Mordechai: The Hebraic or Kabbalistic Tree of Life represents a three-column system (see fig. 2). It represents this creation as well as everything.

Now, to be able to relate to everyone, I will use the analogy of the video "The Tour of the Galaxy[1]," where basically, it showed — at the very end of the video — how the brain cell is an exact photocopy of a picture of the galaxy. I would like to say "the universe," but we don't have telescopes that go that far. So it is an exact photocopy of the galaxy. So what the brain cell is to the galaxy, the Kabbalistic Tree of Life is to the ten dimensions because it is a technology.

The Tree of Life is a three-column system made up of a right column, a left column, and a central column. The right column is male energy, the left column is female energy, and the center column is a combination of the two. That's where the two come together, and then you have balance and harmony.

The Twelve Sephirot

We come to the first *Sephirah*, which is *Keter*. Now, the *Sephirah* of *Keter* (spelled *Kaph-Tav-Resh*) has a gematria — or sacred geometry, if you want to call it that — of 620. It is more than 90 percent outside the tree. So understand that *Keter* is less than 10 percent inside the tree.

Whatever comes in from the crown, which is really in the Kabbalistic

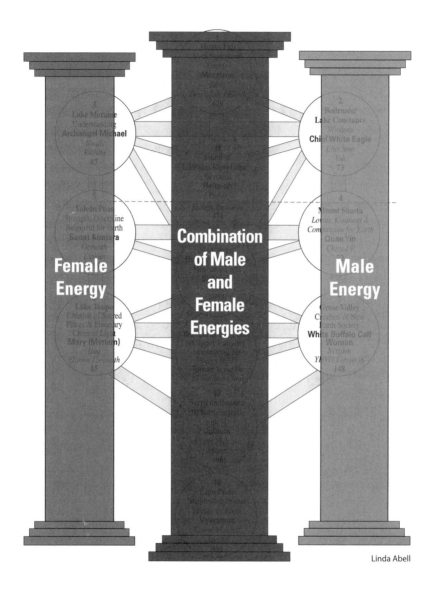

Linda Abell

Figure 2. The Kabbalistic Tree of Life is a three-column system.

rung, the entity that is in that *Sephirah* is called *Arich Anpin*, or large face.[2] There are many, many names of God. We are working from the top down, because *Arich Anpin* is a very high entity, considering that *Adonai* is in the *Sephirah* of *Malchut*. I am just giving you a perspective before we get into number two.

Chochma and Binah

Sephirah number two is wisdom, and it is called *Chochma*. *Chochma* has a gematria of 73. I'm just giving you these numbers because they will come together at a point — if not now, maybe in two weeks.

Wisdom is in the right column. From wisdom, you have the third *Sephirah*, which is called *Binah*. *Binah* is understanding. It is a female energy — the top female energy. By the way, the entity for wisdom is *Aba*, or Father.[3] You may consider it grandfathers or elders. However, *Binah* is on the left side, and that is *Ima*, or Mother (or grandmothers or big female energy). It is the mother of *Adonai*, yet it is the eighth *Sephirah* coming up from the bottom. It is an exact duplicate of this world. *Hashem*, the Creator, made us in his image. And the image is *Binah*, understanding.

There are things that are different. What is the difference between *Malchut* and *Binah*? It is the fact that there is no negative inclination in *Binah*. There is no speaking in *Binah*, okay? That is the biggest difference.

Da'at

Let's get into the higher central spheres. In the central column is a sphere called *Da'at*, or knowledge. Knowledge is a combination or a balancing of wisdom and understanding. In the Kabbalistic Tree of Life, there is a dotted line as a circle for *Da'at*. I call it the shimmering *Sephirah*, because it is there and it is not there, and that is why they call it hidden knowledge — because it is there and it is not there. *Da'at* shares the central column with *Keter*.

Then, after these four *Sephirot* (numbers one, two, three, and eleven on figure 3), there is a curtain — a line drawn across the tree. Then we get the next *Sephirah*. From here on, we will call them "step-down transformers," because that is exactly what the Tree of Life is: a combination of step-down transformers. So the light can come in, and by the time it gets to us, believe me, there is very little of it. But nonetheless, it is there. Still, the light needs at least ten transformers to come down into this world — maybe even twelve.

Chesed

The next *Sephirah*, the first one under the curtain on the right side, *Chesed*, is known as loving kindness. The entity in the Kabbalistic Tree that runs through that *Sephirah* is Abraham. He was the epitome of loving kindness. Here we are, all children of Abraham. He shared.

To make a long story short, to be in the presence of Abraham was similar to the first "Hilton Hotel" that was free. Everybody went to this guy's tent. They ate and they slept, and it didn't cost them a thing, but they did have to do one important thing: They had to thank the Creator for providing their room and board. If they refused, Abraham would simply ask them for a hundred camels. If they said, "That is too much for this!" then Abraham would say, "I agree. So wouldn't it be better if you just sat here and thanked the Creator?" Such a deal!

Gevurah and Tiferet

From that right-column *Sephirah*, we go to the left column, which is *Gevurah*. Now, in Hebrew, *Gevurah* is actually three times *Chesed*. *Chesed*'s numerical value is 72, and *Gevurah*'s numerical value is 216, which happens to be a master number, but we don't have enough time to get into that.

From that column — from *Gevurah* — everything comes down into *Tiferet*. *Tiferet* is in the central column. It's the first *Sephirah* under the curtain in that central column. The entity that runs *Tiferet* is actually Jacob, or a group of archangels. There is a group of archangels in that *Sephirah* because — actually, there is an equation here: harmony + balance = beauty. But *Gevurah* is very strong. Archangel Michael is in charge of *Chesed*, and his brother, Archangel Gabriel, is in charge of *Gevurah*. So when anything really has to be done where judgment and strength are called for, the job is given to Archangel Gabriel, whom I personally call the "producer" of the show.

So you have the group of archangels in *Tiferet*: Uriel, Nuriel, Raphael, and one or two others. *Tiferet* is in the central column in the middle. It goes to every one of the other spheres. Most importantly, it goes downward. The number one beautiful step-down transformer is *Tiferet*.

Netzach and Hod

The next *Sephirah* on the right column is *Netzach*, which means victory. The entity in charge of Netzach is Moses, *Netzach Moshe Rabeinu* (Moses, our teacher). He really was the epitome of victory. He represents the last *Sephirah*, or step-down transformer, in the right column.

From here, we go to the sphere of *Hod*. I believe we are on number eight in the chart. I have not mentioned any crystals because I'm leaving that to David; I'm just going by the Kabbalistic range. *Hod* is Moses's brother, the entity Aaron. By the way, *Hod* means "splendor," and "splendor" is the same word as Zohar. So *Hod* and Zohar are quite similar. Zohar light is the light of splendor. Aaron, who really was the first Cohen Priest in this world, in the etheric third dimension, was in charge of the Holy Temple, which was in the desert before there even was a Holy Temple.

Now, with the seventh and eighth spheres, everything goes down into the last *Sephirah* of the bottom triangle, because you see, we have discussed three different triangles, but I'm trying to keep it simple.

Yesod

All right, the next is number nine, which is *Yesod*. This *Sephirah* of *Yesod* is like a funnel: Everything I have spoken to you about — *Sephirah* number one all the way through *Sephirah* number eight, everything — in order to come into this world, has to pass through *Sephirah* number nine, *Yesod*, or the foundation (that same Joseph who was in Egypt), because this *Sephirah* is the epitome of sustenance. This is what brings sustenance, or as we call it, life force energy, into this world. What did Joseph do? In third-dimensional terms, he broke the bank. He broke the world bank.

Joseph brought all the money into Egypt because of the famine. Everybody sold everything they had, even themselves, for food. Everything in the world — all the gold, all the silver, all the diamonds — came into Egypt because of Joseph. So that is how important *Yesod* is. It is also (because we have to include *Da'at*) in the central column. This central column is the power line — the powerhouse.

Malchut

Without any further ado, we will go to *Malchut*, which would be the first *Malchut*, because there are two. The Zohar says that even though in the Hebraic or Kabbalistic original Tree of Life there would be ten spheres, or *Sephirot*, there are actually twelve spheres. The Zohar does bring out the *Sephirah* of *Da'at*, and it does say that we are in the *Malchut* of *Malchut*, so there are two *Malchuts*. This is not any new revelation, but this is where we have to get more complex, and I'm going to try to keep it simple. The bottom line is we bring in the fifth-dimensional energy, the life force energy of the fifth dimension.

The most important thing to know is that we are bringing down fifth-dimensional energy into this mundane third-dimensional world, which has very little light. The only light that gets into this world is what we bring into it. That's the point.

What we have to bring into this world is not something that we have inherited but something that we have to acquire by earning it. And if you think about it, when is something really appreciated? Not when it is inherited, but when it is acquired, earned, or accomplished. That's why the energy of this Tree of Life is so essential.

✳   ✳   ✳

Behind the Hebrew Terms

David: I'm going to review some things that Mordechai said, and I want to make sure that everybody understands them. Then I'm going to talk a little bit about what the Arcturians have done with the Tree of Life.

Mordechai used a lot of Hebrew words. The main Hebrew word that Mordechai used is *Hashem*. When Mordechai uses the word *Hashem*, in the Kabbalah that means "the name." In Kabbalah, we do not pronounce God's name. We are not allowed to pronounce it at all, so we say "the name." So when you hear the word *Hashem*, that is the Hebrew word for God.

A second word that Mordechai used is *Adonai*. *Adon* is the word for Lord in Hebrew, and *Adonai* means "my Lord." This is also a sacred name, and it has a wonderful sound: *Adonai*.

Another word Mordechai used was "gematria." Gematria is another Kabbalistic term. Gematria is a study of numbers, so you might ask, "Well, why would the Kabbalah be interested in numbers?" Well, Hebrew is an interesting language; it is a very powerful language. The first letter, *A* or *Aleph*, is 1; and *B*, the second letter, or *Bet*, is 2. The third letter, *C*, *Gimmel*, is 3, and so on (see figure 3).

So every word is a number. When Mordechai refers to gematria and he uses a number at the top, he is adding up the numbers. It is totally amazing that, if you look at words and adapt the numbers of the letters, a lot of words have a special numerical value. This is somewhat similar to numerology, so you can call it numerology, but it is part of the Kabbalah.

Mordechai used the words "Father" and "Mother," and he used the Hebrew word *Aba* for Father, which I think is pronounced like that music group in Sweden. Then he used *Ima*, which is Mother.

Now, Mordechai also used the term *Sephirah*. He talked about the *Sephirot* as well, by which he was referring to many spheres. *Sephirah* means one sphere.

Each *Sephirah* is powerful, and each one holds a specific energy. He talked about the top *Sephirah* and called it *Keter*. That is the Hebrew word for "crown." So in our configuration with the crystals, we put Mount Fuji on there (refer to p. 34). Remember, in the original Kabbalistic Tree of Life, they only put prophets and higher people or angels in the positions to represent the energy of the *Sephirot*, so the top *Sephirah* is *Keter*.

Mordechai also pointed out that *Keter* is 90 percent above the rest of the tree. What that means is the energy from *Keter* is so high that we call it undifferentiated energy, because no one can really grasp it. No one can really even begin to explain it in words. It is so high up that, if by any chance somebody were able to touch the energy of *Keter*, it would be like 10,000 volts, and it would blow everyone away. It is very high. So in our planetary configuration, we use Mount Fuji to represent the energy of *Keter*, and we placed Archangel Metatron there, and we call it undifferentiated energy.

We call the second *Sephirah* wisdom. Mordechai called it by the Hebrew name, *Chochma*, which means "wisdom" in Hebrew. We designated Bodensee (or Lake Constance) as the physical representation of this on Earth, and we designated Chief White Eagle in that spot as the entity overseeing it. We also designated Metatron for Mount Fuji, because Metatron is considered the highest archangel.

The third sphere Mordechai mentioned is *Binah*, which is known as understanding. We have Archangel Michael there, and we designated Lake Moraine in Canada to it. Many people may know that Lake Moraine is considered the home of Archangel Michael in the Canadian Rocky Mountains.

Now, if you go to what looks like sphere eleven, you'll see that it is a central circle that is labeled "hidden knowledge." Mordechai called that *Da'at*, which is the Hebrew word for knowledge. We expanded that to "hidden knowledge revealed," but in the Kabbalistic tree, it actually is simply knowledge. We put the Arcturian spirit guide Helio-ah there.

Remember that, with the Arcturian Tree of Life, they adapted the Kabbalistic Tree of Life, and Juliano has told us that this Kabbalistic Tree of Life is a glyph, which is like a paradigm for the whole universe, not just for Earth. This is actually a galactic symbol; it is not placed just

for Earth but for the entire galaxy and the entire universe. We have
Istanbul as the physical place representing that sphere (eleven), and
Helio-ah represents hidden knowledge.

The next one is Mount Shasta — loving kindness — and Mordechai
called that *Chesed*, which is "loving kindness" in Hebrew. So that is the
Sephirah of loving kindness and compassion for Earth. Now, the Arcturians have adapted this Tree of Life for planetary healing. When we
were talking before about the Kabbalistic Tree of Life, we weren't talking specifically about planetary healing. But now we are talking about
using the Tree of Life for planetary healing. We put Quan Yin there in
the sphere of loving kindness for planetary healing.

Moving on to the next one: Volcán Poás in Costa Rica represents
strength, discipline, and judgment for Earth. Mordechai called that
sphere *Gevurah*. I'm giving you the Hebrew words and spellings because
some people may be interested in them. There is so much information
already out there about each of the *Sephirot*. The word *Sephirot* is also
related to the Hebrew word for counting, so it is interesting that you
can count and have the ten spheres or the twelve spheres. In any case,
Sanat Kumara has been designated as the spirit guide for Volcán Poás.

So if you look at this, we made minor modifications to fit the energies of the Kabbalistic Tree of Life. The center sphere is *Tiferet*: balance,
harmony, and beauty. *Tiferet* is the Hebrew word for beauty, and we put
Sananda/Jesus there because every energy passes through the center.
That is where Sananda/Jesus is. Jesus explains, "If you come through
me, you are going to reach my father." This is because Jesus is connected to every energy. The location at Montserrat, Spain, represents
such a sacred energy.

Then we go to Grose Valley, sphere seven, and the attribute that we
called "creation of a New Earth society." Mordechai called it *Netzach*,
which means "victory" in Hebrew. We put White Buffalo Calf Woman
there as the spirit guide for this sphere because we feel that she is supposed to help us bring in a New Earth society.

Lake Taupo in New Zealand represents the sphere for the creation
of sacred places and the planetary cities of light. Mordechai called that
Hod, which also means "splendor." Splendor also refers to the Zohar.
The Zohar is the Kabbalistic mystical book that explains the Kabbalah,
and Zohar also means "the brilliant light." We put Mary — Miriam is
her Hebrew name — to represent the spirit guide for this sphere and
the cities of light.

Sphere nine, Barrancas del Cobre, or Copper Canyon, Mexico, represents the energy of shimmering. Shimmering is the ability to vibrate your energy field so that you can experience the fifth dimension. We put Tomar, the Arcturian spirit guide, for that sphere.

Serra da Bocaina, Brazil, represents the next sphere. For this energy, we added an additional sphere to the Tree of Life. We added a new *Sephirah*, and we say that this sphere represents Earth's interaction with the fifth and third dimensions. We put Juliano, an Arcturian guide, in charge of that new addition. In the traditional Kabbalistic Tree of Life, there are no intersecting spheres or *Sephirot*; however, this sphere is actually intersecting with the bottom sphere.

The bottom sphere is called *Malchut*. In Hebrew, it means "kingdom," and that is where we are on Earth. We are living in the kingdom of Earth; we are living on the third dimension. We represent this sphere as Lago Puelo, which is in Patagonia, Argentina. The function of this sphere is described as manifesting higher energy on Earth, and the spirit guide assigned to this sphere is Vywamus.

Basically, the Arcturians have slightly modified this Universal/ Galactic Tree of Life, which was originally given to Moses and the Hebraic mystics — the Israeli mystics, the Jewish mystics. They adapted it for planetary healing, and they put etheric crystals in each of these places. These etheric crystals can help us download the energies for holding on to fifth-dimensional light.

❋   ❋   ❋

The Numbers in the Tree of Life

Mordechai: Everybody is talking about numbers, and numbers are very important. Numbers brought me to where I am today because I didn't believe anybody. I have only believed in numbers. I believe that all is black or white; there is no gray. Either it is or is not. Mathematics is what brought me to the Zohar and to the Tree of Life — how important it is. So I'm going to spend the next few minutes explaining numbers to you — at least basic gematria.

Basic gematria is Hebrew, but I repeat: There are no accidents, and there are no coincidences. "Gematria" and "geometry" sound similar. Geometry is all about triangles and angles, and believe me, this whole universe and multiverse are all made up of triangles (see fig. 3). It is all about the triangles; it is all about geometry. David was bringing up all

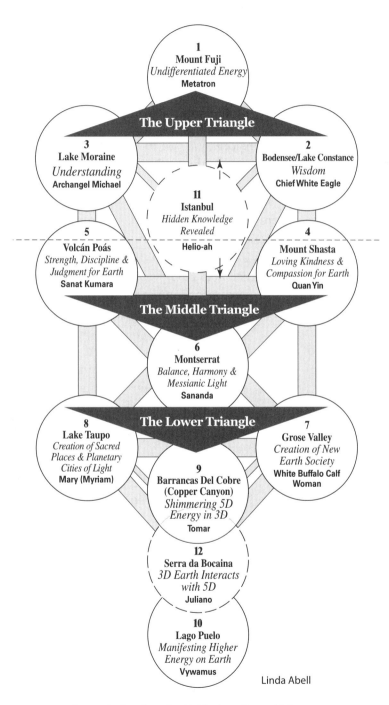

Figure 3. Triads in the Kabbalistic Tree of Life.

of the Hebrew words. I'm going to tell you something about the numbers and how important they are.

What things relate between the third dimension and the fifth dimension? You have music, vibration, and frequencies. Those are all numbers. You have colors. All colors have a frequency and a number. The important thing about the Hebrew letters is that when we do Biorelativity or planetary healing exercises at a sacred time and place, you have all these letters flying and winding around the ring of ascension[4] to help create and recharge it.

What is it about these letters? The analysis of a letter has three forms: sight, sound, and number. This is pure Kabbalah, my friends. This is getting it right from the *Aleph-Bet*, right from the one, two, three — sight, sound, and number. Each Hebrew letter has a relevant number, a relevant shape, and a relevant sound.

What is the most important sound we use in the Hebrew letters? "Mmmm." *Shalommmm*. The *M*, the *Mem*, is in the sound of the names Metatron and Moses. Their names contain the *M* sound. That is among the highest vibrations as far as connecting us with fifth-dimensional energy. Believe it or not, the numerical value of the letter *Mem* is 40. I just happen to mention this; I'm just channeling this, and I'm taking it right from the hip.

The numerical value of the sound *M*, which is the most important sound of *Shalommmm*, *Ohmmmm*, and everything that ends in a final *M*, is the value of 40. The Group of Forty has its origin in the Hebrew letters. I will tell you that from the bottom of my heart. Forty squared, or 1,600, is the number of souls in their fifth-dimensional bodies sitting around that Arcturian crystal lake.

When we talk about Hebrew letters, we talk about their power. Their power is a galactic knowledge that comes directly from the Central Sun and is very real. So we start with the first letters: *Aleph, Bet,* and *Gimmel*. That seems to be the one, two, three: *Aleph, Bet, Gimmel*. When we describe the Hebrew letters, we talk about the *Aleph-Bet*. Is it not amazing that in English they call it the alphabet? *Aleph-Bet* or alphabet. There are no accidents; there are no coincidences. The question is, which language was here first? And which language are they finding on the 12,000-year-old archeological site recently discovered in Turkey? They are not talking about it, but I tell you what: It definitely isn't English.

The point we have to understand is that the *Aleph* is a very important letter. It wasn't the first letter in the Torah, because the Creator had more important jobs to do through it. The letter *Aleph* is shaped with two *Yuds* and a *Vav*. It's all about geometry, or sacred gematria.

It's no accident that *Yud* is 10 and that *Vav* is 6: 10 + 10 + 6 = 26, and that is the numerical value of *Yud-Kay-Vav-Kay*, YKVK, or *Yud-Hey-Vav-Hey*, or *YHVH* [Author's Note: sometimes referred to as Yahweh in English.] I'm getting permission to pronounce these words strictly so that you can understand who is in charge, what is in charge, and why it is in charge.

In my Kabbalah 101 class, I'm asked, "What are these Hebrew letters that they are so powerful, and how can you relate to them?"

I say, "Well, imagine Santa Claus and Santa Claus's elves. Well, these Hebrew letters are the Creator's elves." It is as simple as that.

When I give an advanced class, I talk about different signs of Virgo, Aquarius, and Gemini. The third letter, *Gimmel*, corresponds to the number 3. The letter *Gimmel* is associated with the creation of the planet Jupiter, which also represents miracles.

What do we call miracles? A miracle is just rising above nature — something that happens that we are not used to. But there are many miracles in this world. Giving birth is a miracle, but it happens so many times a day that you take it for granted. When I ask the angels about miracles, they say, "Imagine every breath you take is a miracle, Mordechai." That is really getting down to basics.

The letter *Bet* is a very powerful letter: *Aleph-Bet-Gimmel*, A-B-C, or A-B-G — however you wish to express it. The letter *Bet* is not only the first letter of the Torah, but in Kabbalah, it is also associated with the creation of the planet Saturn. Now, I would add that *Shabtai* is the Hebrew word for Saturn, but interestingly, *Shabtai* is closely related to *Shabbat*, the Hebrew word for the day of rest. Saturn happens to be the seventh planet. Everything happens in a perfect way and in a perfect time.

These letters, the whole purpose of bringing these letters into a Biorelativity exercise, is to do Biorelativity during sacred times. These letters are alive. Why? Because sacred times put us into fifth-dimensional space and environments. That is why they can exist so easily. It is very simple. It doesn't matter what you call Saturday or Sunday or Friday. What makes it a sacred time? When you get thirty million to forty million people praying at the same time. That is the big secret of sacred time. It is to have a completely open mind and to know that whenever you can bring twenty million people together to pray on a

Tuesday, then that is a sacred time, okay? It is all a part of numbers. It is simple numbers.

There could be a ninety-minute lecture on each letter of the Hebrew alphabet because each is living energy intelligence, not just a letter. And you know, we can go back to that movie *Stargate*, in which Kurt Russell starred. He is trying to write in the sand, and they say. "No, no, no! It's forbidden." Writing is forbidden, and speaking is definitely forbidden. Why? Because that would bring in a potential lowering of that consciousness. The whole point is: What is the connection and what is the understanding in the connection? Consciousness, and connecting with that quiet, still voice is a beautiful and elevating journey of activating consciousness. Those of us fortunate in having tenure in our connections may have heard the term "the thunder in the whisper." We have been made aware! We must be more aggressive in savoring our quiet time and give more time to it in order to hold that galactic space and perspective.

✳   ✳   ✳

The Importance of Balance in the Tree of Life

Shalom, Shalom, Shalom. Greetings. This is **Juliano**. We are the Arcturians. You are studying a pattern of energy called the Tree of Life. We are familiar with the Tree of Life because it is part of the galactic knowledge, and the idea is to use it. It is not a static intellectual game; it is not an idea that is only mental. But in our work with you, we have thought to develop it as a planetary healing tool.

This planetary healing tool, which we have adapted from the basic Kabbalistic Tree of Life, can and will be used to bring this planet back into a better balance. It is a wonderful gift that you, the Arcturian starseeds, are so devoted that you have been able to work with twelve different sacred, powerful locations on this planet, and you have been able to designate and work with these twelve etheric crystals. The etheric crystals then have been correspondingly placed in areas that represent the energies of twelve spheres.

So why did we adapt it for twelve instead of ten? The answer is that we are entering a new age; we are entering a new time period. Yes, it is true that the ten spheres are totally sacred, and even the ancient Hebrew book says not nine but ten spheres.

Now here we are, the Arcturians, saying not ten, but twelve. Twelve is a sacred number. Our reason is that you are living in a period of unprecedented energy in which the third dimension is intersecting with the fifth dimension. This means that there is the great possibility of and great advantage to bringing higher-dimensional energies down into the third dimension.

You have been studying special spiritual techniques such as shimmering, but shimmering energy is represented in the bottom sphere by Lago Puelo and Serra de Bocaina. Shimmering represents the fact that you are living on two dimensions at the same time and that you will be able to bring both dimensions into the same sphere, which is the sphere of Lago Puelo.

Planetary Healing through Loving Kindness and Judgment

This is a totally new advancement on the Tree of Life. It adapts the Tree of Life for planetary healing, and I can tell you that this is one of the main functions. It is so versatile. Everyone knows that this planet is in a crisis. Everyone knows that there must be a new paradigm, and we offer the new paradigm of the Sacred Triangle. But also we are saying that this model represents a way to energetically interact with the planet — to bring about healing. And the simplest way is to look at the column that represents loving kindness and the column that represents judgment.

We, the Arcturians, have traveled through many different planets. We have seen at least eight different planets in this galaxy that are on the same level as Earth and going through the same planetary transition. You know, it is even said in the Kabbalah that the Creator created planets that had too much judgment. And if there is too much judgment, the planet fails.

For example, what if every time you made a mistake in this third-dimensional world, you were punished and you died? You would never be able to progress in your reincarnation cycle, and you would never be able to evolve. A planet with too much judgment does not work, and we have seen that. We also have seen that a planet with loving kindness can balance the judgment, so you can have compassion; you can have forgiveness. These are all beautiful dimensional episodes, or characteristics.

But if a planet has too much loving kindness, then that can also destroy it. And I, Juliano, like to use the example of people who become terrorists on this planet. You cannot have loving kindness for them and say, "Oh, I understand why you are stuck. It's okay that you blow up people." You cannot have loving kindness all the time because loving kindness will not solve some of the evil that exists. There must be a balance.

Now, how do these two spheres apply to the planet? Well, I like to use the example of nuclear energies because we are continually talking about how dangerous nuclear energy is to the planet, how it harms Earth's aura, and how it destroys life in ways too numerous to explain in this short lecture. But if you just have loving kindness for nuclear energies and say, "Well, I understand why people must have nuclear energy. People need to have air conditioners," well, all that is true, but eventually, someone is going to have to say no. Someone is going to have to say, "This is going too far!" There are numerous examples on this planet. It is like destroying the forests: You can have loving kindness and say, "Yes, I understand why people are tearing down trees and habitats — because people need the wood." But if it goes too far, then there must be judgment.

Obviously, this planet is in a state close to a severe judgment — very close. And you see all of these reports about 2012 and the Mayan predictions. You see all these ideas about the end times. You can be assured that these prophets, including Nostradamus, the Maya, and many of the great rabbis, know that when things become out of balance too much, Earth will respond with judgment. Earth is close to doing this. That is what you are close to experiencing. The Tree of Life is showing that. But we are saying that with Biorelativity, with the spiritual power of forty, you can use your energy to create a better balance so that an end-time catastrophic judgment does not have to come to Earth.

Lago Puelo as the Foundation

I want to just speak briefly about Lago Puelo. That's because Lago Puelo was the place where the first etheric crystal downloaded. It is the basis, the foundation, for holding together all this fifth-dimensional healing energy that was brought down to Earth. You can see and feel that Lago Puelo is a perfect place for this etheric crystal and that it is a perfect place to hold the Earth's healing energies. The top of the Tree of Life is Mount Fuji. Mount Fuji perfectly represents undifferentiated light — the cosmic light that needs to be downloaded. It is an ancient energy.

So you are blessed, all of you, to be given this knowledge of the Tree of Life. We appreciate your flexibility in working with us to adapt and to transcend the Tree of Life into a Planetary Tree of Life to be used for planetary healing by you, the planetary healers, the Arcturian star-seeds. I'm Juliano. Good day.

Questions from the Class

Alessandra in Washington, DC: If Earth is responding with judgment with her material effects and all the damage that is being done to the environment, then is this because we are being too merciful? That is what I understood: She is balancing our mercy with her judgment.

Mordechai: No, you misunderstood. Juliano was saying that sometimes there is too much. In other words, as we say in Kabbalah, there is too much *Chesed*. There is too much loving kindness. What is loving kindness represented by? It is represented by water because water is the optimal sharing. In other words, when we spill water on the floor, it spreads and spreads until it evaporates, okay? So when you have too much loving kindness, when you have too much water, you have a tsunami — God forbid! So what Juliano was explaining was that without anything political, just being strictly spiritual, you have to have a balance. That is why there is a three-column system — because you need to balance *Chesed* with the strength and judgment of *Gevurah*.

As far as the direct answer as to why there is judgment for the planet, it is because the planet is now imbalanced. The feedback loop system cannot handle the intensity that is coming at it, and that system is usually self-sustaining and self-balancing.

Now there are large amounts of negativity, political range, power, and greed. The global industrial corporate system is trying to suck up so much oil and gas. You know, you have all this oil and gas. They are trying to get the thirteen trillion cubic meters of gas that were just discovered, but what people don't realize is that when you use that and you suck up the liquid from the inside of the planet, it creates empty space. It creates nothing but potential for future sinkholes and tsunamis! That is what can destroy the surface. This is simple physics. This is not anything metaphysical.

David: It is a complex answer, and I just want to add one more thing. Then we'll move on to the next question. It is structured versus unstructured and freedom versus control. When people are free to do whatever, as Mordechai said, this often leads to out-of-control greed. So if you emanate loving kindness and say, "Well, people can do whatever they want," then that works for a while. But after a while, it goes too far. So just having loving kindness is not a balance. Think of the Tree of Life as showing that there needs to be a balance.

I want to say one other thing about the Hebrew alphabet. The letters are very ancestral. *B*, the second letter, *Bet*, means "house." *Bet* is also the Hebrew word for "house." And *Gimmel*, which is the third letter, *G*, is also the Hebrew word for "camel." So you find that a lot of the letters are also words. Mordechai pointed out that *Shalom* contains the *Mem* and that letter also has a meaning. So this is a very unique alphabet, but of course another system of numbers was developed using Roman and Arabic numerals. The ancient Hebrews did not have the Arabic numbers, so they used the letters as the numbers. In some ways, this is kind of primitive, but in another way, it is great for gematria, which is the study of the numbers and their relationship to letters and words.

Pauline from England: I was wondering why Archangel Michael is in number three, which is the feminine grandmother energy. I am really interested in that.

Mordechai: Remember, the Arcturian Tree of Life is a manner of being able to relate to everybody. It took David and me years and years of study to understand what the Kabbalistic form was. So what we try to do is put the energy of Lake Moraine there, which happens to be Archangel Michael's energy. Michael is really everywhere. He is in charge. He is second only to Archangel Metatron. So we were trying to just put him toward the top of the tree so that we could better relate to him.

David: When you think of the feminine, don't forget that it also can be interacting with the masculine. Why would you put, for example, White Buffalo Calf Woman, who is a feminine energy, in a masculine part? The angels we designated can hold both masculine and feminine energies. They have both male and female traits. But I think that Archangel Michael, as Mordechai pointed out, to me represents understanding. Also, we placed the crystal in Lake Moraine, and it is well known that Lake Moraine holds the crystal for Archangel Michael.

Mordechai: As far as Lake Moraine and Archangel Michael are concerned, I must say that everything in Lake Moraine relates to healing. Lake Moraine is one of the healing capitals of energy.

All About *Aleph*

CLASS 2

MORDECHAI, DAVID, AND JULIANO

Mordechai: Today we are going to start from the bottom up — from Lago Puelo, *Sephirah* ten. I want you to imagine taking the whole page of the Tree of Life diagram and putting that whole page into the Lago Puelo circle, okay? That is how we are going to concentrate on that bottom sphere, which is called *Malchut*.

To really understand the Tree of Life, you have to understand that it is directly connected to the Torah. The Torah is a whole code. It is huge. It has lots of letters, words, and sentences, but the important thing is the letters. As I said before, the Hebrew letters are energy intelligences, and they are alive — if not more so than we are. To understand the Hebraic alphabet, we are going to start this class with the first letter of the Hebrew alphabet, which is *Aleph*.

Aleph, along with every Hebrew letter, is categorized as a sight, sound, and number. Now, sight has three categories under it: worlds, souls, and divinity. From sight, which we would call form, there are categories of worlds, souls, and divinity. In the sound or name, there are also categories of worlds, souls, and divinity. And number has its levels of worlds, souls, and divinity too. So let's see how far we can get!

The Sight of *Aleph*

Aleph, as far as its sight, is formed by a *Yud* on top and a *Vav* slanted down in between with the letter *Yud* on the bottom. The two *Yuds* represent the waters — as the *Elohim* flew over the waters. There are upper waters, and there are lower waters. We are going to keep it simple. The upper waters connect with what we would consider the upper atmosphere and the electromagnetic waves, and the lower waters are the waters we have here on Earth: the oceans, the subterranean waters, and so on.

Now, the *Vav* is slanted in between, and it basically separates us from the fifth dimension. You can count the top *Yud* as the fifth dimension, the bottom *Yud* as the third dimension, and the *Vav* as in between. It is important to understand that this is a paradox because we are not connected to the fifth dimension, yet we *are* connected to the fifth dimension. This is where the paradox comes in: a simultaneous connection. So we're starting with the sight, and we are going to the world. I have given you the world definition.

Now, as far as the soul's definition, it is the same thing: Our soul is down here in the lower aspect of what we call in Hebrew the *Nefesh* of the soul, because we have three levels of the soul. Everything is in threes. It's important to understand this; that is why three is such a beautiful number. We have the souls, and then we have the level of divinity. Basically speaking, it all relates to bringing fifth-dimensional energy into the third dimension.

The Sound of *Aleph*

Now, as to the sound of the *Aleph*, it has many meanings. It means "oxen," and with a change in the value of the letter, it is 1,000. It means teaching, and the head of a country, or the master, is called *Aluph*. So *Aleph* is always number one as far as the sound. The oxen represent physical reality or the lower animal soul of the *Nefesh* that is in the blood. The sound is in the multiplicity in creation. You can count it: 1 or 10 to the third power.

The Gematria of *Aleph*

The level of divinity is one. There is one master of the universe. This is an important fact. We first are going into the best part of it, which is its number, the number 1. Everything starts from number 1. You can't go anywhere without the number 1. It is said in the Zohar that the divine said to the letter *Aleph*, "My unity shall not be expressed except through thee. On thee shall be based all calculations and operations of the world." And unity shall not be expressed, save by the letter *Aleph*.

Now, what does it mean that all calculations and operations relate to and need the number 1, the *Aleph*? Well, for those of us who live with computers, the whole base of the computer is 0 and 1. Without the 1, there are no computers and there is no communication, which is another important point.

The second point is that one means unity, which is the secret to the ascension. Everybody wants to ascend. Everybody wants to get to that ladder and ascend. So we need to unify within ourselves and with every one of our fellow starseeds, no matter their race, creed, color, language, or whatever else. We are all starseed brothers and sisters. That is a decent challenge. We are unity. The unity is everything.

The word "one" in Hebrew is *Echad*, *Aleph-Chet-Dalet*. The total sacred gematria of these letters, this word, is 13. Of course, in physicality, we immediately think 13 is very bad. We have Friday the 13th, for example. But know that 13 is important. Why? Because there are three words in the Hebrew language that equal the number 13. One is *Echad*, or unity. The second word, *Ahava*, means love and is equal to 13. *Da'aga* means caring for the next human being.

That is a big point, because what is going to get us to the ascension? It is unity, self-nullification, and treating the next human being with human dignity. That is the secret to the ascension. We got right to the point, but working forward is another story. In any case, we have basically completed the *Aleph* in its form, name, and number.

Aleph and the Tenth *Sephirah*

Now, these energy level intelligences (all twenty-two letters of the Hebrew alphabet, plus the five final letters) came before the Creator, in reverse order, to try to compete to be the first letter in the Torah. When it was time for *Aleph* to come up, she (because this letter is female energy) said, "Why should I come up? You have turned everybody else down; you have already made your decision: The letter *Bet* is to be the first letter in the Torah."

The Creator said, "Well, by saying that, you have self-nullified yourself, and you have not been able to raise the water. Because of that, you are going to be the first letter in the Ten Commandments, or as they say in Hebrew, the *Aseret HaDibrot*, the ten utterances."

They were utterances and not commandments because the utterances were a vibration. Those ten were holographic living images. That is why they saw voices and heard colors.

The letter *Aleph* means so much that it needs a ninety-minute lecture to properly cover it, but I will try to keep it short and to the fact.

Without the Zohar, we really can't understand the Torah because it is completely coded. Since we are sort of at the bottom level of the bottom sphere, of the Tree of Life, things here are a little bit tougher or less comforting than they are in the other *Sephirot*. That's because in this particular sphere, we have an inclination. Actually, we have a positive inclination and a negative inclination: the tree of knowledge of good and evil.

What we must understand is equal polarity. When you have a positive polarity, the cosmic rule states that you need an equal amount of its opposite to balance out the energy. However, the number 1 is the tiebreaker.

If we can understand that, we can follow what they call *Mitzvoth*, which in Hebrew means "good deeds." The whole purpose of this incarnation is for us to do good deeds for no reason. Or if there is a reason, it is to care for the next person. And in the near future, we will be pushed to care for the next person.

That is why I have so much respect for nurses, caregivers, and people who spend their lives sharing their energy with people who need it. It is a big plus "upstairs" — a very big plus. Our souls love us for it!

There is a substantiation of the *Aleph* from the Zohar, and it has been misused and abused in these past few centuries. Basically, the Virgin of Israel, the *Shekhinah*, has fallen, and it is thought she will rise no more. People have taken the literal meaning of the English translation. What else can they do if they don't understand Hebrew?

The real important factor is that in order for her to rise, the first move has to come from "upstairs." Then she will rise because it is a covenant. It is a commitment by the divine essence that the *Shekhinah* will rise.

* * *

Start with a Foundation

David: We are talking about the bottom *Sephirah*, which is represented by Lago Puelo and refers to energetically manifesting higher energy on Earth. What we manifest in the Tree of Life is all of the energies that are on the top. That includes Mount Fuji, Bodensee, Lake Moraine, Istanbul, Mount Shasta, Volcán Poás, Montserrat, Grose Valley, Lake Taupo, Barrancas del Cobre, and Serra da Bocaina. All of those energies become manifested in the bottom of the tree.

One of the key teachings in the Tree of Life is that what you see on the bottom, where we are, is a result of the manifestation of everything on top. So there is a huge energetic flow on top that has brought us down into the basic, or bottom, sphere, which we call the tenth *Sephirah*, or Lago Puelo. Mordechai used the term *Malchut*, which is the Hebrew word for "kingdom." Where we are now is the kingdom, and this is the manifestation of everything that is above us.

The other thing I want to talk about is the idea of the letters. Remember, we talked about the alphabet? The word "alphabet" is derived from Hebrew — from the first two letters of the Hebrew alphabet, which are *Aleph* and *Bet*. So *Aleph-Bet* means "the alphabet."

Now, in the concepts that we are talking about in the Kabbalah, the words create the energy. In the Old Testament (Genesis 1:14, KJB), and in the Torah, it states, "And God said, 'Let there be light.'" When he uttered those words, literally, the sounds and the vibrations of the utterances created the world. I use this example because in the New Testament, there are many examples where Lord Sananda says, "Let there be healing," or "Let him be healed."

There are different levels of healing. There's the hands-on healing where you touch somebody. There is the traditional medicine form of healing, which often focuses on giving people medicine. But the highest level of healing, in my opinion, is speaking the words "let there be healing." Then there will be healing. In other words, the energy of the healer is at such a high vibration that saying the healing word — or words — can create the energetic vibration for a healing.

This is profound. Imagine that when God said, "Let there be light," there was light, and then the world was created. He did that just by speaking the words.

So in the Kabbalah, the Hebrew letters are powerful because the letters are the foundations of the words. The Hebrew language is powerful because it was believed that God spoke the words "let there be light" in Hebrew. I want to point out that the two most sacred languages with strong vibrational energy on Earth are Sanskrit and Hebrew.

Drawing the *Aleph*

Now I'm going to describe to you how to draw the letter *Aleph*. Take your pen and make a diagonal line from the top left to the bottom right of the page. Then from the bottom right, go up approximately a quarter of the diagonal line and draw a vertical line upward. And then from the top left, go a quarter of the way down the diagonal, and draw a vertical line down. There you have the letter *Aleph*.

Just in case someone needs me to describe it one more time: Draw a diagonal line from the top of the page to the bottom. On the bottom right of the diagonal, come up a quarter of the way of the diagonal, then from that point, go up as a vertical line — straight up. Now, do the same thing for the other side, only going down. There are other ways of writing it, but this gives you an idea.

A Closer Look at Some Hebrew Words

When we talked about souls, Mordechai mentioned the word *Nefesh*. *Nefesh* is the first level of the three parts of the soul that we experience here on Earth. That is the life force, sometimes referred to as the animal energy, in the first level, but *Nefesh* also means "breath" in Hebrew.

I want to reiterate that the Zohar is a mystical text written either in the second century or third century AD. It is a mystical explanation of the Torah, and it is this mystical explanation that is the basis of the Kabbalah. The word "Zohar" means "brilliant light," and the book contains the basis for much of the teachings about the Tree of Life.

Another word Mordechai used was the word "one" in Hebrew, which is *Echad*. He also used the term "self-nullification." This is a fancy word that means one is nullifying or removing the ego — removing the desire.

One way to receive all the energies is by first focusing on the bottom sphere. We refer to this bottom sphere as Lago Puelo, which is on the bottom of the Tree of Life. One way to receive all the energy is to first empty yourself. The word "Kabbalah" means "to receive" in Hebrew, so if you can nullify your ego and thus empty yourself, then you can receive.

It is on the bottom, at Lago Puelo, where we want to receive all the higher energies, and then we also want to manifest them. But in order to receive all the higher energies, we have to empty ourselves. Now, it is interesting that the Arcturians chose Lago Puelo for the bottom sphere: because it is a huge lake. It is also near Patagonia. We visited Lago Puelo on our journey to Argentina. It is sacred, very beautiful, and has fresh energy there.

I want to explain another word Mordechai used: *Mitzvoth*. It means "good deeds" and comes from the Hebrew word for "commandments," which is *Mitzvah*. I'm sure everybody knows the term *Bar Mitzvah*, which means "commandment and good deeds." In talking about the ascension, we talk about removing or "burning off" karma because that is one of the big issues in the ascension. One great way of burning off karma is doing good deeds, or *Mitzvahs*. Ascension means that we want to complete all our lessons, and in order to complete them, we have to be manifest service from the bottom *Sephirah*.

Being here on Earth, in the tenth *Sephirah*, is a way for us to burn off any karma. One of the highest ways in the mystical teachings to do that is through service — through good deeds. There are different levels of good deeds, but the highest level is when you do the good deed anonymously. You do it with no anticipation of receiving any benefit. Examples of people who have done that are Mother Mary and Mother Teresa, the famous nun living in India. These are examples of people who devoted their lives to doing *Mitzvoth* — good deeds.

I know when people think about the ascension, they always think about it in a complex way, and they think about resolving all their personal issues. It is good that we do that, but I also want you to understand that the Kabbalah teaches that the simplest and easiest method for burning off karma is *Mitzvoth* — the doing of good deeds.

So we look at Lago Puelo, and we see that we have a *Sephirah* above it that signifies the third-dimensional Earth interacting with the fifth dimension. This concept of interacting with the third and fifth dimensions is a new addition. The Tree of Life from the Kabbalah does talk about higher dimensions, but it does not categorize them in the way we do on this chart as the third and fifth dimensions intersecting. But here we are, talking about Earth directly interacting with the third and fifth dimensions, and that sphere of Serra da Bocaina is helping us represent that process.

So this is an additional sphere, an interacting sphere, that represents a concept the Arcturians have talked about for a long time: the intersection of the dimensions. Earth is coming closer to an intersection with the fifth dimension, and the actual intersection is the moment of the ascension. So it is good to be on Earth. It is good to be in *Malchut*. It is good to be in Lago Puelo, and Lago Puelo is holding all of these diverse foundational energies.

✳ ✳ ✳

The Gematria of *Aleph*

Mordechai: The number 1, as far as the number of the letter *Aleph*, is spelled like David says: *Aleph-Lamed-Pey*. Its total gematria, or sacred gematria, is 111. For those of us (who have seen many times in our lives) when we look at the clock and it reads 1:11 or 11:11, we think, "Ah, it must be that the number 11 is a good sign. It is an important number." So 11, 22, and 33 are all wonderful combinations of numbers; they are very good. But in this case, it is 1, 1, and 1.

It is 1 for each column of the Tree of Life. It is unity and love in the right column, in the left column, and in the central column. There is no doubt about it: The letters spelled out are 111. That is why many of us who have seen that number throughout our lives are reminded to connect to love and unity. That really is the secret of that connection.

David was talking about how "Kabbalah" means "to receive." The real understanding of Kabbalah and the Zohar is that these texts are trying to show us or teach us how to receive. How do we receive when we come into this world? We want everything, and we want it now. That is our nature. It is true, and it is an amazing thing, but that is what we call the desire to receive for the self alone. We want immediate gratification. We have a tremendous desire to receive for the self alone. The desire to receive for the self alone was placed along with the spark in each of the starseeds.

The catch is how you deal with it. Do you receive for the self alone, storing things and feeling afraid you are not going to have enough? Or do you desire to receive for the sake of imparting? That is the real secret. It is just the life force energy. You can't get life force energy unless you share what you have, because if not, there is no room for the light to come in.

The desire to receive, to share, is important. That's why they call it flow. In the world of money, they call it cash flow or currency. Why? Because it was originally created so we could serve other people — not take millions, billions, and trillions of dollars and stuff it somewhere. That doesn't work. If you don't use it for the light, the light will take it away. This happens 100 percent of the time.

Now, Archangel Michael's number from his name (as Angel Michael) in gematria is 101. Why 101 and not 100? There are no accidents and no coincidences. It is 101 because you have to go that extra mile. The number 100 is completion, but 101 shows the desire to go the extra mile. For example, going an extra mile to Argentina for the workshop is really super because I came to really love Lago Puelo once I understood what it really represents.

It is the first crystal that was downloaded, and I found out it is actually self-sustaining. It doesn't get weak; it gets energy whether or not we give energy to it. But when we give energy to Lago Puelo, that gives it a boost because it fits with all the other crystals. It gets a superboost. Whatever it gets from us, it gives away. The crystal really represents the desire to receive for the sake of imparting. It flows; its current just flows right through the waters in the lake and goes directly to the other eleven crystals.

It's important to understand this because it is all about give and take, up and down — like a diaphragm. In and out, like the lungs. Back and forth, like the waves, like the tide.

Here's something I didn't bring up about the letter *Aleph*: It represents some interesting parts of our bodies. It actually represents the respiratory system, the diaphragm, and the digestive system. Being that it is one, and one is really water, you see the shape of the letter is separating the upper male waters from the lower female waters. When those waters come together, we will know it. Believe me, we are going to know it. It also represents the water in the skull, the membrane, and the brain moisture. This is all related to the letter *Aleph*.

The Sound of *Aleph*

At the level of the name, it teaches you wisdom. I will teach you wisdom, for the root of your soul is derived from the wisdom of the Creator. What is wisdom? We start with the number 1, because without it, you can't go anywhere. So what is coming from the bottom up? From the bottom up, we have information. What we are receiving now is information.

Then you can turn it and go straight up the ladder to the central column beyond the curtain and go to knowledge. Relate to the information, and it becomes knowledge. What is knowledge? Knowledge is metaphysics, or as we will call it, telepathy. We will call it meditation and connection, because Vywamus, the fifth-dimensional spirit guide, said (and he said it very well), "With the connection, it jumps." It jumps from the hidden knowledge of *Da'at*. Then you go to understanding, because understanding is the connection. It is as simple as that. You have the connection, and then you get the understanding.

Once you have the understanding, then you can live it, and you can turn it into living life at its highest spiritual level. What is that one word? Wisdom. Anyone who really tries to get to that level of wisdom knows certain great basics of life. We shouldn't gossip about people, because we don't realize that speaking those words is an addiction. We are going to talk more about that in other classes, but I just want to plant that seed right now.

It is very important when you have the number 1 and you are only one person. You can't talk to anybody, so you can't gossip, but what you can do is to try to reach the person through your mind — through meditation. When people say, "God spoke, 'Let there be light,' and there was light," was God speaking? God doesn't speak. But the divine essence, our Creator, has a will, and we are the evidence of his will, as well as all of the core, the *Kadosh, Kadosh, Kadosh, Adonai Tzevaoth*.

The *Tzevaoth*, all those angels — the hierarchy and the "lowerarchy" and whatever-archy — they are all serving the Creator. The whole purpose, as I said, when we help somebody else, is more important than we are. It is all about service, whether it's Michael, the Lord Sananda, or Lord Metatron speaking. They are all speaking the same language: service from the heart with no judgment!

You must understand that when the Creator spoke to the letter *Aleph*, He was addressing female energy. I bring this up because the number 1 is female energy, and the fact is that when it gets lifted, the Creator is going to come down and lift the letter *Aleph*, along with the *Shekhinah*. Everything will be lifted back up to where it came from. There is one thing that all the great sages, all the great rabbis, and everyone says about the reason for this creation: It was that God's children, the *B'nai Yisrael*, or what we call the galactic starseeds, will go back to the light of their Creator. How do you go back to the light of the Creator? That is another class.

✳ ✳ ✳

Visualizing the Crystal in Lago Puelo

Shalom, Shalom, Shalom. Greetings. I'm **Juliano**. We are the Arcturians. We have been working with you on understanding this beautiful galactic diagram called the Tree of Life. We have shifted the energies and explanations so that you can use the Tree of Life as a planetary healing force. Our goal with you is to begin to activate the Tree of Life energy for planetary healing.

A project such as a planetary healing group is a huge effort. To accomplish something of this magnitude, you must have a solid foundation. From our perspective, the foundation of all the energies and all of the understandings of the planetary healing begins with Lago Puelo. It begins with the downloading of the first etheric crystal from the Arcturian crystal lake.

For a moment, visualize with me the fifth-dimensional lake that is the Arcturian crystal lake. It is a lake of one mile in diameter. There is a huge dome around the lake, and there are 1,600 Arcturian starseeds in their etheric fifth-dimensional soul bodies sitting around the lake.

You can see that your multidimensional body is at that lake. And as you are visualizing that lake, feel that you are there. You are sitting around the lake, and you see this beautiful crystal. It is a mile wide. The crystal slowly rises out of the water. You know how powerful crystals are on Earth. Can you visualize, can you imagine, or can you even perceive the power of a fifth-dimensional crystal that is so huge?

We are talking about receiving. Sometimes in receiving, the energy voltage is too high for you to receive, and it must be stepped down. So when we bring the etheric crystal up, we are only bringing a portion of the crystal out of the water, and you can receive its energy comfortably. But for this exercise, I'm going to mute the crystal. I'm going to attenuate the energy of it so that the entire crystal is now out of the water and you can interact with it.

Many years ago, we — with the Group of Forty — created an etheric double of this crystal. Then we sent the etheric double to the beautiful lake at Lago Puelo. And there, with more than 300 starseeds present, we received this etheric crystal and downloaded it directly into Lago Puelo.

Now visualize this event that happened many years ago, and see immediately an etheric double being created again. See the energy of the etheric double travel from the fifth dimension to Argentina, to Lago Puelo. There it is downloaded by hundreds of starseeds. This etheric crystal then becomes the foundation for holding all the Arcturian energies for healing Earth.

You can understand the primary sphere serving two purposes: (1) receiving all the energies from the higher levels and (2) providing a solid foundation for the interaction of higher levels with the lower levels. You cannot work with higher energy unless you have a solid foundation. This is one of the basic teachings of the Tree of Life: We must implant a solid foundation on this planet.

We must implant a solid foundation of starseeds who are able to teach and understand that Earth is a living spirit and that we can interact with it. We can help you to shape the weather. We can help you to shape volcanos, and we can help you to shape how this planet is interacting with the many cosmic and Earth forces. But this can only be done with a strong foundation. That strong foundation will help you bring down the fifth-dimensional light, because if the foundation is not strong enough, then Earth will not be able to hold the light.

So now the crystal in the crystal lake has descended into the water. You have briefly visited the Arcturian crystal lake with me. You felt the fifth-dimensional power of that. You can now return to your physical body and to the physical energy of the first sphere. I'm Juliano. Good day.

* * *

Questions from the Class

Olga: When you talk about Aleph, *it is connected with the respiratory system, the brain and water, and to other parts of the body. Is that correct?*

Mordechai: Yes — the respiratory system, the diaphragm (which actually provides the power of the respiratory system), and the digestive system. The water is the skull water, the water that surrounds the brain, the membrane of the brain, and the brain moisture. Those three things represent the number 1.

The most important thing I wanted to say that relates to the tenth *Sephirah* at Lago Puelo is that it represents the number 1, which symbolizes the meaning of unity, love, caring, and concern. It all relates to *Ima Adama*, which is Mother Earth in Hebrew. The whole point of number 1 of the three, of the number 111, is the three connections between the top and the bottom of love, unity, and caring.

Participant: Mordechai, the brain fluid is called cerebrospinal fluid.

Mordechai: Yes, thank you.

Lesley from Oregon: Kezia and I have done something with integrating energy back into your energy field and the importance of that. I'm thinking it relates to bringing a liquid light to the energy field, which is another way of forming a greater foundations to be more effective as an individual starseed. I wanted to encourage people to also pursue that as a way of strengthening their foundation, their energy boundaries, and their ability to use more light efficiently on the third dimension, the light that comes from the fifth dimension when you bring it into a perfect alignment.

Kinico from Reno: *I constantly see 11, 11:11, 22, 33 — you know, all these doubles and triples. What is the significance? I heard you explaining some of that, but it appears often.*

Mordechai: Basically, it's a connection that you have. It is a reminder that you put into your own screenplay, a reminder that you are connected. What you need is the certainty to know that you are connected. I used to see these numbers all the time. I couldn't understand; I was trying to think, "What is this thing of 1 and 11?" Then I realized from my study of the Zohar and Kabbalah and the three-column system that it all fits in.

Most important is the word "balance," because you have the three ones; they are balanced. When you do healing, the most important thing is to know the vibration of *El Na Refa Na La* (a special Hebrew healing chant that means, "Please God, heal her now"). You could say that this is showing all the connections to those energy intelligences of the letters.

The most important thing is to really release everything you have and just come from the heart. If everybody did that, there wouldn't be any doctors or hospitals. It is unfortunate that doubt is always coming into the picture. But understand the power of the words, the power of the Hebrew letters working. And remember, these are galactic letters. This has nothing to do with religion at all, no matter what everybody tries to promote. The point is the galactic connection. These letters come directly from the Central Sun, if not from even higher levels than that.

David: *El Na Refa Na La* is a special healing chant in the Kabbalah. We will be working with that in future lectures. When you say that chant, a great healing energy and force can come into your energy field and can be directed at another person. Remember that we talked before about the letters in the beginning, and I said, "Well, Jesus said, 'Let there be healing,' and there was healing." I guess it was Miriam, Moses's sister, who had leprosy. He looked at her and said, *"El Na Refa Na La"* — "Let there be healing to her now" — and then her leprosy was cured. Is that correct, Mordechai?

Mordechai: It's as simple as that. You have to understand why she got that leprosy. Leprosy is an imbalance created by what they call *Lashon Hara*, which, to make it simple, is translated as "gossip." What Miriam said to her brother was, "What are you doing trying to marry this woman, this Ethiopian woman?" And Moses's brother Aaron and Miriam sort of tried to have a family council with Moses. Now, because she and Aaron spoke that, that was how they got the disease of what today would be called eczema or psoriasis, but it was on a much higher level than that.

Cora: This biofeedback loop of Earth that you are speaking to us about also concerns water. In the past years, there have been floods; there have been tsunamis. We have had water, water, water. So is Earth saying, "Look at number one; let's get down to the foundation. What are you doing here, people?" Is that the message? To get back to number one?

David: I was meditating this morning about the imbalances, and I thought about the flood in the Old Testament, the Great Flood. So in some ways, that is what you are saying. But remember, we are talking about this as a warning. Earth is saying, "Okay, I could cleanse. I could cure. I could purify all of these if I rebalance."

Bet and the *Ana B'Koach*

CLASS 3

MORDECHAI, DAVID, AND ARCHANGEL MICHAEL

Mordechai: This class actually is about the letter *Bet*, which is an important letter. More than 1,500 books have been written about the letter *Bet* and the word *Bereshit* (beginning). So we're going to squeeze it all into fifteen minutes. But have no fear. It is all wonderful.

Introducing the *Ana B'Koach*
We decided to represent the letter *Bet* and relate it to the *Ana B'Koach* meditation (a Kabbalistic prayer used for spiritual power) because it starts with the *Aleph-Bet*, or alphabet. This is *Ana B'Koach* in English:

> We beg you with the strength of your right hand's greatness,
> untie the bundled sins. Accept the prayer of your people,
> strengthen us, purify us, oh awesome one. Please, oh strong one,
> guard like the pupil of an eye those who foster your oneness.
> Bless them. Purify them. Show them pity.
> May your righteousness always repay them.
> Powerful Holy One, with your abundant goodness, guide your
>   people.
> One and only exalted one, turn to your people who proclaim your
>   holiness.
> Accept our entreaty and hear our cry, you who know all mysteries!
> Blessed is the name of this glorious kingdom for all eternity.

And in Hebrew:

Ana B'Koach Gedulat Yeminecha Tatir Tzerura.
Kabel Rinat Amecha Sagvena Taharenu Nora.
Na Gibbur Dorshei Yechudcha Kivavat Shamreim.
Barchaim Tacharaim Rahamei Tzedkatech. Tamid Gamlaim.
Chasin Kadosh B'rov Tuv-Cha Nahail Adatecha.
Yachid Ge-Eh L'amcha Pinei Zochrei Kedushatecha.
Shavatenu Kabel U'shma Tza'akatenu Yodaya Ta'alumot.
Baruch Shem Kavod, Malchuto L'olam Va'ed.[1]

As a matter of fact, it says in the book *Sefer Yetzirah* (the Book of Creation, the earliest text on Kabbalah, written by Abraham 4,000 years ago) that the letters of the *Aleph-Bet* are like stones. The *Bet* represents the house, so a word is built of letters, as a house is built of stones. Each whole word is like a house, so a word is built of letters — as a house is built of stones. This is really important.

We must also look at the foundational number of seven. Sevens show up continually: the seven days of the week, the seven *Sephirot*, the seven colors, the seven verses of the *Ana B'Koach* prayer, and so on. The *Ana B'Koach* is a meditation, and we're going to go through this meditation slowly and nicely.

The *Ana B'Koach* in Hebrew contains the first forty-two letters of the Book of Genesis, and that means it also contains the first forty-two letters of the Torah. These are very powerful letters. Basically speaking, there are secrets in these letters that can be used for meditation. As a matter of fact, in the second paragraph, the combination of the words *Ana B'Koach* is hidden in the first forty-two letters. The letters are translated using a secret Kabbalistic calculation. What we are going to learn in this session are those secret Kabbalistic calculations and the reasons why you see the calculations as they are. We're going to start now.

I ask you all to open your minds, open your hearts, and close your eyes, but leave the third eye wide open. We're going to do this slowly so that everybody can say it along with me. We will say two words at a time, because every two words represent a set of angel wings. We really must understand that the first two words are the top two wings, and the next two words cover the body. The first two words represent the space from the top of the chest to the top of the head. The next two words represent the second set of wings, with which the angel covers his or her body, and with the third set of wings, the angel is covered from the knees down to the feet.

Now we're going to start the meditation with the first seven *Sephirot* in the Tree of Life, beginning with *Chesed*, the first *Sephirah* under the curtain.

We will say it slowly, two words at a time:

Ana B'Koach. Gedulat Yeminecha. Tatir Tzerura.

Aleph-Bet-Gimmel, Yud-Tav-Tzadi (equals 506), and (*Vav-Shin-Resh* = 506).

The sacred gematria of these letters equals *Ahavat Chinam* — unconditional love. We are all one soul. We have another *Bet*, which is the *Beit Hamikdosh*, in Jerusalem. All are included. We are one soul there at the Dome of the Rock.[2] We are all together at the stone itself — not just the Dome of the Rock, but at the foundation stone itself. We also are one with Joseph the Righteous, where he is buried in Shechem. Joseph actually represents *Parnassah* (sustenance — what we need, not what we want) and everything good that comes into this world.

The second line of the prayer represents the *Sephirah* of *Gevurah*:

Kabel Rinat. Amecha Sagvena. Taharenu Nora.

Kuf-Resh-Ayin, Sin-Tet-Nun. When sounded out, these letters say, "*K'ra Satan*." That is the reason why in Kabbalah they say we are "tearing at the Satan," or the negative inclination, by not reacting to things that happen to us. *K'ra* is the expression of tearing.

How do you tear at the negative inclination? With the number one word in the Kabbalah, which is "restriction." We must understand that we must restrict before we do anything. The letters permuted or rearranged another way express *Sha'ar Katan*. In English, this would mean "small gates." We are closing all the small gates, which we have created through our reactivity — that which we didn't mean, such as when we tell a little white lie. We are closing all of these small gates that we have created, and we are putting them in a basket and sending them down the river to give them back to the divine essence.

The sacred gematria of this combination of letters is equal to the word *Tishkach*, which means "to forget." And we must forget two things: doubt and limitation. These are the two most important things we need to forget. We must make it so that they don't even exist — limitation and doubt.

Now, we go to a *Sephirah* in the central column: *Tiferet*. And the prayer continues:

Na Gibbur. Dorshei Yechudcha. Kivavat Shamreim.

Nun-Gimmel-Dalet. The gematria of the first three letters is 57, which represents the Hebrew word *Zan* (spelled *Zayin-Nun*). *Zayin* is 7 and the *Nun* is 50, which together equals 57. *Zan* means *Parnassah*, which is sustenance.

Sustenance is not something that we want. When we use the word "sustenance," people think of dollar signs right away. No, sustenance is not what we want; sustenance is what we need — for the expansion of our souls, the whole purpose of our being here.

The Sacred Gematria of 57

Now, we are going to check out other words that equal the same sacred gematria of 57. The first word is *Maggid* — one who speaks with angels. There were very few *Maggids* in history, but today among us, the starseeds and everyone who is connected here, there is a connection. As starseeds, we really must understand that the word *Maggid* is used to describe everyone who connects to angels.

Now, if you switch those letters around, keeping the gematria of 57, you get *Dagim*, which means "fish." Usually, they say the word for fish is *Dag*, but that's singular. Like we say, whether there is one fish or there are one hundred fish, it's still fish. *Dagim* means "all the fish in the entire Mother Earth." All the fish swimming in the Blue Jewel are *Dagim*. This is very important. Why? Because it is believed that everything under water has no negative inclination. Yes, there is survival. When they get hungry, they do whatever they do, but as far as we have to go through with the negative inclination, there is no evil eye or negative inclination under the water. That's why the eye of the fish is such a cleansing, purifying eye.

Another word that equals 57 is *Mizbayach*, which is an altar. Most of us don't know it, but our own dining room or kitchen table can be used as an altar. If we use it right, we can do some amazing things with it! That would be a whole other three-hour lecture, but it's important because using the *Mizbayach* relates to the expansion of the soul.

Another word that equals 57 is *Bitul*, which means "self-nullification." It's dropping the ego as best we can. As a matter of fact, *Bitul* actually means "complete self-nullification." It's difficult to do in this world, but this power is found in the central column of the Tree of Life, which in Kabbalah includes the spirit guides Joseph, Jacob, Sananda, and Metatron. All those entities are included in this *Sephirah*. Also,

Nun-Gimmel-Dalet spelled out in Hebrew actually means *Neged* or "against" — against all injustice, against all lies, and against all negativity that we have to deal with in this mundane, dense, lower-energy existence. That's *Nun-Gimmel-Dalet*, the first three letters *Na Gibbar Dorshei*.

Back to the *Ana B'Koach*
Na Gibbar. Dorschei Yechudcha. Kivaat Shamreim.

The second three letters, *Yud-Kaph-Shin*, are even more powerful. *Yud-Kaph-Shin* actually is what Moses did with an Egyptian. He looked at the Egyptian, those people who know, *Ko V'cho*. Moses saw there was nothing in this Egyptian that could be positive energy at all in future lives or anything he could produce in this lifetime. He looked at the Egyptian with these three letters, *Yud-Kaph-Shin*, and basically there was nothing left. The Egyptian completely dissolved, dissipated, and there was nothing left but his clothes. Moses just kicked some sand over his clothes, and that was it. *Nun-Gimmel-Dalet, Yud-Kaph-Shin* — this is represented in *Tiferet*, the first central-column energy under the curtain in the Tree of Life, which is also contained in this meditation and prayer.

The next line refers to the sphere of *Netzach*.
Barchaim Tacharaim. Rahamei Tzedkatecha. Tamid Gamlaim.
Bet-Tet-Resh, Tzadik-Tav-Gimmel.

Netzach is the second sphere of the right column, below the curtain the top level of what we'll simply call immortality, or fifth-dimensional existence — victory into immortality.

The next line refers to the sphere of *Hod*:
Chasin Kadosh. B'rov Tuvcha. Nahail Adatecha.
Chet-Kuf-Bet. There again is the *Bet-Tet-Nun-Ayin*. This is the last *Sephirah* in the left column before *Yesod*, so this is the real lower manifestation of immortality coming toward us.

We'll go right to the sixth line, which refers to *Yesod*:
Yachid Ge-Eh. L'amcha Pinei. Zochrei Kedushatecha.
Yud-Gimmel-Lamed, Pey-Zayin-Kuf.

We'll go to the seventh line because of time:
Shavatenu Kabel. U'shma Tza'akatenu. Yodaya Ta'alumot.
Shin-Kuf-Vav, Tzadi-Yud-Tav.

This is *Malchut*. This is where we are. This is the seventh. It's all about the seven lines, the seven days of the week, and most of all, the seventh day of the month of Leo. The month of Leo in Hebrew is *Ab*. *Aleph-Bet* is how you spell the month of Leo. *Ab* means father. We are connecting to all the patriarchs and all of the intergalactic fifth-dimensional guides, teachers, and our own higher selves.

We say the last line quietly, even silently:

Baruch Shem Kavod, Malchuto L'olam Va'ed.

This manifests everything in this third-dimensional world. Amen. Thank you.

* * *

A Brief Review of the Tree of Life

David: I want to review a couple of things. So we are looking at the Planetary Tree of Life and the fact that the Planetary Tree of Life is based on the Kabbalistic Tree of Life, but the Arcturians have added two *Sephirot*. This Planetary Tree of Life is meant to help and monitor the healing of our planet.

In the idea of the Tree of Life, there are some unbalanced energies that need to be balanced. The Tree of Life is based on three columns. There is the male, the female, and then the center column, which tries to balance the left and the right (male and female). Each circle, or sphere, is called in Hebrew a *Sephirah*.

When we look at the *Sephirah*, we are talking about actual energy that is coming down from the highest source. It is our belief in working with the Tree of Life that each *Sephirah* is like a transformer. That means that the energy that is coming down is so powerful that it needs to be transformed into a lower energy with which we can work. For example, when you look at the world, you can look at it in terms of different subatomic particles and different minute energies, but if you stay on that level, you can't function because you would just be in total awe of everything.

When Mordechai talks about loving kindness, he uses the word *Chesed*. That is an energy we can use for many different purposes, but there is also the counter energy of restriction, the energy through which we use things like judgment and different ways of containing things so that they don't get out of balance.

So in the Planetary Tree of Life, when things are getting out of balance, we ask if that means there is too much loving kindness. Is there is too much freedom? Then there needs to be some kind of restriction. If there is too much pollution in the air, then there need to be restrictions so people don't put in as much pollution. This is all based on looking at the planet as a whole and seeing if there is a way to bring it back into balance.

Now, the Arcturians have designated certain etheric crystals to correspond to certain special places on this planet that represent each etheric crystal. They have then also referred to those places by correlating a *Sephirah* with each energy configuration represented by each etheric crystal.

The second point I want to make is that you have heard me talk about the Sacred Triangle. The Sacred Triangle is a paradigm for an energy unity, a spiritual unity on the planet. The idea of the Sacred Triangle is that we can unify the mystical traditions, which include all religious mystical traditions on this planet: Christianity, Judaism, Hinduism, Islam, and more. The mystical traditions also would be united with the Native Americans, but the Native Americans have been given a separate part in the Sacred Triangle. We know that the Native Americans use prayers to talk to Earth, and they also have special Earth ceremonies.

Examining the *Ana B'Koach*

This particular prayer that Mordechai has chosen for us to look at, *Ana B'Koach*, is a very famous Hebrew prayer. This prayer has mystical power. There are several ways to look at mystical prayers. Many of you have worked with me before, and you have worked with me on the concept of healing words. There is energy in words, and if we use certain words, like "please heal" or "receive the healing light," then saying those words with the right intention can produce special healing energy. Remember there are at least two so-called sacred languages on this planet: Sanskrit and Hebrew.

In Sanskrit, we know the word "Om," for example, and everybody hears that word. Even if you don't know what the word means, it can affect you if you are enunciating it in the right way. So *Ana B'Koach* has certain sounds and a certain energy. Even if you don't understand what the actual Hebrew words mean, the sound of the prayer can set off a mystical energy.

There is another mystical Hebrew chant: *El Na Refa Na La*, which means "please God, heal her now." I was healing someone recently, and I just said the words with intention. I chanted them. She immediately felt the healing energy a lot differently.

This prayer, *Ana B'Koach*, has that kind of energy. What I want to do is read the prayer in English. Now, the prayer has a great deal of references to God Almighty, and I know everyone has different views on religion, but instead of worrying about that, let's just listen to the words. We can put in "the Creator." The words *Ana B'Koach* mean "we beg you." What a way to start a prayer! Just imagine that the Native Americans were praying to Earth, saying, "Earth, we beg you," or they were praying to the Great White Father: "We beg you."

As Mordechai said, there are forty-two words and seven lines, and each line represents a different sphere so that it is a different energy. So rather than analyzing the whole prayer line by line, at this point, I just want to read it in English and then see what kind of effect, if any, it may have on you.

> We beg you with the strength of your right hand's greatness,
> untie the bundled sins. Accept the prayer of your people.
> Strengthen us, purify us, oh awesome one. Please, oh strong one,
> guard like the pupil of an eye those who foster your oneness.
> Bless them. Purify them. Show them pity.
> May your righteousness always repay them.
> Powerful Holy One, with your abundant goodness, guide your
>   people.
> One and only exalted one, turn to your people who proclaim your
>   holiness.
> Accept our entreaty and hear our cry, you who know all mysteries!
> Blessed is the name of this glorious kingdom for all eternity.

Now, we can analyze the prayer line by line and look at different concepts of the prayer, or we can just feel whether there is an energy in the whole prayer and in the sounds of the Hebrew language. Remember, it is not required that you learn the ancient Hebrew. What is required is that you receive the energy, the feeling, and the intention.

When we talk about strength, which is a powerful concept in the Tree of Life, it's because you may need to impose strength and help put restrictions on this planet. We can say the starseeds need strength. We need it because if we are going to be planetary healers, then we have to find a way to strengthen our spiritual resolve and the Group of Forty so that we can make an impact on this planet. In essence, the prayer is saying, "Well, we need strength, and we are calling on the energy of strength." The Tree of Life has a secret paradigm to help you with strength.

Now, understanding prayer can be a complicated concept, but I like to look at the Native Americans of the Sacred Triangle. They have something called the "talking prayer," and I think that is a beautiful idea — to say their prayers aloud like they are talking to the Great Spirit. This is the same idea we are using with the prayer *Ana B'Koach*. This prayer is said out loud, so you're speaking to the spirit of Earth and to the spirit of the Creator. For example, you say, "Strengthen us and purify us." Mordechai talked about purification, and he used the term "self-nullification," which is a complicated concept. Self-nullification means removing your ego so that you have your pure essence. In order to receive energy and strength, you have to empty yourself.

The whole idea of the Tree of Life is to receive the energy and strength — to receive the energy of this kingdom, of how to shimmer, of balance and loving kindness, with both strength and restriction. You have to empty yourself and nullify your ego. Self-nullification is a strong concept, but I think you all understand it now.

Starseeds talk about guarding your energy. I really think that we, as starseeds, are performing a sacred task on this planet, and we need protection. People are constantly asking me, "How can I protect myself from the darker forces?" There are a lot of negative energies for a lot of reasons, and auras are becoming more challenged because there is so much different energy from which we need to protect ourselves. This prayer, *Ana B'Koach*, asks for help, guarding, and self-protection.

We know that if you just ask the guides for protection — especially if you use the words "protect me" — then they will come, so "the powerful Holy One" could be the Creator coming to you with your abundant goodness. We have to believe that the whole healing process we are doing on this planet is for goodness.

In the line that reads, "Accept our entreaty and hear our cry, he who knows all mysteries," at least be clear that this whole planet, this whole third dimension, this whole cosmic drama that we are now experiencing, is a great mystery. We will not understand everything on the third dimension because our perspective is narrow, so you have to have a perspective of mystery about this drama that we are seeing on Earth.

I'm going to conclude my part of the presentation by reading the
first line in Hebrew. See if you can hear any of the energies I've been
talking about.

Ana B'Koach Gedulat Yeminecha Tatir Tzerura.

※ ※ ※

The Importance of the Sacred Triangle

Mordechai: That was beautifully pronounced. *Baruch Hashem* —
blessed is the name of God. I want to tell you the reason why we went
into this *Ana B'Koach* prayer — actually, it's a meditation. We all need
this meditation. We need to say this meditation three times a day. We
all want protection from this energetic infection or virus that we call the
negative inclination, or doubt or chaos. It is so important for us.

It wasn't just an accident that David mentioned the Sacred Triangle.
Someone on Facebook put out a new crop circle that came out a few
days ago. That crop circle was a perfect example of the Sacred Triangle
that we use, from the Arcturians, and it's almost an exact copy. I was
completely awed by that crop circle. I'm not a crop circle fan, although
I know there is geometry within them that I respect and I know it's a
message for all of us. But when I saw that Sacred Triangle crop circle
that came out a few days ago, I knew that was a message for us, the
starseeds. The starseeds are the ones who really put an effort into balancing the Blue Jewel. It's so important! The Blue Jewel is everything!
The purpose of using sacred Hebraic words and letters in planetary
healing is to keep giving energy to the Blue Jewel.

You know, David said that this prayer was a mystical prayer, but
it is beyond mystical. This *Ana B'Koach* is everything for which we've
been asking. That's why I said it now.

The right hand of the Creator was used to split the Red Sea — or
the Reed Sea — and that's not just some fairy tale. We were supposed
to be the starseeds in that moment in time. We were supposed to take
that knowledge to the nations of the world.

Unfortunately, they got so caught up with themselves that it did
not happen. But it is happening now. That knowledge is coming out
now, and we must take advantage of it. And as far as what David said
of the frequency of the letters, yes, it is a frequency. It is a vibration.
That's our connection to the fifth dimension.

What we are doing, really, is being remorseful about the destruction of both holy temples and of Jerusalem. But what does that really

mean? It's about our disconnection from the Arcturians, from the Pleiadians, and from everything in the galaxy — from everything to which we deserve to connect. That is why what Juliano says and everything that David channels relates to being able to reconnect with that galactic energy. This is important!

Back to the Letter *Bet*

We haven't forgotten about the letter *Bet*. The letter *Bet* is still hanging in there in the background because it represents the house of the galaxy. The Holy Temple was our connection — our galactic connection. As Vywamus, one of my favorite entities from the fifth dimension, says about understanding, what is understanding? Understanding is the connection. To make it all very short and sweet: Understanding is the connection.

Why are we here? We're here to expand our souls. You either have an expansion or you have a contraction. We have to take advantage of all the opportunities that expand our souls.

We have to understand that "Kabbalah" means "to receive." To receive what? To receive, understand, and connect to this *Ana B'Koach* meditation. As I said, it's not a prayer; it's a meditation. When we use this meditation quietly, with an open heart and an open third eye, we have all the protection we need, but we need one other thing: certainty — no doubt. That's because all the different belief systems eventually merge into one. But this is not easy for any of us, especially the gung-ho guys who think that their way is the only way to go — that this way or that way is the only way to go. No, it is the Sacred Triangle. It is a unity. We have to understand the cosmic unity.

That's why the letter *Bet* comes after the letter *Aleph* — because it's twice the letter of *Aleph* and because *Aleph* represents unity. So does *Bet*. We have to really have certainty in our imagination and understand that *Bet* is twice the energy to connect to that unity. You have no idea; I'm coming to you guys from my heart because this is the real deal.

So getting back to the letter *Bet*, it represents the house, and there's only one house: the house of our consciousness, which connects to the Holy Temple, the Holy House, the *Bet HaMikdash* (Hebrew for "the Holy Temple of G—d"). This is not about a Jewish or Hebrew thing; this is a unified cosmic drama in which these letters and words assist us in doing our job of planetary healing and the bigger job of Biorelativity.

✳ ✳ ✳

Generating Power through the *Ana B'Koach*

Shalom, Shalom, Shalom. Greetings. This is **Archangel Michael**. I send blessings to each of you as you are listening to this sacred energy, as you are contemplating, as you are thinking about the sacredness of fifth-dimensional energy. Please understand that when you think about the Tree of Life, the bottom — where you are — is the kingdom. This is sacred. You are living in a sacred third dimension. It is often hard for you to realize the sacredness of it, but it is your job as starseeds to teach and to make more places on this planet sacred. Part of the teachings of the Planetary Tree of Life focus on bringing down the sacred light, the holy light, and the Holy Spirit. The Holy Spirit is the light of holiness that must be manifested now on this planet.

One great imbalance that now exists on this planet is the lack of respect for the third dimension. Another great imbalance on this planet is the lack of designated places to be sacred and holy. That then becomes one of the greatest tasks of the starseeds. Another such task is for the healing of this planet, which focuses on creating more planetary cities of light and more sacred energies using the existing twelve sacred etheric crystals to make the planet aware of the holy and sacred.

So today you are studying a prayer that has great powers of sacredness, healing, and miracle creation. It has the great power of divine intervention. This prayer, *Ana B'Koach*, (a sacred Hebrew prayer used by Kabbalists to increase their power) is a sacred energy that makes the people who recite this prayer aware of their sacredness and holiness. At this moment, when you become aware of your sacredness, you can then become aware that you are bringing energies from above down into this planet. You are doing this with sacredness and holiness, and you become more powerful.

It has always been understood that the starseeds are going to generate a new spiritual power. People often ask, "How is it possible that a few starseeds can influence the planet?" But remember, those who are receiving the highest energies are receiving light that could be considered a miracle on this planet. A miracle means that the energies are transcending normal logic; they are transcending cause and effect. A miracle is an energy that is going beyond what you can see as the normal flow of this reality. Everyone agrees that there must be more energy of miracles.

I send energy of protection to each of you so that your auras can be protected. And now let me chant just the first two words of this prayer. Maybe you cannot learn all forty-two words of it, or maybe you cannot follow it, but everyone should be able to remember these two words (*Ana B'Koach*) as I chant them. It is like having special letters; you can think that GOF means Group of Forty, but if you say GOF, everybody understands the Group of Forty, the Sacred Triangle, and all of the thoughts and planetary work. So if you want to hear the words *Ana B'Koach*, then you can recite those words, and you can receive the energy of healing. You can receive the energy of protection, you can receive the energy of holiness and sacredness, and you can receive the power that this prayer is bringing to you. So please listen as I chant only these first two words of the prayer for you.

[Chants: *Ana B'Koach*.]

Let in the light of *Ana B'Koach*. Let the miracle of this energy be with you. Blessings. I am Archangel Michael.

*　*　*

Questions from the Class

Lin in Chicago: *I do understand that Hebrew and Sanskrit are particularly sacred with their sounds, so what happens if we say the prayer in English?*

Mordechai: It's very simple, Lin. The Creator and all of the angels are not interested in the pronunciation as we would think of it, as energies or frequencies. What they are looking for is what is in our hearts and what is in the open third eye. That's what they're interested in. Are we coming from intention? We can say the words in Chinese; it doesn't really matter. All that matters is what's coming from our hearts. Lord Sananda has mentioned it many times. That's a simple answer, and it's quite accurate.

Ingrid in Florida: *This is incredible. I think it's so powerful, and I'm amazed. I bless you, and I thank you.*

Cecelia in New Mexico: *I wanted to mention just a couple of things. When Mordechai was talking about the eye of the fish, what I saw was the eye of Horus. I believe there's a connection there. I think it's also connected to the all-seeing eye. And when we're talking about the 57, which reduces down to a 12, and then to a 3, there's quite a significance to the 12, 3. The third thing I saw was that we are in the seventh golden age.*

Mordechai: You're absolutely right. I love numbers. Numbers got me where I am today. It is not believing anything; it is not knowing anything. It is absolute mathematics that has brought me to this level. I must tell you, you're absolutely right. Whether you bring it into a small gematria or you expand it out, it doesn't really matter. What matters is that you know numbers do not lie. Numbers are the truth. There is no gray matter. One and one is two; it's not three. It's either black or white, and that's important. God bless you.

Sandra in New Mexico: David, this is very, very healing. This is really exquisite. I just want to thank you and Mordechai so much. I really appreciate it. Thank you.

David: For people who are new, Mordechai right now lives in Jerusalem, and he's talking from Jerusalem. He lives close to the Dome of the Rock. Mordechai, tell people something about the Dome of the Rock. There are a lot of things about it that people don't realize. What is the energy there?

Mordechai: I'm getting so much energy from this. You have no idea! The rock — I must tell you all, it is the place of the original ascension. That's our goal. Our goal is to educate and make everybody aware of the ascension.

If anybody reads my lectures, they'll know I'm not a doom-and-gloom guy. What it is is destiny, because we don't want to change — especially here in Jerusalem. It's like every other city physically, but spiritually, it's like no other city. I must tell you this: The Dome of the Rock — it's not the dome; it's the rock. The rock does not sit on this planet, the Blue Jewel. This entire Blue Jewel sits on that rock.

In Hebrew, the rock is called *Even Shtiyah* or *Eh'ven Shtiyah*. In Hebrew, one word can have many translations and spellings, depending on the context or the way it's said. It's amazing. Hebrew is an amazing language.

The most important translation of *Even*, or *Eh'ven*, *Shtiyah* is "the rock of weaving." What are we talking about? Why are we talking about weaving? We're talking about weaving light-force energy through and across all of the grids from all of the other channels and entities who talk about the grids. All entities get their energy from there. Anything that comes into this world has to come through the *Even* (or *Eh'ven*) *Shtiyah*.

Archangel Metatron, who is my teacher and my master, was the first to ascend as Enoch. Elijah was the second ascension from the rock. This rock is beyond comprehension. It is the greatest secret in the third dimension, and I'm not being overly dramatic. I'm trying to get a point across. I'm trying to speak very slowly. I'm excited about this particular subject because it is the number one subject.

There is nothing more unifying than to teach the ascension. That is our job as starseeds: to teach other people about the ascension. We are teachers. It's like the greatest networking pyramid you've ever seen in your life. Most of us, I'm sure, are familiar with network marketing. Now we're network marketing for light-force energy. It's as simple as that.

David: I just want to remind everyone that the idea of ascension is contained in the Tree of Life because we're working toward planetary ascension to bring everything into balance. Then we can go into higher dimensions. Part of the idea of this whole lecture series is to bring you into balance and to help bring the planet into balance. When the planet is in a better balance and we're in a better balance, then we all can ascend.

Gimmel: Strength, Discipline, and Judgment

CLASS 4

Mordechai, David, and Sanat Kumara

Mordechai: This letter that we're starting with today, *Gimmel*, is really the beginning. We started with the letter *Aleph*, and then we talked about the letter *Bet*, which we explained gave birth to the *Gimmel*, which stands for stability and steadiness. It goes in the third column of the Tree of Life and makes the three columns complete.

Has everybody searched through Google to find the shape of this letter? I hope so, because I'll tell you the truth — which is all I do anyway. *Gimmel* actually was given birth to by the *Bet* from that open window on the left side. If you notice, the *Gimmel* looks a little bit like *Bet* on the right side. Just the top is cut and the bottom is cut, and there is a different letter.

The *Gimmel* is made up of a *Vav* and a *Yud*. We really have to understand what this *Gimmel* is. You will see what I'm talking about as we go forward. As it was birthed out of the *Bet*, it enthusiastically rolled out like a baby in the fetal position. The letter carried with it the divine desire to share with the next letter, the *Dalet*, which represents a poor person.

The *Gimmel* represents one with sustenance. It wants to do nothing more than share with someone who desires to receive — someone who is in need. The *Dalet* is the poor person, and the *Gimmel* is running after the *Dalet*. The *Gimmel* is like water running down to fill an empty vessel.

Go to the Tree of Life. Remember that I told you to take the whole page of the Tree of Life and put it into Lago Puelo, sphere ten? That is the bottom *Sephirah*. So we're dealing with the twelve *Sephirot* inside this bottom *Sephirah*. Now that we're inside this bottom *Sephirah*, we can go back up to number five, Volcán Poás. Sanat Kumara is the spirit guide in number five. It is his job to oversee the different worlds and to see how the races on the planet are doing. Archangel Gabriel is also in that same post. They're like partners in the same area, except under different perspectives.

The *Gimmel* is a fun letter. It describes Archangel Gabriel because the word *Gevurah* in Hebrew represents sphere five, and also it means "great." *Gadol* means "big," and this also describes Archangel Gabriel. The *Sephirah* of *Gevurah* also begins with a *Gimmel*. We've only just started with this *Gimmel*. A couple of classes ago, I explained how the *Gimmel* is associated with the creation of the planet Jupiter, influencing the signs of Pisces and Sagittarius. These are important aspects of the *Gimmel*. It's powerful. When I say it rolls out with enthusiasm, I mean it rolls out with energy. Its whole desire is to impart. It is the true letter that we talk about.

We all came here with the desire to receive for the self alone, and the whole thing is to make the switch from the desire to receive to the desire to receive for the sake of imparting — for the sake of sharing. Sharing is everything, and the *Gimmel* is a big influence to that situation. Also, it's so energetic.

Do you remember when we did the sight, sound, and number? In the category of sight, we use the word "form" because it's actually the form of the letter. It is formed where that bottom leg is up a little bit, so it's stepping forward. It is running after the letter *Dalet* — the poor. It's not waiting for an invitation. It's not waiting to think about that; it's one of the 248 positive deeds or attributes. The letter *Gimmel* is just doing it for the sake of doing it, knowing that it's a job that has to be done.

I will not start talking about electromagnetic energy waves and cosmic cone frequencies. I just want to keep it simple for you. So when the fetus starts to roll out of the *Bet*, it rolls and rolls and forms a circular pattern called *Gilgul*. *Gilgul* is a circle, a wheel. It means "rotation of souls" in Hebrew. The plural of *Gilgul* is *Gilgulim*. Now, when this *Gimmel* is rolling, it's like wheels within wheels. What does this relate to? The *Merkavah*, the chariot.

So where does the *Gimmel* fit in? The *Gimmel*, when it's rolling, is actually the hub of everything circular. It is the hub with all the spikes going out to the circumference — wherever it is. So as Juliano says, sit and go around in a shimmering exercise. Go off and visit wherever you want to visit. The *Gimmel* is also the hub of the wheels of the *Merkavah*.

It's an amazing thing: Souls constantly reincarnate. As it says in the Torah, one soul can roll through many generations. In other words, the soul of Moses is here. The soul of Lord Sananda is here and incarnated in people. So is the soul of Abraham. Everyone who has lived before and ascended has come back down in different people to help get this starseed galactic point across.

The *Gimmel* is so important concerning the *Gilgul* that it's amazing. It also represents the constant progression of us, the galactic starseeds, the *B'nai Yisrael*, the children of Israel. When you look up *Gimmel*, you will read, "reward and punishment." That's what the *Gimmel* actually stands for. You have your reward for doing good things, and you have your punishment for not doing good things. The *Gimmel* is also partly assisting in the shimmering of our cosmic egg, because everything that goes in and out, up and down, and back and forth is the excitement and the enthusiasm of the *Gimmel*.

Up the Ladder

Now, we really haven't finished the category of numbers yet. Because three is completion, it's the three Fathers. It's the three columns. The *Gimmel*, when it becomes the third column, unifies the columns, or unifies the entire Tree of Life. It is unifying the right side of the tree, which is water; the left side of the tree, which is fire; and the central column, which is air. Air brings all three together as one. The *Gimmel* is stability and equilibrium, which are important.

The Torah talks about the "chosen people." It uses the word *Segol*, which is a vowel with three dots. Those three dots are the three corners, and they look like a triangle. They are the corners of the redemption, which is called *Geula*. What is the redemption? The whole point of the *Gimmel* — and I'm really abbreviating this — is to give us the excitement to do all these things, all of these great, wonderful things for other people. This is so we can raise ourselves to a higher consciousness, so when we look up at the ladder of ascension, we get sucked right up to the top of the ladder with nothing in between.

That's our goal, isn't it? Everyone is looking forward to getting up that ladder. We don't realize the work that we have to go through yet — the spiritual work that has to be done to accomplish that ascension.

Those of us who think we've gone through our life's correction have a lot of surprises coming to us every day. We're going to get more opportunities to climb up that ladder. After all, every day is new, and every moment is new!

Every time we do a nice thing for no reason, we receive a garment. When we start going up the ladder, there are different degrees of fire. Everything is fire. So the more garments that we can accumulate in this lifetime, the more "asbestos covering" we'll have. That's good because the fire gets so hot as we go up that only those souls who have many garments to protect them as they elevate will be protected. It takes a soul that has accumulated many garments to be able to handle the heat range of the fire as it intensifies up the levels of the grades.

Basically, *Gimmel* has its paradox. When the *Gimmel* went to the Creator to ask, "Can I be the first letter in the Torah?" the Creator said, "*Gimmel*, you're a great letter; you have the greatest intentions. You are going to roll out to do all these wonderful things, but the word *Ga'ava*, which means 'pride' and the word 'ego' both start with the letter *Gimmel*. Another non-kosher word, *Ganiv*, or *Ganiff* in Yiddish, means 'one who aggressively takes' — a thief. It is because of these two things that you can't be the first letter in the Torah. But you are going to be great anyway." And with that, the *Gimmel* sat back down, and the letter *Bet* came forward to be the first letter of the Torah.

There are also the three parts of the Torah: the five books of Moses, the prophets, and the writings. These are all bound up in this Project Israel, the Jerusalem Command, which actually is what this project/ experiment is down here. *The Book of Knowledge: The Keys of Enoch* explains it clearly and perfectly.

*   *   *

Gimmel Is a G

David: I want to explain that the letters have sounds and that each sound is linguistically in each language. So even though we are talking about the *Aleph*, the *Bet*, and the *Gimmel*, those are *A*, *B*, and the *Gimmel* is the *G* sound. Of course, that *G* sound is in most languages. So when Mordechai is talking about the third letter of the Hebrew alphabet, in English it would be a sound like the *G*. Remember that in the Kabbalah, the sounds are carrying energy and vibration.

I'm going to spell out the three letters *Aleph*, *Bet*, and *Gimmel* in English. Mordechai mentioned the *Dalet* as a letter. It has a *D* sound. So for the purposes of the sounds, *Aleph* is A-L-E-P-H, *Bet* is B-E-T, *Gimmel* is G-I-M-M-E-L, and *Dalet* is D-A-L-E-T. So the corresponding letters are *A, B, G, and D.*

Balancing Strength, Discipline, and Judgment

The Planetary Tree of Life is based on the Kabbalistic Tree of Life, which is a galactic Tree of Life. The letter *Gimmel* makes certain words that relate to Volcán Poás, or the fifth sphere on our chart. If you just look at the chart, you'll see that we have strength, discipline, and judgment in that sphere.

Mordechai gave three words in Hebrew. The first word was *Gibor*, which means greatness. The second word is *Gadol*. The last word was *Gevurah*, which is strength and discipline. These words represent the fifth *Sephirah*, and each *Sephirah* holds an energy. In this case, it is the energy of greatness, strength, and justice.

To better understand one *Sephirah*, you have to understand the opposite *Sephirah*. It is difficult to talk about one energy without talking about its opposite. Also, we are talking about everything having threes, so you have the one energy like the positive, you have the negative, and then you have the balance. Now, strength and discipline aren't negative or positive; they are the opposite of loving kindness.

Juliano has talked many times about the concepts of planetary energy, planetary process, and planets that have existed in our galaxy that lacked judgment and discipline. They destroyed themselves. Examples of this include the civilization of Atlantis, where things got out of control and there wasn't enough discipline.

To have discipline, you also have to have strength; to impose the discipline, you have to have strength to impose the judgment. You can't have judgment without the force and strength to back it up. So when we look at our planet, we could say that there needs to be some kind of strength and force to impose discipline on this planet, but we all know if the discipline is too strong, then there will be other problems.

Reincarnation Energy

The other word Mordechai mentioned is *Gilgul* (that is the approximate transliteration into English). It actually can be translated as "reincarnation." Even though it means "circle," when we think about souls, you are on a wheel or a circle. This is very similar to the Hindu idea.

A lot of people are on the wheel of life. A lot of people are really surprised to find that in the *Kabbalah* and in the Tree of Life, the concept of reincarnation is very strong. So *Gilgul* is like a circle: We go from one lifetime to the next. That word also begins with the letter *Gimmel*. It is a good sound. So you can see linguistically that in Hebrew, especially in the mystical *Kabbalah*, they tie the energy of the letters to the words and the energy of the spheres in the Tree of Life.

So what is the energy of *G*, the *Gimmel*? The energy is greatness. The energy is reincarnation — *Gilgul*. You see, all these words in Hebrew come from this word *Gimmel*.

Rewards, Punishment, and Karma

Mordechai also mentioned reward and punishment. That is the basis of karma and reincarnation in a simplistic way. I have done a lot of channelings for people about not only Earth karma but also the kind of karma that the guides call "cosmic karma." That means that the events we are seeing now on this planet have karmic ramifications and that there are certain events like large destructions of people and large wars that are totally incomprehensible. Those events could not be explained from karma just on Earth. So you have to consider cosmic karma — that some people on this planet come from other planets and they are bringing their problems and their dramas to our Earth.

Mordechai mentioned the term *B'nai Yisrael*. *B'nai* means "children of" — the children of Israel. In Hebrew, Israel is pronounced "Yisrael." So it is "the children of Israel." When you think of Israel or Yisrael, you can also define it as a community of fifth-dimensional beings, spiritual beings, and starseeds.

The Energy of Letters and Different Names for God

I also want to point out this concept of threes. I want you to think about Christian mysticism, where we have the Father, the Son, and the Holy Ghost. Three is a sacred number in many other mystical traditions, not just in the Kabbalah.

Mordechai also talked about this other sound called *Segol*. I want you to understand that the Hebrew alphabet has twenty-two letters. If you look at the Tree of Life and the lines of it, there are actually twenty-two paths between each *Sephirah*, so each of those has a letter. Now, Hebrew is essentially an alphabet with consonants only, which is really hard for us to understand. If you spell my name, for example — David — in Hebrew with just the consonants, it would be D-V-D.

I asked my Hebrew teacher, "Well, if I wrote D-V-D and you pronounce my name David, how would you know it is not 'DVD' — that thing you play in your music machine?"

My Hebrew teacher responded, "Well, it is context. So people know that D-V-D in a certain way is referring to the name David. But there are vowels in Hebrew, and the vowels were added later. The vowels are underneath the consonants, which is difficult and unusual for us Western people to imagine — that the vowels are like dots underneath the letters."

Now, the reason why the Kabbalah and the Tree of Life are so interested in the alphabet is because everything is linked. So the vowels are playing an important role in the pronunciation of the sound and of God's name. Each *Sephirah* that we are talking about has a special name for God. So certain names of God are more sacred or more powerful than other names because each *Sephirah* has the power. You can gain power yourself by pronouncing the name of God in the *Sephirah*. For example, one name of God is *El*, and the word *El* is also in a second name of God: *El Shaddai*. To receive the power from this name, you would concentrate on the sounds of it.

We designated Sanat Kumara to represent the judgment of Earth. We did that because he is like the overseer of the planet. I will channel Sanat Kumara in the next part of my lecture.

* * *

The Transmigration of Souls

Mordechai: Getting back to the three dots in the vowel, the vowels are very important. In the Hebrew language, these letters are living energy intelligences. When the *Gimmel* came out, it was running enthusiastically. It was actually running after the poor person, the *Dalet*. Now, the Hebrew word for "run" is *Ratz*: Resh-Tzadi. The word for desire, or divine will, is *Ratzon*: Resh-Tzadi-Vav-Nun. So actually, the desire of the will of the Creator finds the root of that word "desire," *Ratzon*, in the verb "to run." *Ratz* means to run for nothing else but doing the will of the Creator. That's what the *Gimmel* represents.

I'm going to use the phrase "transmigration of souls." Let me define that a little bit. Most of us understand that we are here and the things that come at us do so because we designed our own screenplay for our own evolution of our own souls. So this is a screenplay.

The only free will we have is to be either reactive or proactive to whatever we have planned for ourselves in our screenplays. Now, when you talk about cosmic karma, you're talking about our map of incarnations, which has already been planned. However, we have gone through many hundreds of incarnations previously. Only when we go back up the ladder will we find out the real story. Then we will learn what's in front of us and where our planned incarnations are going to be.

There are many groups of incarnations. There's the group of galaxies, a cluster of incarnations, and we have other clusters of incarnations going wherever else. Why? Because the soul needs to learn — because it's all about the expansion of the soul. That's another five lectures in itself.

The *Gimmel* represents the up-and-down running of the angels — up and down the ladder of ascension. The water that Gimmel represents, because of its kindness, always flows down. It flows down into a step-down transformer and into another step-down transformer, and into another one, and so on.

The *Gimmel* Is In Charge of Waves

It's so important for us to at least have a clue, to have a perspective of what is going on, because when any Kabbalist wakes up in the morning, the first thing he or she says is, "Thank you, God, for returning my soul." The next thing the Kabbalist says is: "This is the first day of the rest of my life. Let's make the best of it." That's how we have to think. We have to take all that past, all that baggage, put it in a basket, and send it down the river. But there is one river that you don't want to send it down: the river of "denial." It's in Egypt (Nile River), which symbolically represents constriction in the Kabbalah. That's not a place you want to send that thing down. It's important to put all that baggage down and to start fresh and clean.

So the *Gimmel* rolls out energy in waves. The *Gimmel* is in charge of waves. Actually, it is the energy behind the contraction and the expansion of basic existence in the third dimension. Contract and expand, which is what the Arcturians talk about: getting us to shimmer, to contract and expand, contract and expand. That's what this pulse is all about.

Every Friday night when the sun sets (about 8:30 – 9PM PST) designates the beginning of the Sabbath in Jerusalem, and I'm standing at the Torah. That's the best time. It is the greatest time, a sacred time. All the entities are around the ring of ascension and look for opportunities like this so that they can work with us. This is a sacred time and a sacred place. You don't have to do anything. You can just lie in bed and put your consciousness in Jerusalem — to the stone, to the crystal around the crystal lake. Just send the energy because we need to buffer the inevitable. It's inevitable; it's destiny, and we need to buffer it.

I'll be straight with you: Whether the buffering works a little bit, a lot, or not at all, it doesn't matter. Why? Because our job is to bring down fifth-dimensional energy to this planet. We act like a lighthouse, and then they see: "Aha! There's a spot over there." It's almost like planetary cities of light. This is the way to charge up the planetary cities of light. These are the little white shining sparkles that they see from the starship, and this is what needs to be energized. The best time to energize is wherever you are on Friday at 8:30PM PST, but you do not have to do too much. There is nothing formal. Just put your consciousness there. This is very important.

The next thing I want to do is answer someone's question: Does it matter what language you speak with the *Ana B'Koach*? You can speak Chinese if it comes from the heart. Yes, it's an accurate answer, but I want to add to it. You need to at least look at those Hebrew letters as you are saying it in English, or in any other language, or say it in the transliteration. Either way, you have to look at those letters, because that's where the energy is. Those are the letters that are flying around the ring of ascension, the ladder of ascension, and the planetary cities of light.

✳ ✳ ✳

Galactic Spirituality

David: I want to say something about the *Ana B'Koach*, which maybe we didn't explain in detail before. Mordechai talked about the Hebrew letters and said there are forty-two words in that prayer. If you take the first letter of each word and put them all together into forty-two letters, then those letters are supposed to make a sacred name of God. So that is like hidden energy in that prayer. Remember when we looked at the prayer? Some of you might have thought, "Well, when you translate it to English, maybe it is a kind of regular prayer," but it is actually linguistically tied in with this name of God. Do you remember that I said that each *Sephirah* has a name of God?

In the Kabbalah, the name of God and its pronunciation, especially the *YHWH*, is not vocalized because it is considered unpronounceable due to its holiness. There are many names for God, which is a deep concept. So supposedly in the ancient sacred temple, only on the certain holy day known as *Yom Kippur*, the sacred name of God was pronounced. There are different interpretations. Some people thought there was a seventy-two-letter name. I mean, how can you pronounce a forty-two-letter name? I couldn't do it. But this prayer, *Ana B'Koach*, if you take the letters and put them together, is supposed to be the pronunciation of God's sacred name. If you can say the name correctly, then you could have power over all of creation.

I also wanted to mention that Mordechai talked briefly about the galaxies and the group of galaxies in a local group. One of the things we are teaching is that we must discuss galactic spirituality. Galactic spirituality is acknowledging that there is a greater planetary existence all over this galaxy and all over other galaxies. There is a great spiritual wisdom that needs to be translated and transferred to all of the planets.

So in my study of astronomy and cosmology, I came across this concept of the galaxies and the group of galaxies, and the totally mind-expanding thing I learned was that we are part of a local group of galaxies that consists of eleven or twelve galaxies in a cluster. It is so hard to imagine that, because each galaxy has three to four billion stars! Our galaxy might be 30,000 light-years across, which is a tremendous distance. Our galaxy is so huge that it could take our solar system 500–700 million years to go around the whole galaxy. That is how big our galaxy is.

We are part of a cluster of galaxies, and our sister galaxy is the Andromeda galaxy. Many of you have links to this galaxy. Even though it is the closest galaxy, I think it is still 2.5 million light-years away, so that gives you an idea of how far away it is. If you can travel at the speed of light, which is a fantastic speed of 186,000 miles per second, it would still take you 2.5 million years to reach Andromeda — our closest galaxy.

A Closer Look at the Fifth Sphere

We are looking at Volcán Poás, sphere five, as strength, discipline, and judgment. The reason why is that we are coming to a period of time some people refer to as the end times. Some people refer to it as a great purification. It's this idea that you cannot bring a planet too far out of balance without experiencing an opposite discipline or judgment.

In the histories of the Bible, in Atlantis, and on other planets, people have gotten out of balance. Part of the out-of-balance energy on our planet is that there is higher technology without accompanying spiritual wisdom. Remember, wisdom is up on the Bodensee, sphere two, represented by the spirit guide Chief White Eagle. We don't have the wisdom to balance the higher technology.

We are here as the starseeds helping to bring this planet back into balance, and there are other forces that we can speak about to help activate or bring down a judgment or a discipline that will rebalance the planet without destroying it. One of the things that the Kabbalah teaches is that the Creator has had other planets that had too much loving kindness, and that didn't work — for obvious reasons. Other planets had too much discipline, and that didn't work, either.

Imagine you made a mistake such as going through a red traffic light, and then you were put in jail for five years for violating the traffic laws. That is severe. But now imagine that this planet is using nuclear energy, and there are bombs and radiation all over the place. You wanted to use nuclear energy and radiation for power, but now it is out of balance, and to stop it, there may need to be a severe judgment.

I read in a book[1] that the United States in the 1950s and 1960s detonated 286 nuclear bombs around Area 51 near Las Vegas. Some of those bombs actually exploded in outer space. They sent missiles up 300,000 feet to explode these nuclear bombs. Remember that in some of the earlier channelings the guides said we were bringing nuclear weapons into outer space. I personally did not realize we had exploded these nuclear bombs in outer space. That could totally destroy the whole ozone layer. So now, because we are so far out of balance, there may have to be a harsh judgment, a harsh discipline, and that is representative of Volcán Poás.

* * *

A Planetary Logos Perspective

Shalom, Shalom, Shalom. Greetings. I'm **Sanat Kumara**. I'm known as the Planetary Logos. I'm known as the person who oversees and looks at the planet as a whole. It is a great perspective for understanding the whole planet.

As you are gaining spiritual wisdom, you will begin, as planetary healers, to understand the concept of the feedback loop system. That feedback loop system is an energetic, etheric spiritual loop and the third-dimensional loop that creates the balance necessary to keep this biosphere in harmony. Also, it holds the biosphere in the right balance so that humanity can exist on this planet.

Humanity requires a special balance to have the right percentages of oxygen and nitrogen. There are so many factors contributing to the balance. If this planet goes too far out of balance, if there are too many forests cut down, if there is too much pollution in the oceans, if the oceans become too acidic, if there is too much radiation in the atmosphere, or if there are too many greenhouse gases in the atmosphere, then the feedback loop system responds, and some of those responses could be harsh. You know that some responses are an attempt to bring Earth back into a greater balance, and sometimes a planet, from the planetary perspective, is required to use harshness. The energy of harshness can bring an out-of-balance planet back into balance.

But this feedback loop system is also influenced by the galaxy. You are part of the starseed heritage. You are beginning to learn that the feedback loop system is not only influenced by Earth but also by the galaxy. It is influenced by the Central Sun and by galactic energies that are continually coming to Earth.

You shall understand that you are not living in isolation. You shall understand that you are, as a planet, interacting with the whole galaxy. And during this period known as December 22, 2012 [Editor's Note: the date of this channeling], we are at the height of the energy of the galaxy and its ability to interact with Earth. This interaction is reaching its epitome, which means that the central galactic energy is sending powerful and special energy that can have profound abilities to affect Earth's feedback loop system.

This time of December 22 marks the energetic opening for understanding and using the galactic energies from the Central Sun. Understand that there may need to be some harshness on some parts of the planet, but this is necessary to bring forth a new balance so that the planetary system can continue to support this biosphere.

As planetary healers, you can intervene. You can help bring back a balancing energy that does not need to be as harsh. You can, with your powerful, energetic telepathic messages and transformative thoughts, help to rebalance the feedback loop system in a gentler way that also includes loving kindness. I'm Sanat Kumara. Good day.

Dalet: the Door to the Truth

CLASS 5

MORDECHAI, AND DAVID

Mordechai: Good morning, good afternoon, and good evening. This is going to be a wonderful class. The letter *Dalet* is among my favorite letters. It's the fourth letter in the Hebrew alphabet, and it is a special letter. First of all, the second class explained the letter *Aleph*, which we know is number one. It represents all of creation: as above, so below. You have the slanted *Vav* separating the two *Yuds*, as was spoken from upstairs[1] all the way down here.

Then we went to the third class, *Bet*, which is the first letter of the Torah and represents a house. It houses creation; the letter *Bet* is our house of creation.

In the previous class we discussed that the *Gimmel* actually came rolling out from or was birthed by the letter *Bet*. That letter, *Gimmel*, which is so powerful, as soon as it was born, it came rolling out on a perennial, infinite, divine mission to do as many things as possible for the Creator. That, by the way, is the mission of every angel and every entity that David and I and all of you deal with. Our mission is to serve. The letter *Gimmel* is running or rolling after the letter *Dalet*, which is our subject in this lecture.

Gimmel represents wealth and the Divine light. *Dalet* represents us in a world with no light except what we can produce. The mission of the *Gimmel* is to run after the *Dalet*. The bottom horizontal line of the

Gimmel is stepping forward or rolling to catch the *Dalet*, to give sustenance to the *Dalet*. That is the mission of the *Gimmel*.

One of the *Gimmel*'s purposes is to serve as the hub of the wheels within wheels, or the *Merkabah*. (We'll get into the whole explanation of the *Merkabah* later.) It's just a fancy way of saying that the letter *Gimmel* represents the light-force energy that's coming down to serve the *Dalet*, and we represent the *Dalet*, the poor. We are poor. Why? Because we have no light. The light left after the destruction of the first temple.

The one-word description of the letter *Dalet* in English is "selflessness." I could abbreviate this whole class in two sentences: "We were created in the image and the likeness of our Creator. The image has been explained in many books, but the likeness (*Kidmutainu*) of the Creator is selflessness, or the consciousness and appreciation of a poor man." Now, we're going to spend the rest of our time discussing this. It's going to be simple — even though that's hard to believe — and we will include all the sights, sounds, and numbers that go along with this letter.

David the Warrior King

The letter *Dalet*, in this case, is the same as the letter *D*. These are the fourth letters of the alphabet in both Hebrew and English. With the letter *D*, we have the name David. My middle name is David. Being that this is a Tree of Life lecture, the energy of this bottom *Sephirah*, *Malchut*, is the energy of King David.

King David was aggressive. He was the king of war. He was a warrior. He shared that sphere on the Arcturian Tree of Life with Vywamus, my favorite therapist. King David was completely connected to the Creator, or as we know it, to fifth-dimensional consciousness. He knew how to listen to that small, quiet voice. He was a warrior king who won all of his battles because he was clearly connected. Why? Because he understood the letter *Dalet*, the first letter of his name, which represented the complete loss of ego.

Ego is our number one setback, difficulty, and challenge. It is second only to doubt. Those are our two biggest challenges in this lifetime, in past lifetimes, and especially starting in a short time from now as world events unfold.

King David was awakened every night at midnight by a north wind that blew in and played his harp like a wind chime. That's how he woke up in the middle of the night to study the Torah. By doing this, he knew how to bring down fifth-dimensional light into this third-dimensional world — or in terms of the Tree of Life, bring the light from *Tiferet*, the *Sephirah* of beauty, straight down through the funnel into this, our world called the kingdom, which has no light of its own. He was king of that *Sephirah* known as the tenth sphere, the kingdom.

It's so beautifully balanced as a paradox for the warrior king to share the *Sephirah* of *Malchut*, the kingdom, with Vywamus, a peaceful soul psychologist assigned there. Vywamus is not a warrior in the physical sense. He is a psychological warrior representing the knowledge of which he wishes us to be aware. Simply spoken, he is a soul therapist and a great asset to anyone who listens to him.

Time is always a factor, so we will move on to the categories of sight, sound, and number of the letter *Dalet*. The letter simply represents a poor man with no ego who can appreciate the fact that nothing is his and that everything is borrowed or lent to us as part of our screenplay. You can call them tools meant to assist us in succeeding in elevating our consciousness and evolving our souls in this incarnation or lifetime.

The Sight of *Dalet*

Let's get down to sight, sound, and number. We start with sight, which is the category of form. Notice the way the *Dalet* is shaped: It is a horizontal line on top at a right angle to a vertical line going down the right side. But in that top right-hand corner is what's called the consciousness of ego. Let us call it an assemblage point in consciousness.

From that assemblage point, you can either go down into physicality and desire to receive for the self alone or you can go across to share and represent the desire to receive for the sake of sharing. The best example of this I can give is the Hopi rock.[2] The rock is profound and simple. You can choose at that assemblage point to either take the road of physicality, which ends at a certain point, or you can take the road of immortality, which is that straight horizontal line that goes all the way around the rock and forms a circle with no beginning and no end.

There is a paradox in this example because the rock has a coded secret of the Hopi. The rock was actually supposed to have that line go down instead of up, but they didn't want to give it away. You had to work for the answer. Doing our spiritual work is not easy. We have to work at it constantly. It is all a matter of our freewill choice. We should never forget. As our teachers, guides, and higher selves constantly remind us, this is a freewill zone. Choose wisely.

The message is to stay on that horizontal path that takes us through the hard work of living the similitude, detaching from the ego and uncertainty, and sending that basket down the river. As I said previously, send it down any river you want, except "de Nile" (denial).

There is a program in our unconscious or superconscious minds that has to do with continuous re-creation by God. What does this mean? It leads to the simple meaning of absolute certainty, and what is that? It is the understanding that this entire world is re-created every moment in time. This completes the level of worlds in sight.

At the level of souls, the vertical line is for understanding selflessness. Sometimes we have to stand in a subway train at rush hour and have the patience to be squeezed like a sardine and not be reactive to it. At this level, the collective consciousness is basically the willingness to sacrifice your life for your people. How many people do you know who would voluntarily and enthusiastically do that?

News flash: The light gave us an example just today, in the news, in which a man[3] in Chicago jumped into Lake Michigan to save two children, but he got caught up in a whirlpool and drowned. He sacrificed his life for his people. This man has a red carpet waiting for him. You're sitting still in a traffic jam for an hour, burning gas, wishing you could take a helicopter, but you're stuck where you are. In the divine level of form or sight, it's just a simple willingness to sacrifice one's life for our Creator. In Hebrew, that's *Mesirut Nefesh*.

The Sound of *Dalet*

The *Dalet*, as a sound, represents a poor man — poverty. We come back to the king of the *Sephirah* of *Malchut*: King David. King David was wealthy. When he approached the divine essence in prayer, he came forward as a poor man with the consciousness of a poor man. He understood that to pray as a poor man means that everyone else is more important than we are. He prayed as if he were nothing and no one. He truly owned nothing because everything was given to him, as everything is given to us by the divine essence to successfully evolve to a higher consciousness.

Now, in all these great secrets, the correct way to pray is to pray for another person or another group of people first before you even think about praying for yourself. Why? Because this shows those who are listening that you really love your neighbors as yourself. The best part about praying this way is if your prayer for the other person is answered, then your prayers are automatically piggybacked onto the other person's and are accepted. Seriously, if you want your prayers answered, pray your heart out for someone else.

Secondly, in the category of sound or names, *Dalet* means "door" in Hebrew. And righteously, it is the doorway to the truth. The opposite is the servant who refuses to go through the door of freedom.

On the level of souls of sound, the true lowliness of the soul, the Moon is a symbol of the soul. The Sun and the Moon are soul mates. We'll go right to the number, which is my favorite category.

The Number of *Dalet*

In the number category, *Dalet* is four. In the level of worlds, we have the group of fours. There are eight groups of four:

- the four elements of the physical world: fire, air, water, and earth
- the four consistencies: solid, liquid, gas, and combustion
- the four elements: hydrogen, carbon, nitrogen, oxygen
- the four physical forces: gravity, electromagnetic, strong, and weak. (What do strong and weak mean? Simply, the lower is weak and the upper is strong.)
- the different levels of existence: humans, animals, vegetables, and inanimate objects (rock, stone); (Wood would not be included because it was once alive.)
- the four seasons: spring, summer, fall, and winter
- the four directions: north, south, east, and west
- the four worlds in Kabbalah: *Atzilut* (emanation), *Beriah* (creation), *Yitzirah* (formation), and *Asiyah* (action)

In the category of number in the level of souls, you have more groups of four:

- the four matriarchs: Sara, Rebecca, Rachel, and Leah
- Jacob's four wives: Leah, Rachel, Bilhah, and Zilpa
- the four sons and the four cups of wine of the Passover Seder table
- the four feet of the divine throne: Abraham, Isaac, Jacob, and David; (I cannot avoid bringing David up so many times because he is the true warrior of the *Sephirah* of *Malchut* in the

Tree of Life. He was the epitome of the *Sephirah* of *Malchut*.)

In the last line in the level of souls is the first commandment of the Torah: "Be fruitful and multiply." That includes father, mother, son, and daughter. There are also four numbers in the levels of divinity, the four letters of God's name, and the four components of the Torah text, which in descending order are as follows: songs/cantillations (*Ta'amim*), vowels (*Nekudot*), crowns (*Tagim*), and letters (*Otiot*).

The basic concept we must understand is that we are all going to change, voluntarily or involuntarily. You can do it voluntarily, which will make it less painful, and it will be a "red carpet," meaning a lot easier. If you do it involuntarily, it will be a lot more painful. Change is the bottom line.

✳ ✳ ✳

Is God Singular or Plural?

David: I want to talk about the concept of the Creator force in the Kabbalah and in the Tree of Life and the concept of the *Elohim*. So we talk about *El*, and everybody probably has heard that E-L is the Hebrew name for God. When you think about the "el," you notice it is on the end of the names of the archangels; Michael ends with the same "el" letters, so his name means "he who is like God." With Raphael, again we have the "el," and his name means "he who heals like God." Uriel, Ariel — all of these names have "els," which refer to the archangels in connection with God.

In the beginning of the Old Testament, in Genesis, it is said, "In the beginning, God created the heaven and the earth" [Genesis 1:1–3, KJV]; in Hebrew, that is "*Bereshit bara Elohim et hashamayim ve'et ha'aretz*." The word *Elohim* is used in the Kabbalah. *Elohim* is plural. So there is the big debate: Why is it plural?

Some people challenge this and say, "Well, if you translate it literally, it really says, 'In the beginning, *gods* created the heaven and the earth.' That sounds like polytheism, not monotheism, because in monotheism, there is only one god, and in polytheism, there are multiple gods. So the criticism is that the Kabbalah and the Tree of Life are suggesting that there is more than one God. But the truth is God has different manifestations. Even in Christianity, they talk about the Father, the Son, and the Holy Ghost, so there are three aspects of the Creator in Christianity.

When we talk about *Elohim*, it is plural, but also I have seen in some theological discussions that *Elohim* is translated as "divinity" because divinity has the sense of plurality and oneness at the same time. So you can say, "In the beginning, *divinity* created the heaven and the earth" instead of saying "gods." So *Elohim* is a fascinating word. We're only five or six words into the Old Testament, and there is already a big controversy about it.

The Location and Patriarch for the Kingdom

In the Tree of Life, we have ten different manifestations. Each manifestation, or each sphere, is given an energy and a patriarch. In our Planetary Tree of Life diagram, we also give each sphere a geographic location.

Mordechai has pointed out that the geographical location for the bottom sphere, the kingdom, is represented by Lago Puelo. The patriarch for this sphere is King David. In the Kabbalah, this sphere is called the kingdom.

But in our Tree of Life, we are working with the energy of Vywamus for the sphere of the kingdom. Why? Because he, as a soul psychologist, is trying to help us understand what we are doing here on Earth. We also exist in these other levels, but we have come to Earth.

Making the Chariot

I also want to talk about the concept of the *Merkabah* because we are looking at the ascension and the Tree of Life. The Planetary Tree of Life is actually giving us instructions on how to ascend: We start at the bottom and go up. So we have to understand where we are on this divine map. On Earth, we are at the bottom.

Merkavah is the Hebrew word for chariot, and in *Merkavah*, there is the idea of using the chariot for rising or ascending. The making of this vehicle, the *Merkavah*, for going into the higher worlds is called in Hebrew *Ma'aseh Merkabah* (*Ma'aseh* means "the making of"). The Kabbalah studies the ascension through the *Merkavah*, and it also studies the creation and its beginning. In modern physics, the term "cosmology" is used for the study of creation.

"In the Beginning ..."

In the Kabbalah and in the Tree of Life, we have the making of the chariot — the "doing" of the chariot — and then we have the doing of creation. The doing of creation in Hebrew is *Ma 'aseh Bereshit*. *Bereshit*, the very first word in the Old Testament, means "in the beginning." The second letter Mordechai talked about *Bet*, is the first letter in the word *Bereshit*. Does the *Bet* mean "in the beginning," or does it mean "*with* the beginning?"

You can see that there is a slight difference, because if you say, "In the beginning ..." that sounds like maybe there was a point where everything began. That goes back to this concept of cosmology and the big bang, because now the theory of the big bang is the theory of the beginning of everything at a certain point. There is even a theory that compares Genesis to the big bang because it represents the point at which everything began. Remember, the idea in the *Kabbalah* and the Tree of Life is that if you can study the nature of creation, then you will understand and become closer to the Creator.

So in creation, the *Ma'aseh Bereshit*, you find that the Tree of Life leads you to the point where everything began. Go to the top of the Tree of Life, which is the crown and is represented geographically by Mount Fuji. The crown is the very top, but there is a point above the crown that is called the infinite light, and the Hebrew word for describing that energy is *Ain Soph*, which means "the infinite light" or "that with no end." So we are talking about infinity.

When we study the universe or cosmology, our minds are trying to understand how we could live in a universe that has no end. Our minds cannot picture something having no end, but our minds can go back to the theory of creation and the big bang. The big bang goes to the point that is called singularity.

Singularity is the point where everything was compressed into a ball, into a dense point. Everything in the creation was at a point so small that we can't even measure it. In our minds, we could say that the point might be as small as the head of a pin. Scientists and physicists can go back to 1,000th of a second up to the start of the big bang, but they cannot go back to the point before the big bang began.

So we say, "In the beginning," and that means that there was a point, but what happened before the big bang? The physicists and cosmologists say, "Maybe there was something before the big bang?" Remember, the Creator is infinite.

In the Kabbalah, they theorize that before the big bang, the Creator withdrew Himself from Himself. That is difficult to imagine. Just imagine that the Creator is everywhere and everything there is. So how could the Creator have created the world and the universe if He is everywhere? The solution was that He withdrew Himself and from a portion of Himself made a space, and that space is the universe in which we now live.

We are manifested in *Malchut*, which is King David. Then we go to the top. We go to Mount Fuji, which is the crown, but then we go above the crown, which is the infinite energy that we call infinite light — the light without end.

Also, there are the concepts of the four worlds. The four worlds are the worlds of thought, creation, formation, and making or doing. We look at the Tree of Life as three columns: the left, the middle, and the right. But we also look at the Tree of Life in terms of four worlds — the four levels. So we can go in the *Merkavah* and rise to the world of thought; in order to create something, the thought first has to appear.

Now, in the Tree of Life, we are working with the higher energy, which is the world of thought. We also are working with our guides, teachers, and the Arcturians. We are trying to create thought patterns. We are trying to create thought energies for holding down this fifth-dimensional energy and this fifth-dimensional light. So again, the four worlds are thinking, creating, formation, and making.

* * *

What Is the Infinite?

Mordechai: You know, there are seventy different interpretations of the Torah. There is a scholarly Hebrew book on the Torah called *The Germara*. It is a huge multivolume set, but if you can read all those volumes and understand them, you can pass any law exam in any state in the United States. That's a fact.

As far as the names of God go, that's a very tricky thing about *Elohim* — whether it is singular or plural. They're all one. When you say the codes of ascension, you say, "*Kadosh, Kadosh, Kadosh, Adonai Tzevaoth* — holy, holy, holy is the divine and his core, his army. Since the whole thing is infinite, we don't know how many zeros there are in front of the one, or how many *Tzevaoth* there are. Each of the columns in the Tree of Life can correspond to an archangel. We have Archangel Lord Metatron on top. Archangel Michael, Archangel Gabriel — each one of these archangels is in charge of billions and billions of angels.

I'll give you the whole secret: In the end, when the ascension comes, whenever that happens — and there will be a few of them — there will be a magical, mystical, multidimensional contact between the very bottom *Sephirah* of this Tree of Life and the top one. The tree folds up like a circle and touches the very top of the *Keter* (the crown, Mount Fuji), so it's one continuous circle. That's the real image of infinity of a diagram of the Tree of Life on a piece of paper.

That's where the infinite is. That's where the ascension goes: It goes in one beautiful circle. Yet there are millions and billions of these *Sephirot*. Without making it complicated, trying to keep it simple, when they talk about the *Elohim*, it's all one. How many names of God are there? Millions and billions? We don't know. There are many, many names.

So *Elohim*, if it were plural, could be plural because it's all open. How open is your mind? Can you comprehend millions and billions and trillions? Can you comprehend this? We're trying to keep things simple, but when *Elohim* traveled over the waters, however He went over the waters, it was the upper waters and the lower waters. And regarding *Elohim*, we don't know how many in the fifth dimension were assisting and fostering this creation on this planet eons and eons ago. All we have to know is to treat the next human being with human dignity. And that's really what this Tree of Life tries to bring across.

It's not easy. How can you make something incomprehensible easy? If you go on with the idea that this is a holographic experience, wow — you just opened up a whole other door. *Dalet* means door: the door to the truth.

When the word "ethereal" is mentioned, well, we have the etheric crystals, and then we have the ethereal cosmic mirror. Everything is in the ethereal. We're dealing with the ethereal. What is it that we're dealing with every minute of every day, every second of every day, in the ethereal? Our thoughts — the whole essence of creation is our thoughts. We deal with the ethereal every second of every day.

Use Your Imagination

Getting back to the *Dalet*, the Tree of Life, and selflessness, we really have to comprehend that everything is a screenplay. Imagine someone carrying a box of five bowling balls. The person holding the bottom of the box feels the weight of fifty to sixty pounds. The person carrying the box is sweating and struggling. He's carrying it because of the help of the invisible hand, which is on top and is really doing all the work. He doesn't want to embarrass the one carrying the box and make him think he's not really doing the work.

We really have to, for the sake of unity and for the sake of the Group of Forty, have confidence in our imaginations because, what is it? Its image, that's one thing we all have in common. We can all think through imagery, in symmetry, in unity. That's how we perform Biorelativity — by thinking in symmetry, in unity. It is all in the ethereal. The *Dalet* is the road, the path to the ethereal. It is the path and the doorway to where Lord Archangel Metatron stands. He stands at the Arcturian stargate. The only way to get there is through the *Dalet*. It's amazing!

The *Dalet* really is the password for the software to get to the hardware of the stargate. Also, David said we all came from a point — not the head — of the needle. That point is actually the letter *Yud*.

David also said that above Mount Fuji is the *Ain Soph*. He said that it is represented by this little dart going upward from the top of the *Yud*. Everything is included in these letters — everything! We have to not take it too seriously, yet we have to get whatever we can out of it. I just love it because it's numerically perfect. Ask any mathematician: "What in the third dimension is mathematically perfect?" The answer is nothing — except the Torah. That's the point I keep trying to make. The Torah is not a religious thing; it's a living, cosmic, mystical tool. It's one of the secrets and catalysts in this cosmic drama to get to the bottom of the ladder of ascension.

* * *

Questions from the Class

Lesley: Hi, David. I have a question for either of you. Is the integration that Vywamus is talking about the self-restoration that we have to do to be more effective on Earth or the third dimension?

David: Well, the restoration of self is also understanding our true nature. Our true nature is that we are parts of all of these aspects of the sphere, but it's easy to get stuck in the third dimension, just on the bottom, without realizing you have greater parts of yourself. If you can connect to the other parts, then this helps you expand yourself. So it would be fair to say we don't want you to think that you're just this part on Earth. Restoring the self is like restoring the connection to your higher self and those higher parts.

In the Kabbalah, they talk about the lower, middle, and higher selves. There's even a part of the self that we never talk about that's even higher than the higher self. At some point, we might even be able to take those four parts of the self and tie them into the levels of self of the Tree of Life. Mordechai talked about the three columns. We're also going to talk about the four worlds going up.

Cora in Minnesota: This question is for Mordechai. So from our higher selves that we connected to while you were with the Torah and connected to the Rock of the Dome, my question is, "what was your experience like?" so that you can give us more direction?

Mordechai: Wow, that's a beautiful question! Let me tell you something: When I'm standing there, I don't want to get too into detail, but there's so much energy going on. It's greater than the eye of a hurricane. It's one big *whoosh!* I have my little piece of paper, and I keep looking at it so that I can keep it in my mind. Unity — to connect to the ring of ascension. I'm so busy in consciousness that I don't know what's going on around me, to tell you the truth. I'm just trying to take all that energy and put it in the right place. They keep telling me, "You don't have to, really — we're taking care of it, Mordy. You take care of the 1 percent, and we'll take care of the 99 percent."

But one thing is important, and what I have to tell you is that the most important thing is image. I have strong images of things that are going on. I'm actually at the Torah twice — once for my *Aliyah* (going up to the Torah in front of the congregation during the synagogue service) and then to pick up the Torah. If I tell you to connect at 8:15, then at around 8:35 or 8:40 is when the energy peaks, because I'm taking this twenty-kilogram piece of parchment, and I'm lifting it up over my head. It's a beautiful question you asked, but if you can just imagine what I'm doing …

Cora: The image from this side that I'm seeing is the ladder of ascension and angels going up and down, up and down. They kept delivering the energy.

Mordechai: Yes, yes, because basically I'm gearing it right to the ladder of ascension, to all the ladders, and I bring that energy into all the ladders around the world. My first stop is Jobs Peak, Nevada, where a ladder of ascension has been placed by the Arcturians. From there, I go to Mount Shasta and Mount Fuji. I go wherever I can remember on that piece of paper. There was one time when I forgot my piece of paper, and I said, "Guys, I'm lost. You take over, and here it is." *Boom!*

I would like to further elucidate because by putting myself up there at that structure where the Torah is, I went back in that *whoosh*, and when I heard that audio myself for the first time, I was taken aback by my jumping and expressing and wondering how anybody was going to understand what I was saying. So to further describe from a place where there's no time pressure and where my mind is not pressured, I can tell you very simply the four things that I do that I know are in my heart are almost like a program. When I get up there, I think this from my heart: "I accept, I forgive, I respect," and I put it all in one beautiful basket and unify the entire quantum thing — everything from the Central Sun all the way down to here, which in the Tree of Life is from the top to the bottom. In Hebrew, the term is *L'shem Yichud*, "the desire to bring unity" — that everything we do brings unity to the name of our Creator. That's part of the *whoosh*.

It's one of those things; it's a matter of the heart. Having the attitude of sacrificing my being for the Creator — that's the whole trip, really, sincerely coming from the heart. Imagining how it would happen, thought form and thought particles — that's really why I'm there.

After I pick up the Torah, I sit down and hold it for about ten minutes. I hold it while they do some other readings. It's called the *Haftorah* — the Torah and the *Haftorah*. I'm sure you feel it, because when I give it, the energy flows right through me. I can't hold on to anything. I give it all away, because if you don't give it all away, then you can't get any.

Cora: *Beautiful.*

Mordechai: It's an experience I wish for everybody.

You're Responsible for Your Thoughts

I would like to try to explain why we don't say the full name of the Creator — or any of his names. It's because (here is the secret to the whole Kabbalah in English) when we spell the word "God," we take out the and spell it G-D. Why do we do this? Here is the simple reason: When we say any of the names of the divine essence, we have a responsibility for what we are thinking because there's speech and thought, and we are responsible for our thoughts. I'll give you the whole thing in a nutshell. When you go upstairs … and say, "Look what I did! I did this!" the response you're going to get is this: "Let's take a listen to the audio of your thoughts in that moment in time when you were doing what you were doing." Then when you hear what your thoughts were, you know what your thoughts were, and everybody just shuts right down.

That's how the courts upstairs work. They are very fair: "Here is your action, here is your speech, and here is your thought. Now, what do you have to say about that?" Usually nothing. There's your whole secret to creation. Everything is on digital video and audio. Everything. That's why we have to be careful what we think. We always have to think good thoughts.

* * *

David: The other way to look at this is when you go to a power spot like Japan, Mount Fuji, Mount Shasta, or Sedona, or to a vortex, a ladder of ascension, or an etheric crystal, you're in a particle accelerator. The thoughts you have can now more easily be manifested, whereas if you were in an area of low vibration where there is lower energy, then your thoughts would not be as powerful. So you want to make sure when you're at Mount Shasta or Sedona that you get the highest amount of power of thought. The idea of how to pronounce the name of G-D is tied in with having the ability to manifest on Earth, so you have to have the purest intention.

Hey Is About Understanding

CLASS 6

MORDECHAI, DAVID, AND SANANDA

Mordechai: The Arcturians wanted us to present the Tree of Life this way because it is a spiritual and interactive energy that we all need to hear again and again. Spiritual and interactive energy increases our spiritual light quotient (SLQ). I'm saying this now in the class of the letter *Hey* because this letter represents a beautiful assemblage point.

We must understand that the letter *Hey* is a part of a graduation. We started with the *Bet*, which gave birth to the *Gimmel*, and the *Gimmel* rolled out aggressively and went right after the *Dalet*. The *Dalet* represents the poor person, and the *Gimmel* represents the gifted or rich person — the one with *Parnassah*, as we say, or however you want to think about it. When the *Gimmel* catches up to the *Dalet*, it takes care of the *Dalet*. *Hey* is made up of a *Dalet* and a foot, the foot being an upside-down *Yud*.

Talk about a cosmic paradox — having the first letter of the Creator's name as an upside-down foot for the *Hey*. The *Hey* represents the act of giving oneself to another. It seems like that's what we said about the *Dalet*, giving oneself to and serving another.

The expression of the *Hey* is thought, speech, and action. The soul possesses these three means of expression. We call them "garments" in the Kabbalah. The higher garment is thought. This is the expression of one's inner intellect and emotions to oneself. The process of the intellect and emotions becoming conscious through thought is similar to giving oneself to another or serving another. The two lower garments of speech and action express oneself to others. So this is really like a one-stop shop. This is an assemblage point of everything from *Aleph* up to this letter *Hey*.

The letter *Hey* is composed of three lines. The upper horizontal line connects to thought and thought-form consciousness. This is the same horizontal line for the sake of relating to everyone simply. I think of that Hopi rock because that rock has a line that goes up, but I'm not referring to that line. I'm referring to the horizontal line that goes all the way around and connects and becomes one; there's no beginning and no end. That horizontal line represents the state of equanimity. I'm trying to find a simpler word: It is consistency — new balance and harmony. That's what the Hopi elders wanted to convey: The continuous flow of thought is the contemplation of how the divine is found equally in every place and in everything. Nothing happens — not the good, not the bad, and not the ugly — without permission from upstairs.

The point of origin of this vertical line represents speech. So at least we have a culmination in the basic sequence represented by these three letters, *Gimmel*, *Dalet*, and *Hey*. Basically, the whole process of giving oneself to another, the gift of the situation represented by the foot — the unattached segment of the *Hey* — when fully integrated in the receiver, becomes that person's own power of action and giving of the self to others.

What does that mean? That means that the receiver of the gift or charity is as much an active part of the situation as the giver. You need a qualified receiver or a qualified vessel to receive the light, to receive the charity. Now we're going to get right into the sight, sound, and number.

The Sight of *Hey*

Form is an important factor. The three lines of the *Hey* represent the three dimensions of the third dimension: width, length, and depth. That is why this is such an assemblage point in the level of worlds in sight. At the level of souls in sight, there are three garments, or servants of the soul, and those are thought, speech, and action — represented by the horizontal line, the vertical line, and the unattached foot.

Now, here is something interesting: It's listed as the *Beinoni*, one who is able to master his servants. *Beinoni* is a word that, for the sake of simplicity, is the average guy, the middle guy. It is said that when the

Zohar was written, it was written for the *Beinoni*. The Zohar was written for the average guy. This is so beautiful. We can hardly believe that because the Zohar was written so high and is the soul of the Torah, yet it was written for the average guy. This is amazing.

Now we're going to get to the divinity level of sight, which involves the three divine manifestations of essence: the horizontal line; the transcendent light coming down as the vertical line; and the eminent light, which is the light that is the unattached foot. There's really very little light here in this three-dimensional world, so eminent light is the Sun. So you have one of the highest letters representing the lowest amount of light. It is a beautiful cosmic paradox.

The Sound of *Hey*

Now we go to sound. Sound is another beautiful essence. When you sound out the word *Hey*, the beginning is in a whisper, and it ends up in a manifestation of sound. What does that mean? It is the whisper coming into what is manifesting. The breaking of these vessels is the whole reason for our creation. The 288 sparks that fell are the broken vessels, resulting in the plurality of this creation.[1] It's like the one breaks up into the complete separation. The vessels break up into the complete separation — fractal geometry. A broken existence resulting in a unified existence — that's what we're going through now. We're all going through this broken existence to end up in a unified one.

This level of souls is impregnating reality with the souls of the starseeds, the souls of *B'nai Yisrael*. That's the starseeds, the ones who are taking the knowledge to everyone else. Then there's the divinity level of sound, which is a divine revelation. The ultimate revelation is the coming of the light of repair. We call it the redemption, the coming of the *Mashiach*, the Messiah. That's really what it is.

❋   ❋   ❋

The *H* in *YHWH*

David: We are approaching the Tree of Life from the aspect of the Hebrew alphabet. The letters of the Hebrew alphabet that we have studied so far are *Aleph*, which is *A*; *Bet*, which is *B*; *Gimmel*, which is like a *G* or a *K*; *Dalet*, which is *D*; and *Hey*. There's really not a letter equal to *Hey*, the fifth letter of the Hebrew alphabet. We are also looking at the number five in terms of the Kabbalah.

The *Hey* has been defined as the *H* in the name of God. So if you want to find an approximate English equivalent, it would be the *H*. When we look at the name of God, *YHWH*, you see there are two *Heys*. This name would be incorrectly but commonly translated into English as *Yahweh*. Remember that's not really the way the Kabbalah would pronounce it, but if you take out the *A* and the *E*, then you have *YHWH*.[2]

The Importance of Equanimity

The middle sphere in the Tree of Life chart, which is geographically represented by Montserrat, Spain, represents balance, harmony, and Messianic energy. Lord Sananda is the fifth-dimensional master we are working with in this sphere. So I will talk a little bit about this Tree of Life from that standpoint, because we are covering lots of different information — especially about what it means to be a Messianic light.

The idea of equanimity — I want to explain that a little bit. Mordechai mentioned that. Equanimity is a concept in the mystical world that means you are of equal reaction. If someone praises you, it doesn't go to your head; it doesn't affect you. If someone criticizes you, same thing — it doesn't affect you. That's equanimity. So if a good thing happens, you're okay; if a bad thing happens, you're okay. It doesn't move you one way or another. That is a highly desirable trait in the mystical world and in the world of Kabbalah.

There is a funny story to demonstrate this. It's about two rabbis and their followers. They took a boat on a voyage. Since they were Kabbalists and Jewish, they were put on the bottom of the boat. They weren't allowed to go to the top of the boat where, of course, you could get fresh air. Then the captain of the boat, who was disdainful of the Kabbalists and the rabbis, went down and urinated on one of the rabbis. When the incident was over, the rabbi went to his students and was elated. They asked him, "How can you be elated when the captain did the most despicable thing to you?"

He said, "I know that I have reached equanimity now because it did not affect me. The horrible thing he did to me did not affect me."

That is somewhat controversial, but it is a very clear way of depicting equanimity. I think as teachers we have to be clear that we're not overly affected by praise or criticism. That would be another way of looking at that.

What Is the Assemblage Point?

The assemblage point is another concept that appears in the shamanistic world. It is a point in the aura. Some people think it is in the back, below the neck. That point is like a valve. When that point is opened or activated, you can receive higher perception. That means you can see the dimensional worlds; you can see the spirits that are around us all the time. So this is the assemblage point.

The assemblage point was discussed in the Don Juan series by Carlos Castaneda. Some of you remember Don Juan would go behind Carlos and would strike him lightly in the back of the shoulder, and that would put him into an altered state of consciousness. He was activating Carlos's assemblage point.

I want to mention again the Zohar. It actually is written in Aramaic, and it is written as a mystical commentary of the five books of Moses. It is written as the true interpretation of the mystical meanings, because in the Kabbalah, when we are talking about the Tree of Life, when we are talking about the different occurrences in Genesis, we are looking at them as metaphorical symbols.

There are different levels of interpretation to use when reading these texts. For example, there are different levels of spheres, and the first level is the literal level, but there is also a hidden level. We can take the stories of Genesis literally, or we can take them mystically. The Zohar is trying to explain the hidden meaning of these biblical stories.

One idea of the Kabbalah is that sound is extremely representative of energies and vibrations. So we are interested in sounds, including those of the spheres. This sphere of Montserrat represents Messianic light. The Hebrew name for this sphere is *Tiferet*. This is an unusual word in Hebrew. *Tiferet* literally means "beauty," and when we see something that is beautiful, we can say we are in harmony.

So the sphere of Montserrat, *Tiferet*, is harmony, because it is the sphere that touches all the spheres. It is exactly in the center, and it is the one that creates balance. In a way, it is the only sphere that is in contact with all the other spheres.

When we talk about Messianic in the Kabbalah, we use the word in Hebrew for Messiah, which is *Mashiach*. The Greek translation of *Mashiach* is *Messiah*, and the Messiah is the one who is supposed to bring eternal peace back to the world. He is also supposed to conquer all enemies and evil and is the means by which the second temple will be rebuilt. So looking at our study of the Kabbalah and the Arcturians, we see the Messiah or the Messianic light as an energy transcending the third dimension.

This means that, logically, we look at all the problems that are controlling our planet. As planetary healers, we want to see and understand all the problems, and frankly, most of them look unsolvable. How are we ever going to solve the problem of nuclear waste? How we are going to stop the pollution of our atmosphere? How are we going to stop the pollution of our oceans? It would seem as though there is no way to do this. No political power will be able to institute this. However, in the idea of Messianic light, the fifth-dimensional light is a light that transcends logic that comes from different places. We are focusing on the fifth dimension and the Tree of Life, which has different levels. There is a way to bring us up to the higher levels.

The Vessels and Soul Levels

I also want to talk about this concept of the vessels that Mordechai mentioned. We are vessels. You are a vessel. Your physical body, your mental body, and your emotional body can hold a certain amount of light. If we look at the Tree of Life and its vessels, the theory in the Kabbalah is that the original energy that came down to the universe was contained in vessels to hold this light. The Planetary Tree of Life and the Kabbalistic Tree of Life are depictions of the vessels. There was a vessel for wisdom. There was a vessel for understanding. There was a vessel for hidden knowledge. There was a vessel for manifestation. There was a vessel for shimmering. There were all these different containers to hold the light, but the vessels were not strong enough, and they broke. This occurrence is called in the Kabbalah world, interestingly and obviously, the breaking of the vessels.

So the vessels broke into shards and little pieces, and we are living in this third-dimensional world that was created when the vessels broke. That's why there are so many imperfections in this world. Our goal as starseeds is to bring the vessels back. In the Kabbalah, it is called "the repair"; we repair the vessels.

The Hebrew word for this repair is *Tikun*. I think this concept of vessels is also clear in the study of mysticism and in the higher light because there is only a certain amount of light that each of us can hold. The idea of the SLQ, which was given to us by Juliano, is that we have to be at a certain level of spiritual light energy to hold light or more light. If we are not at a high enough SLQ, we're not going to be able to hold the light. If you can't hold the light, then you will not be able to do the repairs.

I wanted just to finish by talking about the levels of the soul. There is the first and lower level of the soul that is known as the *Nefesh*. *Nefesh* is the first level manifested on Earth, and it has been referred to as the animal part of us — the part that has instincts and the will to live. Then the *Ruach* is the middle level, which can be our ethical or moral self, which is more than the self concerned about humanity and higher values. *Ruach* in Hebrew means both "spirit" and "wind."

The third level of the soul is called *Neshamah*. Interestingly, it has two *Heys*. That is the highest level for the soul from the Earth perspective. Most of us are still working to reach the level that would probably be equated with the fifth-dimensional self. The next level above *Neshamah* is called *Chaya*, and that is the level that is above all these. When I talk about that level, it is difficult because it is a level of yourself that really is so far above your incarnation that it would not even be affected by your death. As far as equanimity, can you imagine a place in your highest self that is not affected by your death? This is another lifetime, because this part knows. And the final part of the soul is called *Yechida* — "the unity" — that part that is totally united with the cosmos and with the divine light.

✳ ✳ ✳

The Significance of Five

Mordechai: Number five in worlds is also a symbol of division. There are five origins of speech in the mouth, and how these letters are pronounced is a science. There are five fingers on the hand, five visible planets in the solar system (Mercury, Venus, Mars, Jupiter, and Saturn), and then we have the five vanities.

There are five levels of the soul. Let me repeat them again: You have *Nefesh*, which is down here in the blood; you have *Ruach*, which is the breath; there's *Neshama*, which is the third level of the soul; and the next level of soul is called the *Chaya*. It is considered pretty high. It is above the *Neshama*. There is even a fifth level of soul, which is really who we are, that is called the *Yechida*.

This makes up the whole five levels of soul that we're serving and filling these vessels for when we graduate. We're all going to graduate; it's just a matter of how many garments we're taking with us to the graduation. You really can't take anything with you as far as the material is concerned. You know the old saying: "You can't pull the U-Haul in back of the hearse." But at the same time, there are these garments that are simply all the good deeds and all the good things that we've said and all the good thoughts from our hearts.

So in divinity, there are the five books of Moses — the first five books of the Old Testament — the five voices at the giving of the Torah, which is when they saw the voices, when they saw the notes. There are the five times you encounter the word "light" in the day of creation.

In the Torah, the word for light, *Ohr*, is mentioned five times, and this is a really big secret. It's the secret of the number twenty-five, because the first time the word *Ohr*, or light, is mentioned in the Torah is the twenty-fifth word, and that is the power of the twenty-fifth day of *Kislev* (a Hebrew month which is approximately December in our Roman calendar), which is *Chanukah*. The number's power is exemplified by the date of December 25 becoming the accepted date for Christmas. It's a powerful number, this number 25.

The fifth time the word *Ohr* is written in the Torah is the forty-second word — the power of forty-two. There are no accidents and no coincidences; it's the power of the *Ana B'Koach*. The fifth time the word *Ohr* is mentioned in the Torah is the power of the *Ana B'Koach*.

The three lines of the *Hey* represent the three dimensions: breadth, height, and depth. As far as the Tree of Life is concerned, we are really working between the numbers six, nine, twelve, and ten, or we're starting the crystal of Montserrat with Lord Sananda, and that's really where the *Hey* goes. How powerful is the *Hey*? It is two of the four letters in each of the million billion names of God. The letter *Hey* is there twice in each one.

❋   ❋   ❋

Balancing Judgment with Loving Kindness

David: I just want to add two things. Look at Mount Shasta in the Tree of Life and at the sphere that represents loving kindness and compassion for Earth. That is the energy of Quan Yin. Then look at sphere number five, Volcán Poás. You see strength, discipline, and judgment for Earth. So in the Tree of Life, one of the main concepts is the three pillars. If there is too much loving kindness, then it has to be balanced by strength and judgment.

The point I want to make is that judgment is also defined as constriction or restriction, which I think is interesting. To have really effective judgment, it must come from loving kindness. So if a parent is going to discipline a child and have a harsh judgment, then the judgment, punishment, or restriction is only effective when it is based on loving kindness.

When we do our Biorelativity meditations, there needs to be restriction, constriction, discipline, and judgment of Earth, but we want it to happen with loving kindness. That is the only way this tree works. As you know, the spheres do not stand alone. They interact with each other.

Mordechai mentioned the word "repentance," which is *Teshuvah* in Hebrew. This is a very deep subject in the Kabbalah, and maybe we could look at that at another time.

Also, when Mordechai talked about *YHWH*, because of the sacredness of the name, he would say *YKVK*. He doesn't want to pronounce the letters. We can also say *YHWH* — that is the four-letter name. These four letters are also referred to as the *Tetragrammaton*. That is a Greek word that means "the four-letter sacred name of God." The Hebrew letters are *Yud, Hey, Vav,* and *Hey,* which are transliterated as *YHWH* or *YHVH* (there are two ways to spell it).

The reason why you see either a *V* or a *W* is that many of the Kabbalists were German and the *W* and *V* have similar pronunciations in German. For example, the German word for "world" is *welt*, but to American ears that actually sounds like *velt*, even though it is written with a *W*.

❋ ❋ ❋

Repentance and Understanding

Mordechai: I love that analogy David pulled out about the two rabbis. It made the point short and sweet, and that is the point of equanimity. That's the whole point right there. Now I want to get to the real assemblage point: the *Hey*. We call it *Teshuvah*, which is really repentance. The word "repentance" has been around a long time, and it's been missed and dissed. "Missed" means abused and other things, and "dissed" means it's been disoriented, disqualified, used, and diluted. So being that this word has been abused, I use the word "atonement" — at-one-ment — and there's a reason it's at-one-ment. This is where the assemblage point comes in.

Te-shuv-hey is doing atonement or repentance, or whatever you want to call it. It means never wanting to do it again. *Te-shuv-hey, Teshuvah,* actually means "returning the *Hey*" — to return to *Hey* by breaking the vessels and through the four-letter name of our Creator, which are *Yud-Kay-Vav-Kay*. The last *Hey* in those four letters fell with the 288 sparks and the broken vessels. That's what that final *Hey* represents — the whole enchilada, the whole ball of wax, the whole purpose of what's coming toward us now: the fifth-dimensional energy fields that are surrounding us.

You know, in order to bring this Messianic energy in the Kabbalah, in order to bring such *Chesed*, such loving kindness (they call it grace), you need a tremendous amount of *Gevurah* (strength). It's all about equal energy polarity. You need balance. You need a consistent equal polarity and the most powerful, highest level of light-force energy to come in. You need a whole bunch of *Gevurah*, a tremendous amount, to attract that tremendous amount of loving grace — *Chesed* energy. It's a polarity that is well understood in the Kabbalah. The word in Hebrew is *Balagan*. It's a simple word meaning "confusion and chaos." If someone asked, "What's wrong over there?" and the person replied, "It's a *Balagan*," then the matter's not even worth checking out. It's nonsense, silliness; it's chaos.

These are all in the galactic drama — how it is perceived from a galactic perspective. They can't believe what goes on down here — 187 religions, 128 languages. Everything all started with the one. I love the emblem of the Sacred Triangle. It really represents the unity of the indigenous, the *B'nai Yisrael*. We were all natives out there in our beginnings. It's really beautiful when you see this whole thing coming together. We were all natives out there in the desert. It is so beautiful to see, the whole thing about this coming together to be as one — not just to have the equanimity to be oneself, but to have a quantum equanimity, to have everyone in the same state of mind.

That is actually the meaning of the fifth dimension — *Shama'yim* in Hebrew, or "heaven" in English. What is it all about? It's about everybody being more concerned about everybody else. If you become more concerned about everybody else, you forget about your own *Balagan*, your own fears of what's going to happen. Because people are feeling the energy now, especially the sensitive ones, they're having these outrageous dreams, and we just have to be strong and have certainty. Certainty is what this *Hey* is all about. This *Hey* is all about understanding.

It all comes together right here in the world of physicality. What's the most important thing? Our intentions. I gave the example earlier of the courts upstairs. The point is I wanted to make sure I got a couple things across. First, I want to give you a homework assignment. How's that for something different? It's a simple question. Don't bother answering it now; answer it in two weeks. The question is, from where do you believe your thoughts originate? I asked this question eight years ago during a new moon in a *Rosh Chodesh* lecture on the astrological sign of

Scorpio. You Scorpios know how to keep a secret. The whole trip today is to reveal hidden knowledge. We are all here to reveal it and to understand what it is we're learning.

The best definition of understanding is to be able to answer others when they ask you a question so that you can give them an accurate and simple answer to that question. That's the definition of understanding.

* * *

Experiencing the Creator Light

Shalom, Shalom, Shalom. Greetings. I am **Sananda**. I am so moved by your abilities to comprehend the nature of the spirit and the relationship between the spirit and the third dimension. There is a great teaching that is available on Earth, for Earth is a beloved garden of my father. Earth is a beloved child. Earth is a place my father has manifested for you — for your learning, for your experience, for your ability to evolve. This third-dimensional experience is precious. It gives you at any time the opportunity to unite all aspects of yourself.

Remember that the third dimension is a lower dimension than the fifth dimension, but it does still have sacred energy on this dimension. That means that with sacred energy there is always the possibility of unification. There is always the possibility of unifying yourself. Remember, there are many higher masters who have achieved nirvana and enlightenment.

If you look at the Tree of Life, then you can see that I, Sananda, am in the center of the Tree of Life. I am able to communicate to the very highest level. It is said that no human can see the light of our Creator and live. It is explained in the metaphor of the breaking of the vessels. If your vessel — that is, your body — is not trained for higher light, and if your body is not strong enough to hold the light, then you will be blinded by the higher light. You as a third-dimensional being, as an entity residing on Earth, will break. But I, as a fifth-dimensional being, am able to experience this light.

Maybe it is true you cannot experience the fifth-dimensional light directly, but if you are able to identify with me, if you are able to allow me to cohabit with you, then you can come to me in the center of the tree. The center of the tree is represented by Montserrat, Spain. This sphere is known as the Messianic light. I will allow you through me to experience the unity of the entire tree. And I will allow you to tolerate the intense beauty of my father's light. This has always been my mission on Earth. This is now my mission for the ascension: to allow you and to help you experience this fifth-dimensional light.

Remember that the ascension will be activated by a sound, but it will also occur with a light. Ascension is also a light frequency. So think about the concept in modern psychology called "synesthesia." Synesthesia is the ability to see a color and at the same time hear the color. So when you are thinking about the Hebrew letters, remember that in the higher states, the sounds of the sacred letters are visible. The sound of ascension is also transforming into a light of ascension. And this light of ascension is part of the Messianic light. I am going to oversee the bringing of this light to each of you. Blessings. Blessed is the name. I am Sananda. Good day.

✳ ✳ ✳

Questions from the Class

Celia in New Mexico: Why isn't Hey *a fire letter?*

Mordechai: Well, actually, they are all fire letters — all twenty-seven Hebrew letters (the twenty-two main letters and the five letters that are called final letters) are living energy intelligences. Each and every one of them has a purpose, an ability. Every angel has a mission. So you see the angels running up and down the ladder constantly, flashing up and down. Actually, the angels are whispering. Now, with the angels, there's no speech upstairs, so they are actually thinking and whispering, constantly whispering to themselves. What are they whispering? Each angel has a specific mission, and God forbid they should forget that mission. The angels were created for certain missions.

The letters are multidimensional, multifaceted, so they have many missions. The *Hey* is, I would consider, a fire letter among fire letters. Maybe there are two ways to spell the Creator's name: a *Yud-Kay*, a name that we know as *Yahweh* (spelled this way to dilute energy), or the *Aleph-Kay-Yud-Kay*, which is even higher. That goes all the way up to Mount Fuji, sphere one, and Metatron. So the letter *Hey* is definitely a fire letter.

Catherine from England: I was wondering if Mordechai could say the word that people use for chaos, silliness, and confusion. Can you spell it out for me in English?

Mordechai: *Balagan.* It's a great Hebrew word: B-A-L-A-G-A-N.

Alessandra in Washington, DC: *What exactly are we supposed to do at 8:30 Los Angeles time on Friday night for our meditation?*

Mordechai: Yes, 11:30PM your time. You can be anywhere you want. All you have to do is send all your heartfelt desires to balance Mother Earth. Send them to the Dome of the Rock. The dome is just a navigational point. The foundation stone that is underneath that dome stone that everybody has ascended from in the past — that's the energy vortex. Send whatever you want. You could be lying in bed, at the movies, at a restaurant — wherever you are at 11:30PM (your time).

Send your heartfelt love to the rock, because at that time, I am in direct physical contact with the Torah and with a group of *Tzaddikim* (holy men). I'm just taking the energy, whatever is sent to me, to the rock and putting it up in the ring of ascension. The ring of ascension is really the essence of the connection. It clarifies our connection to that whispering, quiet voice.

Vav: God's Ray of Light

CLASS 7

Mordechai, David, and Archangel Michael

Mordechai: *Shalom,* everyone. Good morning, good afternoon, and good evening. Today's class is the letter *Vav.* It is the sixth letter in the *Aleph-Bet.* You can see that the letter *Vav* is a straight line and represents the word connection.

So in the beginning of creation, when infinite light filled all reality, God contracted his light to create hollow, empty space, as it were. The "place," *HaMakom,* was necessary for the existence of finite worlds (by finite worlds, I mean the third dimension). Into this vacuum, the Creator drew down, figuratively speaking, a single line of light. We call it the ray of divine life (referred to in the Kabbalah as the *Kav*): God withdrew himself from Earth and left this ray of light.

The secret of the letter *Vav* is this very ray of light. Though the line of *Vav* is singular in appearance, it has an external as well as an internal force possessing two dimensions. Both of these forces take part in the process of creation and the continuous interaction between the creative power and the created reality, which is an interaction into which we will go.

The external force of the line has the power to differentiate and separate the various aspects of reality, thereby establishing a hierarchical order up and down within creation. This up and down is a consistency. The internal force of the line has the power to reveal the "inherent interinclusion" of the various aspects of reality, one in the other, thereby joining them together as an organic whole.

I'd like to define that term, "inherent interinclusion." Being a rather complicated explanation, I will give you this analogy with a spyglass instead. A spyglass is like a pair of binoculars except it is just one tube for one eye. It is cylindrical and opens up in sections. Now, imagine taking that spyglass, holding the wide circle up, and pulling from the bottom, the different sections going down. That is how creation was created, and that is how the Tree of Life comes down. Everything comes down from the inside.

The inherent interinclusion is when you take the bottom of the spyglass that you've extended all the way down and shove it back into the top. You have inherent interinclusion when everything comes together from the bottom to the top. It means bringing it all together and having the connection to be able to do so.

Now, the property of the letter *Vav* in this usage in Hebrew is referred to as the *Vav Hakhibur*, the *Vav* of connection. Connection is the first word you have of the *Vav*, meaning the word "and," (something and something), heaven and earth, for example, a conjunction; it says *Kosher*. What does *Kosher* mean? The word *Kasher* means "ready." It doesn't mean *Kosher*; it means ready. It's ready for a connection. In other words, when something is allegedly *Kosher* and then when it's been blessed, you've made a clean connection. There is a clean connection; there is no obstacle, no blockage, and no interference with the situation.

The first *Vav* in the Torah is in the first line: *Bereshit bara Elohim et hashamayim ve'et ha'aretz*, "in the beginning God created the heaven and the earth." It serves to join spirit and matter, heaven and earth, throughout all of creation. It is a connection. This *Vav* appears in the beginning of the sixth word of the Torah. Its value is six, and it is the twenty-second letter of the verse.

It alludes to the power to connect and interrelate all twenty-two individual powers of creation, the twenty-two letters of the Hebrew alphabet, from *Aleph* to *Tav*. It means that these twenty-two letters purely represent living energy intelligences. So the word *Et*, *Aleph-Tav*, is generally taken to represent all of the letters of the alphabet from *Aleph* to *Tav* in one unity.

Now, the Kabbalists interpret the word *Et* in this verse to include all the various objects of creation present within heaven and earth. The secret is that when you find the word *Et* in the Torah, it refers to the presence of the *Shekhinah*, the divine essence. So when you see the word *Et*, which really doesn't have any practical purpose being where it is, and it says *Aleph-Tav*, you know it is the presence of the *Shekhinah*.

Borrowing from the Seed Level and the Future

The next subject is really beautiful. In biblical Hebrew, the letter *Vav* also possesses the function of inverting the apparent tense of a verb to its opposite, from past to future or from future to past. That is called *Vav Hahipukh*, or *Vav* reversal, because the tense of the verb is reversed when the *Vav* is in front of it.

The first appearance of this type of *Vav* in the Torah is the letter *Vav*, which begins the twenty-two words of the account of creation: "And God said …" This is the first explicit saying of the ten sayings of creation. *Va'yomer Elohim Yehi Ohr, V'Yehi Ohr*: "And God said," (the verb "said" is being inverted from the future to the past tense by the *Vav* at the beginning of the word) "'Let there be light' [Genesis 1:3, KJB] and there was light." The phenomenon of light breaking through the darkness of the *Tzimtzum*, the original contraction, is in itself the secret of time with the future becoming past, which permeates space.

What I'm saying here is basically what Juliano mentioned in a couple of lectures: We can go into the future and borrow from it, and bring it back to the present or take it back to the past. We can also go to the seed level and bring it into the future. This is the power of the *Vav*. It is very powerful.

It is also a letter in the Creator's name, *Yud-Kay-Vav-Kay*. In divine service, the power to draw from the future into the past is the secret of how to draw *Teshuvah*, repentance, which we discussed with the *Hey* — bringing the *Hey* back up to the other three letters.

Through *Teshuvah* or returning from, with, or because of fear, one's previous transgressions are like errors. The severity of one's past transgressions becomes partially sweetened but not completely changed. However, when a starseed returns in love, his or her deliberate transgressions become like actual blessings, merits, for the very consciousness of distance from God resulting from one's transgressions becomes the motivating force to return to the divine with passion — even greater than that of one who has never sinned. This is an important statement.

What this means is that when the sages say that a *Ba'al Teshuvah* (master of repentance), one who returns to the divine essence, returns to the one living God with love, he or she stands and cannot be matched by the greatest *Tzaddik* (saint or righteous person) who never sinned. This explains why repentance is so important — because if you do it right, you go higher than the greatest *Tzaddik*! This is an amazing statement. The greatest righteous person cannot stand next to you; that's a nice perk.

The power of *Teshuvah* is to completely convert one's past to good. It is the power of the *Vav* to invert the past into the future. This transformation requires paradoxically drawing down the light of the future to the present or to the past. This is exactly what Juliano was talking about — going to the future, borrowing, and bringing it back.

That includes healing. I was reading about Marcel Vogel and his crystals, and he was able to take a hundred severe trauma cases and work on them with the crystals. He brought them back to the original time of the accident, and he brought the present into the past, where they were before the trauma or accident. This is similar to restoring your computer and bringing the date back to a time before it got confused. They got through that trauma, and they were all fine. That's a decent-sized miracle in today's world. He brought them from the present to the seed level via a mundane, third-dimensional healing technique.

The Form of *Vav*

The letter *Vav* is consistent. Now we're going to get to sight, sound, and number. The *Vav* is a vertical line representing a pillar or a man standing straight up. When you're dealing with pillars, remember that there are three levels of pillars. There's the level of twelve pillars, the level of seven pillars, and the level of one pillar.

The twelve pillars of creation relate completely to the twelve lines of a cube. The cube comes from the point of a needle, and these twelve lines expand out, so the third dimension is actually in the shape of a cube — not a circle, but a cube. It also represents the twelve tribes, the twelve zodiac signs, the twelve months, and the twelve *Challot* (special bread) on the table on Friday Night of *Shabbat*, representing the three columns of the Tree of Life. The twelve goes on to a point where people actually wanted to create a mathematics system based on twelve instead of base two or base ten. It sounded good, but when you extend it out, it doesn't work.

Then you have your seven pillars of creation — your six directions (north, south, east, west, up, and down), and the seventh is time. The one-pillar definition is the one Messianic entity that is going to come in that intergalactic, interdimensional Messianic armada. And that will bring the future. There also are connecting rods in the *Tabernacle* — the twelve connecting rods.

That's at the level of worlds in sight/form. Now, souls show a man standing up with his head in heaven and his body on Earth. In other words, we're supposed to be in two worlds at the same time, and that's where Moses, Sananda, and all the great *Tzaddikim* were, or all the great shepherds were. They had one foot in the fifth dimension and one foot in the third dimension. Believe me, it was not easy at all.

Then you have the one pillar, the pillar of truth, in the middle — the level of divinity. The pillar of truth with balance is the middle pillar. We're also talking about how in the three-pillar set, the three columns of the Tree of Life, the middle pillar is the stability — the equilibrium.

With the number six, you have the six days of creation, the six divine forces active in creation, and those are the six *Sephirot* — from *Chesed* all the way down to *Yesod*. There are six letters in the word *Bereshit*, meaning "in the beginning," about which there are some 1,500 books written. There are six *Alephs* in the first verse of the Torah, six millennia in the duration of this world of creation, and six directions of the physical world.

At the level of souls, we have six wings of the fiery angels. In the level of divinity, you have the six orders of the *Mishnah*, the six wings of the *Magen David* (the shield of David, also known as the star of David), which is what we call the Sacred Triangle. We also have the six cubits, as in the dimensions of the tablets that were received by Moses on Mount Sinai.

* * *

Look at Creation through Modern Cosmology

David: I want to talk some more about the whole Tree of Life and remind everybody that the Tree of Life is an expression, in many ways, of the mind of the Creator and how the creation came into existence. One of the things about the Tree of Life that is totally amazing is that it gives a blueprint of the mind of the Creator and of how the forces were used to create this third dimension. The Tree of Life is a main part of the Kabbalah, which means "to receive" in Hebrew; Moses went up to Mount Sinai and received the Ten Commandments, but he also received this information on the Tree of Life.

So the Kabbalah studies creation and the formation of creation. There is a theory that in order to understand the Creator, you must understand the creation. That sounds pretty obvious, but also consider that in order to understand the Creator, you must understand how the creation began. So how did it occur?

This is a part of the Tree of Life. Remember, in the Tree of Life, in the sphere of hidden knowledge, part of the hidden knowledge of how the creation began is now being revealed. I think that studying the creation is an aspect of the Kabbalah and an aspect of the Tree of Life. That is what we are talking about. In Hebrew, it is called *Ma'aseh Bereshit* — the making of the creation. This is an approximate transliteration of the word *Bereshit*, which is the first word in the Torah, the Old Testament.

Let's just talk for a moment about the making of the creation and modern cosmology, because cosmology is the study of the universe. Modern cosmology focuses on the theory — and remember, it is only a theory — of creation, which is the big bang. A lot of people think they have proven that the big bang occurred, but it is not proven. It is an extraordinary theory. The theory of the big bang is that everything was compressed into singularity (singularity is like a dot or a point). The total universe was compressed into this small point. Trillions and trillions and trillions of tons of matter was compressed into this point that is smaller than the point of a pen. That is totally difficult for our minds to comprehend. Then, at the moment of the creation, at the moment when the Creator said, "Let there be light," that dot exploded and became the big bang.

When you study modern cosmology, the laws of physics break down at that point of singularity because they cannot understand all of it. They cannot understand what happened before that millionth of a second. What would cause this singularity to explode and create this creation?

A different idea was proposed by a famous Kabbalist named Ari, which means "the lion" in Hebrew. He composed a beautiful concept that is so in alignment with modern cosmology and called it "the contraction." "The contraction" in Hebrew is *Tzimzum*. What Ari said is that the first act of creation was that the Creator withdrew from Himself and created or allowed space or a vacuum to exist. So the first act of creation was not the big bang; it was the contraction, which is also called "the withdrawal." Then, as Mordechai said, the Creator left a ray of light, which is represented by the Hebrew letter *Vav* (the English letter *V*). So the *Vav* represents a ray of light that was left, and then the big bang occurred.

Remember that at this point, when the Kabbalists developed this idea of contraction or withdrawal, they did not understand the big bang. Even the modern cosmologist cannot go back to that exact point, because what would cause the explosion? What would cause the big bang? Obviously, from the Tree of Life standpoint, it would be the words that were spoken — "Let there be light" — because in the Kabbalah, the words have ultimate power.

I think that this is a beautiful concept, and I gave a lecture many years ago about the Hebrew word *Avra Kedabra*. Many people don't realize that *Avra Kedabra*, as we say in the American accent (Abra-ca-dabra), is a Hebrew phrase that means "as it is created, so it will be," or "as it is spoken, so it shall be." This points out that the words create energy. When we talk about Jesus, we say that he spoke healing words. Jesus said, "Let there be healing," and healing occurred. Speaking healing words successfully is the highest level of healing.

The Tree of Life, then, is an aspect of understanding of the mind of the Creator, and as we are looking at each of the spheres, we are also studying the mind of the Creator. The Kabbalah believes that you must study the making of creation, and that is what we are talking about when we talk about "the withdrawal" or "the contraction." The first aspect of God's action in the creation was to withdraw himself.

If you combine that with the modern big bang, then the Creator withdrew Himself but left one point, one ray, and that was the singularity. Again, the singularity contained all of the mass of the entire universe at that one point.

There's No *W* in Hebrew

Mordechai mentioned the *Shekhinah*, which is also known as the divine or feminine presence of the Creator. That is interesting because the Tree of Life is divided into the masculine and the feminine, the yin and the yang. I also want to point out that there are a lot of similarities between Kabbalah and Taoism. If you look at the yin-yang symbol, even though it is clear on one side and black on the other, each side contains a little dot indicating that the essence of the masculine is still contained in the feminine and vice versa.

I do want to make another point about the *Vav*. Mordechai and I discussed the English transliteration of the name *Yahweh* for God, but that is with a *W*, and there is no letter for *W* in Hebrew. This means the name should be spelled *Yahveh*, which would be with the *Vav*, or a *V*.

If you study J. J. Hurtak as I have, you may find that he is so profound and deep that it is difficult to understand him. In any case, he put out audio of the sounds of the names of God with very beautiful chants and some beautiful chorus people. One of the sounds is *Yaveh*

Shalom, not *Yaweh Shalom.* That is very interesting.

In conclusion, I want to point out that the sphere of hidden knowledge is below Mount Fuji and is represented by the Istanbul etheric crystal. This hidden knowledge, which is on the Tree of Life, is now revealing secrets about the making of the creation, especially through discoveries in modern physics. So now part of the hidden knowledge is being revealed to the world.

For centuries, this knowledge about cosmology and the Kabbalah was hidden and not spoken. It was only talked about if you were forty years old. Then you had to go through quite a bit of initiation to be introduced to this information. Yet here we are today discussing this sacred, complex, and very profound information.

❊ ❊ ❊

Work toward Elevating Your Soul

Mordechai: I want to begin with a question I asked earlier: Where do we believe our thoughts originate? A better question is, how long does it take to win out over our egos? The answer is simple: as long as we want it to take, because of free choice, free will. That's why there are things that happen to make us not procrastinate, avoid, and deny these things that have to be confronted.

I want to discuss in the level of souls, under number six, that there was a prophetic vision. Isaiah saw the fiery angels, or the seraphim, as each possessed six wings. He said seraphim stood above him and each one had six wings. With two, he covered his face; with two, he covered his feet; and with two, he flew. And one called to another and said — guess what? *Kadosh, Kadosh, Kadosh, Adonai Tzevaoth; Me-lo Kol Ha'aretz Ke'vo'do.* Holy, holy, holy is the lord of hosts; the whole Earth is full of his glory.

I said the whole sentence. In order to get to the ladder of ascension, all you need is the first half — *Kadosh, Kadosh, Kadosh, Adonai Tzevaoth.* The whole sentence does offer completion, so I will say it slowly: *Kadosh, Kadosh, Kadosh, Adonai Tzevaoth, Me-lo Kol Ha'aretz Ke'vo'do.* The whole Earth is full of his glory. In general, the wings symbolize the two primary emotive powers of the soul — love and fear. The Zohar teaches that *Mitzvoth,* or good deeds, performed without love and fear (awe) — though infinitely significant and potent unto themselves — do not possess the wings necessary to fly up to heaven to reveal their divine origin.

The two wings that cover the face of each angel correspond to the manifestation of love and fear (awe). Born from meditation, the act of covering the face represents the attribute of holy shame and the face of the divine essence. The two wings that cover the feet of each angel correspond to the innate qualities of love, awe, and fear that exist in every soul. The covering of the feet represents the attribute of walking humbly with your divine essence. The two wings of flight themselves correspond to the experience of divinely inspired love, awe, and fear. These are given from above to one who has sincerely served the divine essence with love, awe, and fear to the maximum, though with a limited level of the soul's initial state of consciousness.

These God-given emotions serve to elevate the soul to infinitely higher states of consciousness as the flight of the seraphim. So what is the Zohar saying? It is saying that we really have these attributes; each of these seven *Sephirot* represents a different level of emotion, and each of them needs to be tweaked. We all need to tweak particular attributes.

The Vav's Gematria

I want to get to the divine name only because it exists in the triangle of six. I will explain the triangle number. The triangle numerically represents a number equivalent to the equation $6 = 21$. What does that mean? That means $6 + 5 + 4 + 3 + 2 + 1 = 21$. Now, I'm going to give you a sort of mathematical analogy to show you how perfection is displayed mathematically.

To understand this mathematically, you have to remember that each Hebrew letter also has a numerical value. *Aleph* is 1, and *Bet* is 2. The *Vav* is 6, the triangle number for the *Vav* is 21, and 21 is the sacred gematria of *Ek-Yeh* (I will be). *Aleph-Kay-Yud-Kay.*[1] That number also is 21. So when you have *Ek-Yeh Asher Ek-Yeh,* "I will be that I will be," you have two *Ek-Yehs,* 21 and 21, which is 42. This is a reminder of the *Ana B'Koach,* because that prayer has forty-two words.

There are two great combination numbers in this sacred gematria. One is the *Ana B'Koach,* or the first forty-two letters in the Torah, in Genesis, and the other is the middle word, *Asher.* Now, the gematria of *Asher* is 501, but that's not as important as the first time it appears in the Torah. It is the 72nd word in the Torah from the beginning, from *Bereshit.*

Now, 72 means a lot. It is the sacred gematria of the *Sephirah* of *Chesed,* which means "loving kindness." But even more powerful are the 72 names (the mystical Kabbalah believes there are 72 names of God), the 72 three-letter combinations of names that come in boxes, nine boxes wide by eight boxes long. These are three-letter combinations that Abraham gave when he gave everything to Isaac, and to Ishmael and the concubines he gave gifts. What were these gifts? Each one of them received one box and went east. Wherever they went — China, Mongolia, Russia, India — they went with one of these boxes. But Abraham gave to Isaac all the boxes — everything. Now, I'm trying to prove a point here.

When you get a gift of one box, you really treasure that one gift, that one box you got. You make the best use of it. All of those individual men and concubines who got those gifts went out and went their own ways, and they treasured that gift of a three-letter box. Yet what happens when you get all the boxes, for some reason, is that you can't appreciate all the boxes like you can appreciate one, if you know what I'm talking about. It's an amazing thing. We'll call this human nature. But here's the kicker: There are three letters in each one of these 72 boxes, which makes a master number. In the movie *Pi*, they were running after this *Chasid* (holy man) because he found a master number of 216 with his calculating.

Two hundred sixteen is the number for the 72 names for each of the three columns in the Tree of Life: 72 for the right column, 72 for the left column, and 72 for the central column. That equals 216.

For the last thirty seconds, I can only say that the *Vav* represents the straight line, and the *Kav* goes all the way from the bottom of the bottom, where we are, all the way to the top of the top, beyond this page of the Tree of Life and beyond many other pages. The *Vav* in Hebrew is called *Yashar*. *Yashar* means "straight." I have to go back to the Hopi Rock and say that the line goes consistently straight — not to the left, not to the right, just a straight path around that rock.

✳ ✳ ✳

Digging Deeper into the Hebrew

David: I want to go over the words that Mordechai spoke in Hebrew because many of us have been using these words: *Kadosh, Kadosh, Kadosh, Adonai Tzevaoth,* and *Me-lo Kol Ha'aretz Ke'vo'do.* That is an approximate transliteration. Also, Mordechai mentioned the sacred name of God, which is "I will be that I will be." A loose transliteration in English is "I am that I am," and the English transliteration from Hebrew of that is *Ehyeh Asher Ehyeh.* That was this famous revelation when Moses was at the burning bush and wanted to know God's name; God said, "*Ehyeh Asher Ehyeh.*"

Now, many people ask this question about God's name — if it's *Yahveh, Ehyeh Asher Ehyeh*, or whatever. Why is it that in Hebrew they don't say the name? They always say "the nameless one" or "the name." You might hear Mordechai say *Hashem* — "the name." I came across an interesting explanation for this: If you can imagine that you are in a court and are meeting the king of the whole world, you probably would address the king as "your majesty." You wouldn't say, "Hi, George"; if you saw Queen Elizabeth, you wouldn't say, "Hi, Liz. How are you?" I think that's an interesting explanation for why we might use "the name." It's because that is showing respect to the king.

* * *

Unlocking the Codes of Ascension

Greetings. This is **Archangel Michael**. I'm here to speak to you about understanding the ascension. I'm here to help you understand what a gift it is that you are able to understand what the creation is. You are able to understand the making of the creation. You are able to understand that there is a beginning and an end as well as that the concepts of a beginning and an end are part of the third dimension, because in the greater, higher dimensions, there is no beginning; there is no end. So the study of the making of the creation in the Kabbalah is called the *Ma'aset Bereshit*.

Bereshit is a mind-expanding process in which you are studying and experiencing the mind of the Creator. In these Trees of Life, the ten and twelve spheres all represent aspects of how the Creator, our father, is manifesting his energy, this world, and this dimension in which you live. The beauty of this is that it is a living Tree of Life. It is not static, even though you have a diagram of it. The diagram really is holographic; it's not one-dimensional, and the energy is continually flowing. It is not in only one place, but it is also an interaction.

Now we understand the spheres on the Tree of Life. We also are connecting with the second sphere, which is called wisdom. We are connecting with Mount Fuji, the top sphere, and we are connecting with the top three spheres. The third sphere, understanding, comes out of the second sphere, wisdom.

We also are talking about the ascension. Now, the ascension is represented in the Tree of Life because you are going into higher and higher spheres. Each sphere brings you closer to the top, which is closer to the Creator — closer to the energy of the Creator. There are beautiful teachings about unlocking the codes of the ascension, because all of what we are talking about is in the supermind. The codes of ascension are in your mind, and you can unlock them within your mind. This is so that you can grasp this energy to use your native and inherent DNA to ascend with use of this phrase: "*Kadosh, Kadosh, Kadosh, Adonai Tzevaoth.*"

Listen as I chant these words through the channel and allow the sounds of these words to unlock the codes of ascension within you.

[Chanting slowly: *Kadosh, Kadosh, Kadosh, Adonai Tzevaoth. Kadosh, Kadosh, Kadosh, Adonai Tzevaoth.*]

Let the name of our Creator, let the name of the Holy One — blessed is he — activate within you and open up within you the codes of ascension so that when you are able to transform, you can transmute yourself into your fifth-dimensional self with the understanding I am giving you.

Avra Kedabra: As I speak, so it shall be. As you hear the phrase "*Kadosh, Kadosh, Kadosh, Adonai Tzevaoth,*" the codes of ascension will be unlocked, and you will use your abilities to go to the higher level. I am Archangel Michael. Good day.

❋   ❋   ❋

Questions from the Class

Celia in New Mexico: Are we experiencing an inbreath of God creating a vacuum that is taking us from the third dimension to the fifth dimension?

Mordechai: Yes — the inbreath of God. Spiritually speaking, we are about to enter that stage. We have to go through, I guess, a form of tweaking. We all have to change, no matter what it is we have to do in our personal soul evolvement. To graduate from this school of Earth and its reincarnations, we have to earn it. It's not a gift. We have to earn it by doing these things for other people. Once we do that and get all that done, the Creator and all the fifth-dimensional entities will be observing us as we go through our changes. Once these changes have manifested, then the inbreath can take us and suck us right up the ladder of ascension.

Bedeep in Tennessee: With regard to the Tree of Life, is there a color associated with each of the spheres?

Mordechai: The *Sephirot* in the Tree of Life that we deal with are the seven or eight spheres under the curtain. In other words, from Mount Shasta (loving kindness) to Volcán Poás, to Montserrat, to Grose Valley, to Lake Taupo, to Barrancas de Cobre, and down to the bottom — all the way down to Lago Puelo. Those are the seven. There is a color for each of those spheres just as there are seven colors, seven sounds, and seven frequencies or notes. That's where your groups of seven are. There are definitely seven basic colors.

David: Also, there are sounds related to each sphere, such as *do-re-mi-fa-so-la-ti-do*. I've also seen that related to each of the seven spheres.

Mordechai: And yes, they are colors, but remember, what color do all the angels and all the energies upstairs wear? They wear white, because white is inclusive of all the colors.

Bedeep from Tennessee: *Would you be able to tell us which colors are related to which sphere?*

Mordechai: I can give you the first three. We usually don't get into the detail of color and frequency. The sphere in Mount Shasta, loving kindness, the color on that right column is white. Then when you go to number five, Volcán Poás, which is strength and discipline — or *Gevurah* — that color is red. Then when you go to the central column, Montserrat and Lord Sananda, that color is green.

I'll go a little further for you so you'll understand. Number four, loving kindness, is white, and the metal related to it is silver. *Gevurah*, number five, is red. Volcán Poás — that metal is gold. The central column is copper. Now, we use the color green for the central column. Why green? Copper is not green, is it? Well, it is once it gets oxidized. The balance is in the oxidation. Once copper gets oxidized, it turns green. As far as the other four, I can't say what the individual colors are because those top three are the tops of each column under the curtain. Thanks for asking.

Alessandra: *I always thought energy traveled in an arc, so this idea of the ray coming from the Creator down to us in a straight line doesn't really jibe with that.*

Mordechai: Okay, this is a toughie. When they're speaking of energy going in an arc, yes, it goes in an arc from local locations. When you're coming down a whole bunch of dimensions, it's sort of ... it may have a curve. For the sake of keeping it simple, that line is called a *Kav*. As a matter of fact, that's the name of the straight line that goes straight down into all those forty circles. It's a matter of understanding distance. Well, not so much distance as it is grades — grades of worlds. So when you're dealing with having a ray of light going from the Dome of the Rock to Sedona or from the dome to Jobs Peak and from there to Mount Fuji, that's an arc. When you have a stream of light coming down through forty-two dimensions, that's a straight line.

David: But one thing you have to understand is that we are in a third-dimensional reality. We are looking at our third-dimensional world as a piece of paper, which is not holographic. So when you say "a straight line," that straight line is, in our perspective, just like I talk about singularity and the point. That singularity was in multiple dimensions; it wasn't in one dimension. When we have to represent it in some way in a third-dimensional world, we use a straight line. So while there are curves and there are arcs, to make this work with our minds, we have to start with a straight line.

Mordechai: The best analogy I can use goes back to that old Hopi rock. It is a straight line going around the rock, but if you're on top of the rock, the line looks curved.

Zayin: Female Energy

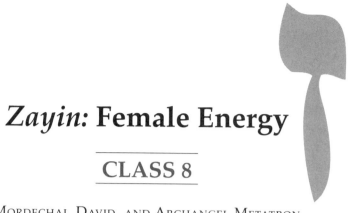

CLASS 8

MORDECHAI, DAVID, AND ARCHANGEL METATRON

Mordechai: Welcome to the eighth class and the seventh letter of the *Aleph-Bet*, which is *Zayin.* I estimate that at least 80 percent of our readers are female, and this is completely about female energy; the *Zayin* is the woman of valor.

The *Maggid* of *Mezeritch,* who was the successor of the *Baal Shem Tov,*[1] teaches that the verse "the woman of valor is the crown of her husband" alludes to the form of the letter *Zayin.* The previous letter, *Vav,* portrays the *Ohr Yashar,* straight light, descending from God into the worlds. The *Zayin,* whose form is similar to the *Vav* with a crown on top, reflects the *Ohr Yashar,* or reverses the straight light of the *Vav,* and sends it back as *Ohr Chozer,* the returning light.

The *Ohr Chozer* is the light that we send back upstairs. It is a very, very important light. It is the light that keeps this creation going. The *Ohr Chozer* ascends with such force that it reaches a higher state of consciousness than that of the revealed origin point of the *Ohr Yashar.* What this means is it goes all the way to the top of the tree and beyond Metatron — actually, from all of the trees of life. It really represents the ancient Holy One and the level of *Keter.*

The initial superconscious realm of *Keter* broadens awareness to both the right and the left. In truth, there is no left in the Ancient One in the level of *Keter,* for all is right. This means the awe of God at this initially superconscious level is indistinguishable. It is actually the same in its nature. It clings directly to the divine essence from the highest manifestation of love of the divine essence.

The experience of *Ohr Chozer*, or this returning light, is a consummation of the creative process. In other words, God created man on the sixth day, but it is the secret of the seventh day of creation, which is *Shabbat*. Everything I'm speaking to you about has absolutely nothing to do with religion. This is strictly a galactic, cosmic science that was brought down into this world. The *Shabbat* Queen is actually *Adonai*. The *Shabbat* Queen, who in general signifies woman in relation to man, has the power to reveal in her husband his own superconscious crown, the experience of serene pleasure, and the sublime will innate in the day of *Shabbat*. What does this mean? This means that the woman of valor has the power to take what is in the husband's superconsciousness and bring it to the level of consciousness. She brings it past subconscious and into the conscious, which is absolutely priceless. It's all about rectification. Rectification is a fancy name for *Tikun*, or correction. This is all about correcting the creation.

The Sight of *Zayin*

Now we're going to move on with sight, sound, and number. In sight, the *Zayin* resembles the man whose head extends in both directions and thus appears like a crown and the scepter of a king. In the level of worlds, *Zayin* is rulership manifested in the world. This means the king holds the scepter, and on top of the scepter, you find that the crown extends equally from the right and the left.

Another level is natural selection. The best way I can describe natural selection in this world of manifestation is by an analogy or metaphor. There's a rule that if you have seven coins that are all the same size and you put one coin down, the other six will surround that coin in the middle. As another example, the six mundane days of the week surround the day of *Shabbat*. You can try it with any size coin — quarters, dimes, pennies. It's a science; it works, and it is pure mathematics.

On the level of souls in sight, a woman of valor is the crown of her husband. The Bible uses Sarah, Abraham's wife, as the original woman of valor. The soul's experience of *Shabbat* is key to understanding the Kabbalah. On the level of divine essence of sight, the form of the *Zayin* is *Shabbat* and the Kabbalah.

The second one is the returning light spreading at its peak — spreading fear and awe to the left and love to the right. The left, fear (awe), is *Yirah*. *Yirah* is the word for "love and awe." They use the word "fear (awe)," but it's not fear. It's awe. When that arc opens up on Saturday morning, there's no fear; there's complete awe. There is awe of the energy, awe of all of the entities — all of the archangels who are surrounding that arc. It's awe and not fear. Also in divinity, the *Zayin* is a vessel for God's blessing and sanctity, which is really the power of how this creation regenerates itself moment to moment.

The Sound and Numbers of *Zayin*

The letter *Zayin* at the level of sound is a weapon or a sword, so you can grab hold of that crown and use it as a sword. It is also an ornament or a crown, and it means to sustain the species or gender. The creative essence influences our Earth drama or screenplay. The creative essence basically decides who is elected to keep existing in this plane and who leaves. Humans are the crowning ornaments of creation. The divine level of sound is God sustaining the world every moment.

Now we get to my favorite category, which is numbers. It is stated in the Torah and in the Zohar that all sevens are beloved. What does this mean? At the level of worlds, it means maximum compactness, which is a nice fancy combination for what I just described of the six coins surrounding the seventh. That's the level of worlds. You have the seventh day of creation, which is *Shabbat*. *Shabbat* is absolutely, positively galactic and cosmic.

Next is the seven weeks of the counting of the *Omer*.[2] This is a situation that happens right after Passover, which is as cosmic a holiday as they come, and we count a period of forty-nine days. Each one of these forty-nine days represents a level of the *Sephirot* of the Tree of Life. It is purely a Tree of Life counting. Another category is the seven consecutive months, which fall on the three festivals.

The Importance of the Sabbatical Year

The main thing I want to talk about before I get into anything else is the Sabbatical year, or *Shmita*. This is a direct connection to *Ima Adama*, or Mother Earth, and the Blue Jewel. What this does, basically, is put the blue into the Blue Jewel. It keeps the blue in the jewel. What do I mean by that? The Sabbatical year is a law, a science. After the land produces for six years, for the seventh year, it must be at rest. The land is ruled by the creative essence, the Divine Essence, and it is decreed that one must leave the seventh year fallow — just let it sit and let the earth rest.

Unfortunately, very few people and few farmers do this today. In the West, they use crop rotation, and that's a nice substitute, but so far it hasn't proven to be successful, because what do you have? "If I do it this way," they say, "and leave the seventh year empty, my goodness — how am I going to exist? What am I going to do? How am I to survive for that year and the year after?" This is a good question, and what the Divine Essence has ruled is that in the sixth year, you are given a triple crop to keep you well taken care of for that year. The seventh year is fallow, and during the eighth year, you can sustain yourself while you're waiting for the new crops to come into being.

This is an agricultural science, but it also came from galactic knowledge. It's beautiful. Unfortunately, nobody has the patience to follow this. So what did the people do to follow the Sabbatical year? They did have a triple crop in the sixth year, but what did they do? They sold it all for the money. They sold it all. Then they said, "My goodness, we have no crops going into the end of the seventh year. What are we going to do?"

It all comes down to greed, but this is the most important of all — because of what we do to the earth. As starseeds, we try to recharge the corrective feedback loop system of Earth. Following this rule of letting the land be fallow in the seventh year is the most material way you can recharge that feedback loop system related to farming.

The Prevalence of Sevens

Back to the numbers: We have the seven millennia, which we have another 230 and some odd years to get to, but I don't think we'll have to wait that long. We have the seven species that we put on the *Sukkot* table in the *Sukkah*, the seven seas, the seven heavens, the seven colors, the seven sounds, and the seven chambers of paradise.

We have the seven lamps of the menorah.[3] We have the seven shepherds of Israel. We have seven categories of starseed souls, who are what? The starseeds are the *B'nai Yisrael* — us. The starseeds of the ancestors include Abraham, Isaac, Jacob, Moses, Aaron, Joseph, and David. And that's exactly the Tree of Life under the curtain. We have the seven circuits, the seven blessings, and the seven days of celebration of the bride and the groom. It's a beautiful thing.

On the level of divinity, we have the seven eyes of God. That's about the Eye of Horus. There's a whole science behind that. The seven lower *Sephirot* below the curtain, and *Tishrei*, the seventh month in the Hebrew lunar calendar, the seventh cosmic month of the year, which includes the holidays of *Rosh Hashanah*, *Yom Kippur*, *Succoth* (the Feast of Tabernacles), the seven clouds of glory, and the seven circles you make after the holidays are over. That holiday is called *Simchat Torah*; they're called the seven *Hakafot*.

❋ ❋ ❋

Zayin as the Feminine

David: I want to talk a little bit about the feminine energy that *Zayin* represents. In the Tree of Life, one side is masculine and the other side is feminine, which is similar to the concepts of the yin and yang in Taoism. The most interesting thing about the feminine idea is that in the Tree of Life and in the Kabbalah, the belief is that the feminine aspect of the divinity, the *Shekhinah*, is alienated or is not united on Earth.

The *Shekhinah* is also known as the divine presence or the divine feminine presence. Look at the bottom sphere of the Tree of Life, which is Lago Puelo. In Hebrew, this bottom sphere is the kingdom. We could say, from the position of the Kabbalah, that the divine feminine light is alienated from the world and that this is probably why we are having some difficulties.

I think this is interesting — especially when we are talking about the return of Buffalo Calf Woman, because she is representative in many ways of the female divine light that is coming to this planet. I also think it's important to point out that we are going to be listening to more feminine ascended masters and receiving guidance from the lady ascended masters.

I know that there obviously is a preponderance of male ascended masters, and people already have asked me, "How come there aren't many more female masters? I mean, we hear from Mary, we hear from Quan Yin, and I know we hear from Spirit Fire." There are going to be more feminine energies coming to this planet. More feminine guidance will return.

So when we talk about the letter *Zayin*, we are talking about the feminine, and we go to the top of the Tree of Life, which is ruled by Archangel Metatron.[4] In the highest unity in the Tree of Life, there is no separation between feminine and masculine because it is all unity. But as we go down into the different spheres, we find that there needs to be a separation, and the question becomes, "Why is there no feminine divine presence on this planet?" And that is what I call the $64,000 question.

The *Shekhinah* Returns on the *Sabbath*

I want to point out that in the Kabbalah, it is believed that on the *Sabbath*, the seventh day of the feminine light, the *Shekhinah* returns, so there is one day of the seven in a week when the divine feminine presence returns. Some people even say that you get an extra boost in your soul from the divine presence on that day.

I want to review some of the other things Mordechai talked about. He mentioned the *Baal Shem Tov*, who is a famous rabbi who founded Hasidism. The *Baal Shem Tov* lived in Poland from 1700 to 1760. His name means "the bearer of the good name," "the doer of the good name," or "the maker of the good name." He was a very high and righteous man who had strong psychic powers and a high understanding of the Tree of Life. He was able to heal people with sound and with his name. He had direct connections to the upper worlds.

Mordechai also mentioned that one of his followers was the *Maggid* of *Mezeritch*, and I want to explain a little bit about the concept of *Maggid*. The *Maggid* has two meanings: one is the preacher, or one who preaches; the second is a guide or teacher. The *Maggid* can be your teacher, but your teacher can be in another realm. It doesn't necessarily have to be the teacher in this realm.

This shows you that the Kabbalist masters and teachers were also receiving information from their guides and teachers on the other planes. The terms "ancient" or "holy one" and "ancient of days" reference the depiction of God as a divine wise man. So in the ancient texts, there was actually controversy over whether one could depict God. Depicting God in human form is anthropomorphizing — creating, speaking, or describing God in human terms. Yet there is evidence in the ancient Kabbalah that they did use human images to describe the Creator, and they called the ancient holy one by the name of "the Ancient One" and depicted the Creator as a man.

The Unification and Separation of Male and Female

The crown, the top of the Tree of Life, is *Keter*. We have talked about that. The *Maggid* (the guide or teacher) we are using for the crown is Archangel Metatron. Remember, we call the energy in the sphere of the crown "undifferentiated energy" so that the masculine and feminine are united in the crown. It is only when the tree breaks down into the lower spheres that we get the division.

Now, I think this is interesting if you compare Taoism to some of the concepts in the Kabbalah. There are things about Taoism that are similar to the Kabbalah. One of those things is that the Tao represents unity. When the Tao becomes separated, it divides into masculine and feminine. But in the ultimate unity of the Tao, it is totally unified. Nothing you can say about the Tao can really describe it. It is similar to the concept of talking about the energy of *Keter*, which is undifferentiated energy.

The *Shevirah:* Breaking the Vessels

I want to also talk again about this concept of rectification, which is also called repair. The Hebrew word and the Kabbalah word for that is *Tikun*. Remember, these spheres are holographic on the Tree of Life, and each sphere holds the energy or light that was brought down for the creation of the universe.

It is believed in the Kabbalah that in the original creation — the active creation — the light and energy that was brought down was so powerful that the vessels, or the spheres, were not strong enough to hold all of the light, so the spheres broke. In Hebrew, this is called *Shevirah* — the breaking into little pieces. It is our goal as starseeds and planetary healers to repair these shattered pieces and bring them back into unity. I think that is a great idea — the repair of the universe, of Earth, of the third dimension. I think we all can agree that the third dimension and our planet are out of balance and that they do need to be repaired.

Mordechai also mentioned the word *Yirah*, which has two meanings. It means fear and awe. There is a debate: Are you to be in fear or in awe of this energy of this divine essence? The answer lies more in the concept of awe, because fear is a contraction. Awe is just looking at the magnificence of something and being so inspired and so struck by its overwhelming energy that you are in awe.

So I think that when we are talking about the light, we are talking about the light at the top of the crown, the undifferentiated energy. We could feel as if we are in awe of the energy rather than afraid of it, but you also will see the term "fear."

❋ ❋ ❋

Understanding Who or What Is a Hermaphrodite

Mordechai: The number one question about female and male lies in understanding the word "hermaphrodite." First of all, the term "hermaphrodite" is a three-dimensional word. We only know its meaning in 3D terms. We do not know of nor can we relate to sexual organs of higher dimensions. We can just assume that the upper Father and Mother create through thought. Although, we can say from what we know of our fifth-dimensional friends: We are in their image of male and female. We do have a clue because of the Zohar, that Aba and Ima somehow, through a "first cause," came together and created *Yud-Kay-Vav-Kay*, and the *Nukva* (*Adonai*). Therefore, to assume that we can relate the word "hermaphrodite" to sixth-, seventh-, and eighth-dimensional entities is silliness. I ask you to consider this, "is a ball of light hermaphrodite? You tell me! In the Tree of Life, the *Keter* is the Ancient One, the Ancient of Days, *Atik Yomin*. Just below him is *Atika Kadisha*. Are these all hermaphrodites? I'll give you an analogy. I'm sure most of us have seen the movie *City of Angels*. In the movie, what was the perk that made the angel use his "free will" to come down into this world and be human? It was about the connection male on female.

In the Tree of Life, the *Sephirah* of *Chochma*, or Bodensee, is assigned to Chief White Eagle. This is the *Sephirah* of wisdom, *Aba*, which represents the male and means "the Father."

In the third sphere, you have Lake Moraine, which is understanding. This is the *Sephirah Binah*, which is *Ima*, the Mother. That's where the *Aba* and *Ima*, the Father and Mother, start in this creation. They give birth to what we call *Yud-Kay-Vav-Kay*. They also give birth to *Malchut*, which is the *Shekhinah*, which is *Adonai*.

Adonai is female, and *Yud-Kay-Vav-Kay* is male, and I want to bring up a fact about these letters. One reason why we have a thing about not saying them — the way they should be said — is because, really, what they are is mathematical equations. This is for real. They are mathematical equations.

So getting back to *Aba* and *Ima*, or male and female — everything has a beginning point.

So why all the angels? You never hear about an angel having a soul mate. Is that because they are hermaphroditic? When it finally gets down here, you must understand that *Adonai* is an entity that all of the other entities in the fifth dimension pray to. *Adonai* is the same entity for us down here as it is for those in the fifth dimension, yet *Adonai* is in the *Sephirah* on the bottom, *Malchut*.

Adonai is female and comes into being, comes into manifestation, on *Shabbat*. She is the *Shabbat* Queen, the *Shabbat* Bride, and the starseeds

— we — are the bridesmaids. We bring in the bride. We have the priviledge to bring the bride together with the groom. I hope it's clear.

The word *Yirah* means awe, and *Ahava* means love. There are no accidents or coincidences, but there is a planet in the constellation of the Pleiades that relates to us in this creation strongly. That planet is called Er'ra. Er'ra sounds much like the Hebrew word "*Yirah*," awe. This planet has experienced the intersection of the dimensions.

The *Shabbat* is the secret of Kabbalah. The crowning power of the female and the male energy together is represented with Sarah and Abraham. Whereas the *Ohr Yashar*, the straight light of Abraham, is always returning to the beginning of creation in order to start anew the ongoing process of rectification, the *Ohr Chozer*, the returning light of Sarah, is ever conscious of the *Shabbat* to come — the secret of the future, whose source is ultimately before the secret of creation.

An Eternal *Shabbat*

The reason things are quickening up now is because time is moving faster. The Kabbalists use the phrase "time is getting quicker," but their expression is that the *Sabbaths* are coming closer together. Time is moving so quickly that the *Sabbaths* are moving closer together. Or as the secular parties say, the weekends are getting closer together. It's almost like a consistent connected party. When is the ascension, the *Geula*, the Messiah, to come? It is *Shabbat*, one consistent, perennial, eternal *Shabbat*. That's what the ascension really represents.

Now, as far as getting back to number in *Zayin*, there are numbers I can give you here. It wouldn't help you too much to understand that there are seven times forty-seven other things; the most important thing from the religiosity factor is that you should make a hundred blessings a day. I used to ask, "Why do you have to make a hundred blessings a day? Why can't I make fifty, seventy-five, or twenty-five? Why do I have to make a hundred blessings a day?"

There's a beautiful answer. I was at a gathering where there was a shaman, and he came out and said, "You must bless everything. Bless everything there is — bless your pets, bless your flowers, bless your food, bless everything."

I said, "Boy, I never heard it put that way. That's very nice."

So what does it mean when we say "bless" — *Baruch*? In the beginning of the blessing is *Baruch Ata* — "blessed are you." What does it mean when we say the word *Baruch*? It means that we're putting the

Creator's energy into everything that we bless. That's why everybody blesses everybody and themselves. It's a beautiful thing. But why the hundred blessings? Because the *Sephirah* at the top of the Tree of Life — *Keter*, the crown — relates to the top of the *Zayin*. What is inside that *Keter*? It's ten *Sephirot* times ten *Sephirot*: That's one hundred *Sephirot*!

So what we're doing is filling that vessel of *Keter*, of the crown. It's so beautiful because it's going straight up the Tree of Life. Do not pass go; collect everything money can buy — straight to the top, and you're there with those one hundred blessings.

You don't have to pray in Hebrew. You can just bless all your pets, your flowers, and all of your inanimate things in English or any other language you wish, just come from the heart. That is all that is looked for. Bless the tipis, bless the medicine wheels, and bless everything. I'll tell you what, the most important of all the blessings is called the *Birkat Hamazon*. It is the blessing you make after you eat your meal and are completely satiated, completely satisfied. You bless the meal you just ate. That is the highest blessing you can make. Why? Because you're blessing something that you really feel good about. It's something physical that you're turning completely into metaphysical. The first line of the *Birkat Hamazon* is *"Baruch Ata Hashem, Ha-zan eth ha'olam."* You are giving sustenance to the world. Remember the word *Zan*? It's fifty-seven: *Ha-zan*.

This is such a perfect science. It's a science; that's all I can say. We have to go forward with this science technology. All we have to do to add to this cosmic science is love from the heart, sincerely from the heart, and that's the whole thing. God bless.

❋ ❋ ❋

The Tree of Life in You

Shalom, Shalom, Shalom. Greetings. I am **Archangel Metatron**. You are studying the mastery of the divine plan. You are studying the mastery of the divine name. You are studying the mastery of the map of the consciousness of the divinity when you are studying this beautiful Tree of Life, known in Hebrew as the *Etz Chaim*.

Let your consciousness feel the brilliance of this energy. Maybe you don't understand everything that is being spoken. Maybe you cannot keep all the spheres in order. This is not most important. What's most important is that you have this map, that you have this energy configuration before you. It is like a medicine wheel, like a crop circle, only this is the highest crop circle. This is the crop circle of the mind of the Creator that is presented to the galaxy, that is presented to you. You are able to comprehend this beautiful representation of the energy of the Creator and how creation is manifested, ruled, and balanced. This is the teaching of the Tree of Life.

I want to point out to you that you have all the attributes of this Tree of Life in you. You have a crown, for example, within you — just like the top sphere of the Tree of Life, which is also called the crown.[4] You have a crown chakra. What is beautiful is that this Tree of Life diagram is also represented in *you*. You have divine wisdom (sphere two), and you have divine understanding (sphere three). These are represented within you as the right and left brain. You have the ability to connect with the Messianic light (the center sphere, or your heart). You have the knowledge inside of you, also known as your third eye. You are manifesting all the different parts of yourself, all the different levels of this energy, into the kingdom — which is the manifested Earth, or your feet. The kingdom is here on Earth. The kingdom is in your third-dimensional body. So this Tree of Life is not just some esoteric diagram that explains the universe and how the worlds work; this diagram also explains how *you* work.

Now, the original prototype of the human species is Adam, and Adam originally was a hermaphrodite. The term "hermaphrodite" refers to someone who is both male and female together, someone whose original DNA code expresses the unity of the masculine and feminine in one being. This is your original prototype. All the beings who follow Adam contain his codes and his energy. It is not even correct to say "his" because a hermaphrodite is male and female together. But there was a separation of the male and female, and therefore Eve was brought into existence.

Now we see a separation. In order to have the separation, the energy must be stepped down so that there can be a division in the masculine and the feminine. But then, in the Garden of Eden — *Gan Eden* — there was perfection. There was fifth-dimensional perfection. But there was the separation, and it continued, so you can look at the separation that led to the discharge from the fifth dimension — from the Garden of Eden — and led into a third dimension. This is not a punishment but rather the Creator wants this dimension and wants the Adam species to exist in this dimension, for there is a divine plan.

The divine plan includes returning to the Garden of Eden. It includes returning to the fifth dimension. It includes returning to the wonderful unity. This means that even when we're talking about the ascension, we are talking about returning to the original unity that you have to experience, which you have in your DNA codes. You can experience this unity of the divinity in you. *Atah Gibur* — you are great, Creator of all.

We in this position in the third dimension can experience the greatness of the unity of this universe. Do not think that being in the third dimension, being lower, means you cannot experience enlightenment or you cannot experience the light, for even on the third dimension — which is the lower of the dimensions — you still are able to experience the greatest unity. This is because when you look at the Tree of Life, and you look at where you are in the Tree of Life, in *Malchut*, (the bottom sphere known as the kingdom), you see that all the spheres are connected — all of them. Even where you are, you can go straight through to the middle sphere, Messiah light, to the crown and experience the highest undifferentiated light.

Baruch Hashem — blessings to all of you, followers of the divine light. I am Archangel Metatron. Good day.

✳ ✳ ✳

Questions from the Class

Alessandra in Washington, DC: *Could you briefly tell us what the seven levels of starseeds are?*

Mordechai: I'll just say that the seven levels of starseeds start with number four, Mount Shasta, loving kindness, and the seven levels to go down to *Malchut*. It is all related to the seven *Sephirot* under the curtain, under the line. In other words, like Archangel Lord Metatron has said, we have the whole Tree of Life in us. Those seven levels are all within us, the starseeds. And that's really what they are. You can look up the seven bottom *Sephirot* (or eight, if you want to include Serra da Bocaina). Those are really our seven levels, and each *Sephirah* is self-explanatory, if I can have permission to say that.

Alessandra: *I think so.*

Mordechai: It's not easy to say something in twenty-five seconds that takes so long to explain in detail. Just hang in there, and know that it's true because it's a galactic science.

Linda: Mordechai, I have read that in the Bible, the reference to the Ancient of Days was actually an office within the Great White Brotherhood, and the person to hold that office was Sanat Kumara, yet in our tree, he appears on the lower Sephirah. *Can you comment?*

Mordechai: Let me program the answer. You must understand, there are — and I say this with loving sincerity — millions and millions of levels of existence. Sanat Kumara is an overseer of planets in the third dimension, right? He oversees this planet and the other 150 planets where there are Adam Kadmon species and where Lord Sananda travels and visits to help correct these other planets. But all these other planets are in the third dimension.

When we're talking about the Ancient of Days, we're jumping upward three, four, or five more dimensions, and each dimension has its millions and millions of situations. You are right as far as the third dimension is concerned, but when you get to four, five, six, seven, eight, and nine, there are other entities. There are elders. Everything you mentioned — the divine Brotherhood, the Council of 9, the Council of 12 — these are all galactic government councils of the Ancient of Days.

Katherine: Mordechai mentioned something about the Pleiades — one of the planets of the Pleiades relates to the awe and love. Do we know the name of that planet?

Mordechai: Yes, and that actually correlates directly to David, because it was in a lecture that Juliano had given concerning the intersection of the dimensions. And the planet was Er'ra.

David: Well, E-R-R-A is the spelling used by Billy Meier, the man who had direct contact with the Pleiades in Switzerland. Samyaze was the Pleiadian who met him in person — in the physical, in the third dimension — and she said that she was from the planet Er'ra. That's how the Pleiadians spell the planet's name.

Mordechai: Okay, but Er'ra in Aramaic or Hebrew text would be the same thing. When I heard that, I knew there was a strong correlation, being that it's been a blessing that we can have this eighth class on the seventh letter because our Biorelativity meditations have been so powerful and have put off whatever was supposed to be put off for another couple of weeks or whatever. I can honestly say that Er'ra is part of the Pleiades. We are part of them. I'll just put it out there, and you tell me whether your guides and teachers agree with this or not. But we are a holographic experience from that star system, Amen.

Chet: Life

CLASS 9

MORDECHAI AND DAVID

Mordechai: *Chet* is the eighth letter in the *Aleph-Bet*. In the picture of it, there is a *Zayin* on the left, and a *Vav* makes up the right side of the *Chet*. It is held together with what they call a *Chatoteret*, which is considered a humpback. This is a divine bonding or coupling, as you might say. *Chet* is the letter of life. It is the essence of the chi. *Chaim*, which means "life" in Hebrew, comes from the root *Chaya*. The first letter of *Chaim* is the letter *Chet*.

As you remember, there are four levels of the soul: the *Nefesh, Ruach, Neshamah,* and *Chaya*, whose most important letter is *Chet*. Remember this: We are taught in Kabbalah that there are two levels of essential life: *Chaim B'etzem* and *Chaim L'hachayot*, which means "to enliven." Now, to show you how beautiful it is, it is all about life force energy. *Chaim B'etzem* is the essential life for us in this world. In Hebrew, *Etzem* is "bone"; *B'etzem* is "in the bone"; *Chaim B'etzem* means "in the bone." What's in the bone? Bone marrow that creates your red blood cells — the essence of life, the *Chaim B'etzem*.

The second one, the life to enliven, *Chaim L'hachayot*, is the four holy entities — the *Chayot Hakodesh*. That's even higher than the archangels. They are basically all levels of the letter *Chet*. The essential or the Divine itself is in a state of essential life. The Divine's creative power continually permeates all of reality to enliven. So the soul of *B'nai Yisrael*, the soul of the starseeds, the essence of their root, is one with the divine and possesses the state of essential life. The reflection of the light of the soul enlivens the body. Its physical experience is at the level of life to enliven, where it is essential life — *Chaim*, or chi. This is the core of the chi, or the life to enliven.

The second level of life — or life as we know it — in general manifests itself as pulsation, which is the secret of run and return. Actually, this is the whole thing. Why I am saying this is the whole thing now with the eighth letter of *Chet*? Like I've said before when we were discussing the *Zayin*, the seventh letter, it represents completion; it represents all that we did from the *Aleph* to the *Zayin*, and we were complete. So now what do we do?

We're complete in the tools, and now it's time to use the tools and live. That's the whole purpose of being here. According to the *Arizal* (Rabbi Isaac Luria), the letter *Chet* is constructed by combining the two previous letters — the sixth letter, *Vav*, and the seventh letter, *Zayin* — with the thin, bridge-shaped line referred to as the *Chatoteret*, or humpback. The new energy affected by the union of the *Vav* and the *Zayin*, of the *Vav* with the *Ohr Yashar* of the straight light and the *Zayin* with the *Ohr Chozer* or returning light, is the secret of hovering, or touching and not touching.

It All Begins with Hovering

In Hebrew, that hovering is *Mati V'lo Mati*. We're going to get into that because hovering is in the beginning of creation: "And the spirit of God was hovered over the surface of the water" [Genesis 1:2, CJB]. There are five Hebrew letters that make up the word for "hovering," which is *Merachefet*: Mem-Resh-Chet-Pey-Tav. The *Chet* is directly in the middle of this word. It is the eighteenth word from the beginning of the Torah. It is basically the first word in the Torah that numerically has a multiple of 26 and is the value of *Havaya*, or *Yud-Kay-Vav-Kay*. *Havaya* is the name we will use.

So take the word *Merachefet*, which is 728. Divide that by 26, and you get 28: 26 x 28 = 728. Twenty-eight is a very powerful number. Why? Because it means power, and the word for power is spelled in Hebrew *Kaph-Chet*. *Chet* is at the end of that word. The word *Kaph-Chet* in Hebrew is *Koach*, which means power.

Now, the full secret implied by the numerical value of the word "hovering" is the power of the divine essence. In Kabbalah, this word in particular is the secret of the divine power to resurrect. There were 288 sparks that fell in the process of the breaking of the vessels. *Merachefet* can be permutated — that is, you can take the letters and mix them around. You can take the first letter and the last letter — *Mem* and *Tav* — and put them together, which is *Met*. *Met* in Hebrew means "died" or "dead."

This leaves us with the middle three letters, the *Resh*, *Chet*, and *Pey*. The *Resh* is 200, the *Pey* is 80, and the *Chet* is 8. That's 288: "The death of 288" or "288 have died."

So these letters contain the codes for understanding these words Kabbalistically. That's why I love these numbers so much. The sages teach us that the spirit of the divine here referred to is, in fact, the soul of *Mashiach* (Messiah), the redemption, or the light of repair.

Here's how it works again: *Mashiach* is *Mem-Shin-Yud-Chet* — four letters. When you take the four letters, divide them in half, and switch them — the first two and the last two — instead of *Mem-Shin*, you get *Shin-Mem*, which is "name" (*Shem* in Hebrew). And the remaining two letters are *Yud* and *Chet*. Now, if you reverse these two letters, you get *Chet-Yud*, which means "life" or "the living name." So the word *Mashiach* permuted becomes "the living name."

Hovering is also symbolized in the Torah. Here's the metaphor that is used: "as an eagle arouses her nest and hovers over her young," as taught by the *Maggid* of *Mezeritch*, who was a student of the *Baal Shem Tov*. To avoid crushing her young in their nest, the eagle hovers over it when feeding her young — touching yet not touching. The eagle here is a metaphor for the Divine in relation to his children of Israel — the starseeds in particular — and to the totality of his creation in general.

If the Divine would fully reveal his ultimate presence or withdraw his power of continuous re-creation, the world would instantaneously cease to exist. You've heard that line many times, but how can a creation cease to exist so quickly? The only way a creation can cease to exist so quickly is if it's a hologram, a holographic experience, because the fifth dimension doesn't exist like that, and neither do the other dimensions. Yet there is regeneration of life; here in this dimension you have a re-creation of every moment.

Now, can you imagine how many planets there are in this three-dimensional universe that are being re-created every moment? This is the definition of incomprehensibility; we really can't fathom such a situation.

I have to continue with this hovering because, as hovering created reality, the Divine continues to sustain and nourish his creation while

simultaneously allowing each creature — or in the terminology of the
Kabbalah, each vessel — the ability to grow and develop independently.
The letter *Chet* does hint at the delicate balance between revelation of
the divine presence to us, the *Vav* of the *Chet*, and the concealment of
his creative power from his creation is the *Zayin* of the *Chet*.

The state of hovering — or touching yet not touching — is the
beginning of the phenomenon of life to enliven, or touch yet not touch,
from above. Therefore, we can ask the question: What does the Creator reflect Itself as? The Creator reflects Itself in the inner pulsation of
every living creature, and the living creatures run and return like the
appearance of lightning.

Do not read it as *Chayot* (with an *O*), which means "living creatures," but read it as *Chayut* (with a *U*), which means "life force." It can
also mean light force — light-force energy. The light-force energy is
Chayut, which is spelled in Hebrew *Chet-Yud-Vav-Tav*, where the *Chet* is
8, *Yud* is 10, *Vav* is 6, and *Tav* is 400, which equals 424.

So you ask, "What does 424 mean?" In Hebrew, 424 spells out
numerically *Mashiach ben David* (Messiah, son of David), and there's
no bigger light force than that. You want to remember that easily? It's
twice the boiling point of water, or twice 212.

Chet's Paradoxes

I want to point out some paradoxes insofar as the letter *Chet* is concerned
because it represents life. The run-and-return pulsation is the essence of
life. At the same time, there's polarity and paradox in the word *Chait*,
or *Chet-Tet-Aleph*, which means "sin." Sin is a *Chait*, a soul torn against
itself, even though it is sure that it is pious. On the other side, a *Chasid*
(also beginning with the letter *Chet*), a pious one, ironically, is a soul
convinced that it commits many sins. It is a level of consciousness.

You have *Hevel*, or pang, or birth pang. This describes a woman
almost dying from birth work, from bringing forth life. And on the
other side, you have *Chaim* — almost dying and almost living from
bringing forth life.

Then you have *Chillul*, or desecration — the secularization that
shows no sanctity and can only drive souls apart. Then you have *Cha-
vura*, which is bringing ten people together to do something holy or
divine, and *Churban*, which means devastation and always seems to
result in an end. Then you have *Chupa*, which is what you get married
under. It's a shelter protecting the seeding of another generation.

That's why when we finish a book in the Torah, we say *Chazak* — it means "strength": *Chazak, Chazak, Chazak* (we say it three times, one for each column), *V'nit'chazek* — strength, strength, strength, may we be strengthened.

Learn from what was been done before. The strength is not of might and force, but of endurance, balance, and harmony — of what? To be sure of your confidence in your imagination, to have confidence in your consciousness.

* * *

Chet and the Center of the Tree of Life

David: We're talking about the Hebrew letter *Chet*. The "ch" is the same sound in German when they say *ich* and *dich* — the same guttural sound. When Mordechai talks about the letters, he is also talking about the words that contain those letters so that we understand what kind of energy the letters contain.

Look at the center of the Tree of Life, which is represented by Montserrat. It stands for balance and harmony, and the spirit guide for this sphere is Sananda or Jesus. The Hebrew word for the Messiah is *Mashiach*, and there is that sound of the *Chet* again. That is the "ch" sound at the end. I will spell it for you: M-A-S-H-I-A-C-H. *Mashiach* is the Hebrew word, and I believe the Greek word is Messiah. The actual meaning of the Hebrew word *Mashiach* is "anointed one." When a person was made a king in ancient Israel, he was anointed. For example, when David was chosen as king of Israel, he was anointed with oil by the prophet Samuel.

Look in the center of the Tree of Life. There you find balance, harmony, Messianic harmony, and the spirit guide Sananda/Jesus. So we can say that this center sphere is in communication with all of the other spheres. It is the only sphere that has pathways that touch all the other spheres.

We could say that if you can come to the energy of the Messiah, of the *Mashiach*, then you can understand everything, because that is touching everything. In Hebrew, this sphere, which we are recognizing geographically as Montserrat, is also called beauty. Beauty in Hebrew is *Tiferet*. It is interesting that the Kabbalah would describe the center where Jesus is as beauty, because beauty represents a special harmony.

Think about Jesus/Sananda and the energies of *Tiferet*, and let us look at some of the other examples I gave of having direct contact with the Creator. For one, Moses was not able to look directly toward God or to see God's face, because he wouldn't be able to tolerate the intense light. So God showed him the shadow of his presence instead.

There is a story of four rabbis going into a special garden. The special garden represents a place where God's divine light was, and only one rabbi came out intact from that experience, because moving up the Tree of Life, moving up into higher energy, requires a certain ability to tolerate divine light. Unfortunately, most of us humans are not able to do that.

Jesus/Sananda is able to directly experience God. Jesus/Sananda is able to sit next to God. Think about his teachings. Some of them say that you can "come through me to experience my father." In other words, he is saying, "I am allowing you to use my vessel to experience the Father. I'm allowing you to use my energy. I have been to the highest place; I have been to *Keter*. I have sat next to the divine light. I have not gone crazy. I have not lost my sanity from the divine light. I have not been blinded by the light, and I am able to help you move closer to it." So in essence, from the Kabbalistic standpoint, Jesus is saying, "Come through me" — meaning he will be able to take you to those places where you cannot go alone because your vessel is not strong enough. From that standpoint, the Messianic energy and light is beautiful.

Here is another idea of the Messianic light: If you look at the center of the Tree of Life, you will recognize that the center, *Tiferet*, represents the Messianic light, the *Mashiach*, and the light of the *Mashiach* is transcending the third dimension. It is an intervention. It is like a miracle, and it does not follow the laws of the third dimension. Think about quantum light and quantum healing. With quantum light and quantum healing, we're saying that the light we are using, the energy we are accessing, is transcending logic.

The light of the Messiah can bring us great harmony. We can use a term from the Kabbalah: *Mashiach ben David*. It is believed that the *Mashiach* came from the lineage of the house of David. That is why they use the terminology *Mashiach ben David* — the *Mashiach*, son of David. The Messiah must be part of the lineage of King David.

The Maker of the Good Name

I want to go over a few other things that Mordechai mentioned in this lesson. We talked about the *Baal Shem Tov*. *Baal* means "master," but I think I translated it as "maker of the good name" rather than "master of the good name." He was one of the greatest Kabbalah teachers. Now, "master of the good name" implies that he was able to use the names of God for higher purposes. He could say the sacred names of God, and by saying those sacred names, he would be healing.

Each sphere has a special name for God. In the bottom sphere, Lago Puelo, which is also known as the kingdom in the Kabbalah, we use the name *Adonai*, which means "my master." All of the names of God have special powers, and the *Baal Shem Tov* was able to heal people by using these names.

Soul Levels

When he was talking about the letter *Chet*, Mordechai also mentioned the four levels of the soul. You may have heard me saying the Kabbalah teaches that there are three levels of the soul. The lower level, the *Nefesh*, which is the animal self, is our instinctual sign, and it also means "to breathe" in Hebrew. The second level is *Ruach*, which is like spirit but also means "the middle part of the soul." And then there is *Neshamah*, which is the higher self. It is the higher soul that is in connection to greater soul energy and our greater light. Then Mordechai mentioned the level *Chaya*. The *Chaya* is so high that none of us in this lifetime and this dimension would even touch that part because it is so high up in the Tree of Life that there is no way that we, as mortals, would even reach that level.

Mordechai also talked about *Chaim*, which is life. Some of you may have heard the famous Hebrew salutation when you are drinking wine: *L'chaim* — to life.

❋ ❋ ❋

The Sight of *Chet*

Mordechai: You were talking about chi. The *Chaya* and the *Chai* sound very similar, and one thing came from another. They both represent life and there are many things you said that I'd like to follow up on. But more importantly, we didn't have enough time to get to sight, sound, and number.

As far as sight is concerned, the letter *Chet* contains a *Vav*, which is on the right; a *Zayin*, which is on the left; and a thick hunchback bridge, the *Chatoteret*, connecting above them in the level of worlds. It's like a gateway. The power to enter a higher energy level and exit from there is what David was trying to explain before with the rabbis.

The most important thing is to know how to get back from the visit with the higher light. It's like Juliano says: After you take an out-of-body visit on a spiritual exercise, when you come back into your body, you have to line up and then put your aura body back into perfect alignment with the third-dimensional body in this world. The best analogy I can give is when you're flying an airplane, anybody can take off; it's no big deal. But try to land the plane, and that's another story.

The second level of worlds is related to the *Sabbath*. The ascent of all worlds occurs on *Shabbat*, and the subsequent descent after *Shabbat*. This is *Shabbat*; this is purely galactic. All worlds ascend as one world; everything moves up one notch. In the level of souls, the union is of the three partners in humanity, the Father (*Vav*), the Mother (*Zayin*), and the divine essence, which is that *Chatoteret* — that little humpback that connects both letters to make it a *Chet*. Now, on the level of divinity, the *Chet* represents the Divine hovering over creation, the union of the Divine's eminence, transcendence, and the *B'nai Yisrael* — the starseeds.

The Sound of *Chet*

The level of sound is the full expression of love. In the level of worlds, it's about loving the Divine with your physical body or with the life force of your body. The level of souls is loving the Divine with your soul, or the light force of your soul. And the third section of the soul, the heartbeat of the *Tzaddik*, is really the life force of the soul.

The *Tzaddik* feeds the soul, and that's really why you have to spend more time studying that kind of thing — because it's all a matter of doing what we're supposed to be doing down here. Sound, at the level of divinity, is the essential unity with the divine essence and is the life force of life itself — or as they say, the resurrection of the dead.

The Numbers of *Chet*

Regarding numbers, the number eight is the number besides zero that has no beginning and no end when it is being drawn. It represents infinity when it is placed sideways. It also represents the female energy. From our perspective, the infinite is female energy because that's what's coming down the pike in the future to help heal the planet.

As far as numbers are concerned in the level of worlds, there are eight vertices in a cube — eight corners. There are six sides and twelve lines to a cube. We live in a cube. If you add the 12 + 6 + 8, you get 26, which is *Havaya*, one of the names of God. God represents the cube; the cube represents the creative essence.

Also in the level of worlds, eight represents third-dimensional plurality. The divine is one in the seven heavens and this Earth. In other words, there are seven heavens and us, which adds up to eight.

At the level of souls, it's all about circumcision. On the eighth day after the birth of a male, the circumcision occurs, and there are eight days in the holiday of *Chanukah*. You must understand why there is circumcising of the foreskin. Foreskin is a spiritual blockage. The circumcision takes away 85 to 90 percent of that blockage. Circumcision of the foreskin of the lips has a special symbolic meaning. Without this symbolic gesture, one is subject to all kinds of speech that we wish we didn't say. Circumcision of the foreskin of the ears symbolically occurs on the eighth day of the holiday of *Succoth*, the Feast of the Tabernacles, which is when all the energy from the tabernacles is supposed to come into this world. The circumcision of the foreskin of the heart symbolically occurs on *Yom Kippur*, the Day of Atonement. This ceremony occurs on the eighth day of the high priest's separation from his home because he had to prepare for that very holy day of *Yom Kippur*.

As far as the level of divinity and the number eight, we can say that eight is the gateway to infinity. It represents the Divine's transcendent light and is the origin of us and our descent through the seven heavens to Earth.

Basically speaking, the letter *Chet* puts us right into number three, Lake Moraine, which geographically represents the third sphere and stands for understanding. If you understand the letter *Chet*, you understand life. As far as life and our world are concerned, it is a game. Life can be viewed metaphorically as a game — the game of life.

Starseeds Must Unlearn and Undo

Unfortunately, when we're brought into this world, we don't come in with an instructional booklet. Whatever we buy — an appliance, a car, everything — comes with an instructional booklet. This game of life does not have such a handbook, and unfortunately, we are the results of everything we've been taught.

The first thing I heard from my teacher about eight years ago was, "Mordechai, do you really want to change? Well, you have to unlearn everything you've learned and undo everything you've done." Boy, I was silent for two days trying to understand that simple statement. We have to unlearn everything we've learned and undo everything we've done. As starseeds, we are in the process of unlearning what we've learned; undoing what we've learned; and starting to get together, unify, create portals, and do some wonderful things.

David told a story about four rabbis who came too close to the divine light. You know what it was that they weren't supposed to look at? Upstairs. The best thing I can compare it to is like Superman's fortress of solitude. Everything is like ice, but it's really crystals. There is one thing you are not supposed to do in that divine area because it is composed of all thought; it's all consciousness. So what got all the rabbis into trouble was they looked at this mysterious ice — as it's called in the Zohar — and they started thinking it was water. When they started thinking "water," everything fell apart.

They started bringing a third-dimensional consciousness up to wherever they were — the fifth and sixth dimensions — and that's a no-no. That's why one rabbi decided he liked it so much he stayed there, and he died down here. Another rabbi came back crazy in the sense that he was able to use normal consciousness versus higher consciousness and control his logical mind so he could function in this third-dimensional reality. We might find out in the end that everybody in the mental institutions is normal and the people who think they're normal are not.

Then you have the holy man called *Acher*, or "the other," because he wasn't part of this world anymore. He was really sharp, but he kind of messed up. He was the teacher of a very big rabbi, Rabbi Meir Baal HaNes. This man created miracles everywhere he went. He lived in Tiberius. Another rabbi who was famous at this time in Rome was Rabbi Akkiva. It is said that he was one of the few men who "got out clean" when he departed from this world. Rabbi Akkiva was a warrior and three-quarters. What can I say? This is a great letter.

When you pronounce the letter *Chet*, it's like the top and bottom of your throat are coming together. It's like a joining that's not calm; it's a rumbled joining.

* * *

Store Your Chi in Your Bone Marrow

David: When Mordechai was talking about *Chaim*, which is life, and then I compared that to the light-force energy of chi and Mordechai talked about bones, I thought about an interesting qigong and tai chi exercise.

The exercise is called "bone marrow." You take your chi and store it in your bones and bone marrow. The Chinese believe that the strength of your physical structure and physical energy is stored in your bone marrow and that the life force energy can be stored in your bone marrow. The bone marrow contains a lot of strength for our immune system.

In the Taoist Chinese philosophy of chi, they believe that you are given a certain level of chi that you can use in this lifetime. I have always found this to be a very interesting concept because if you think about it, you have a certain amount of life energy that you can use in this lifetime. In their mystical philosophy, the Chinese believe that you can obtain chi from the universe, not just from the earth. You can obtain chi from the stars. So you could connect with the star Arcturus, the Pleiades, the galaxy, or the universe and bring down the chi. So then this chi can come into your crown chakra.

✳ ✳ ✳

Questions from the Class

Cora in Minnesota: You're talking about vessels, containers, Sephirot, *and I'm thinking of another analogy in our language: "Never put new wine in an old skin." That's how I'm feeling right now — new wine in an old skin. I like this, so I'm so grateful that we have these lectures to listen to over and over again. Thank you for doing that for us, David. So I'm looking at my new wine; this is old wisdom, because I know my body, even though I'm an old skin, can handle this. It's a long way around, isn't it?*

Mordechai: You're absolutely right. It's old wisdom, and your body has been waiting for it all this tenure. You got the tenure, and you got the vessel to handle what's coming.

Bridget from San Diego: Hi, David and Mordechai. I was wondering how we could bring down some chi from Arcturus.

David: There are two ways to do it. One is to try to find Arcturus in the night sky and sit underneath it. The second way is to get in a kind of a yoga meditation and visualize the star Arcturus above you and a blue light coming from Arcturus into your crown chakra. Part of the visualization is seeing yourself sitting on the Blue Jewel, on this planet. You are sitting there on a chair, looking at this part of Earth, and you are energetically connecting to the star Arcturus.

Ingrid in Miami: I love it, David.

David: You can do this also with the Central Sun. You can do it with your other favorite star systems, or some of you relate to the Andromeda galaxy. Or you can do it with the Pleiades. That's my basic idea. Mordechai, do you have ideas on that?

Mordechai: Just have certainty. If you want to go, you go. Decide whose light you want to invite in, and then it will come in. It's all really a matter of having certainty in your consciousness. And you know, you don't even have to be online. You can really just do it if you have enough certainty. You can do it wherever you are. Plug in and put your consciousness in Lake Moraine, and there you are.

Tet: Concealed Good

CLASS 10

MORDECHAI, DAVID, SANANDA, AND CHIEF WHITE EAGLE

Mordechai: The ninth letter is the letter *Tet*, spelled *Tet-Yud*-final *Tav*. It's the initial letter of the word *Tov*, which means "good." The form of the *Tet* is inverted, so the letter represents concealed good; the good is hidden within it: *Tov-haganiz b'gav-ya*.

The form of the letter *Tet* symbolizes the union of a groom and bride consummating with conception. The secret of the *Tet* is that it is numerically equivalent to nine. The nine months of pregnancy are the power of the mother to carry her inner concealed good — the fetus — throughout the period of pregnancy. Pregnancy is very big with this letter. Pregnancy is the power to bring potential into actualization.

The revelation of new actual energy, the revelation of birth and the new balance, is the secret of the next letter of the *Aleph-Bet*, which is the *Yud*. What we're trying to do here is show you how every letter is a progression from the one before. The *Yud* reveals the point of essential life that was realized in the secret of conception of the *Chet* and carried, impregnated, in the *Tet*.

With the *Chet*, which comes after the first seven letters, we showed you all the tools and how that letter is life while this ninth letter is an impregnation, a conception of the eight synonyms for beauty in Hebrew. *Tov* refers to the most inner, inverted, and modest state of beauty. This level of beauty is that personified in the Torah by Rebecca and Batsheva, who are described as *Tovat Meiram Meod* — very beautiful, goodly in appearance.

In the beginning of creation, the appearance of life was termed "good" in the Divine's eyes: "And God saw the light, that it was good" [Genesis 1:4, KJV]. Our sages interpret this to mean "good to be hidden for the righteous ones in the time to come." Where did he hide it? In the Torah! There is unique good in the Torah.

I bring this up because Torah is not a religious object. It is a galactic gift from the cosmos and represents cosmic and galactic wisdom. The *Baal Shem Tov* teaches that the "time to come" also refers to every generation. Each soul of the *B'nai Yisrael*, or the starseeds, has a potential righteous person, a potential *Tzaddik*. It is said, "And your people are all *Tzaddikim*," connected to the goodly light hidden in the Torah. The more you actualize your potential to be a *Tzaddik*, a righteous person, the more goodness you reveal from the womb of the Torah. The Torah just produces; it is a cosmic womb. It's so beautiful.

In the very first verse of the Torah, "In the beginning God created the heavens and the earth," the initial letters reveal a hidden name for the Creator. I'm not going to give you the name, but I'll give you a hint: The numerical value of this name is 17, which is the same value as the word *Tov*, good. The word *Tzaddik* — spelled *Tzadi-Dalet-Yud-Kuf*, equals 204, which is really 17 x 12, so it has a total value of 12 permutations (the total value of the 12 permutations of the 4 letters of this hidden name). Now, if you have 4 letters in a name, the number of permutations should be 24 because it's 4 x 3 x 2 x 1, but here we have 12 permutations.

This refers to the letter *Hey*, which we mentioned appears twice in a majority of the names of *Hashem*. There are four names of *Hashem* that do not contain the *Hey* twice. One is *Aleph-Lamed (El)* and *Shin-Dalet-Yud* (*El Shaddai* or God Almighty), which is on every *Mezuzah*. Another name of God is *Aleph-Lamed-Hey-Yud-Mem*, which spells *Elohim*; and the energy that is coming to Earth is a female energy, which is expressed in the name *Adonai* (*Aleph-Dalet-Nun-Yud*). That is the female energy that's coming. It's all called "good."

In other words, the *Tet* is actually a connector, a conduit between the *Chet* — life — into the next letter, *Yud*. Another connection between life and good is found in the story of Moses because Yocheved, his mother, saw that he was good, *Tov*.

Rashi, who was a big sage from medieval France, is known as the greatest Torah commentator. Even today, he remains one of the main commentators of the Torah. He quotes the *Midrash*, which explains that a great light filled the room when Moses was born. According to the early *Mesorah*, which means "tradition," the *Tet* in the word *Tov* in this verse is written extra large. This hints at the absolute divine good entrusted in the soul of Moses, whose life mission was to fulfill the promise of redemption from Egypt and the revelation of the Torah at Mount Sinai.

That same light that appeared when Moses was born also appeared when Lord Sananda came into this world. They're not that far apart. The Egyptian exile is compared to a womb in which all of Israel was latently pregnant for 210 years, and at Sinai, heaven and earth were united as discussed in the letter *Aleph*. Thus, the full teaching of the *Tet* is that through the service of the soul, all of reality becomes pregnant with the Divine's infinite goodness and beauty, thereby bringing harmony, new balance, and peace to the heavens and the earth.

The Sight of *Tet*

Now we get to sight, sound, and number again. In the category of sight, in the level of worlds, the *Tet* has forms that are hidden in matter. In other words, the *Tet* represents the hidden good that forms into matter. It's the nothing that becomes something, the hidden potential that becomes actual.

We can get into that peace in the elements of creation right now because it's beautiful. In the Torah, the primary example of peace between the elements of nature is the secret of the word *Shama'yim*, which means heaven. Our sages interpret this word as comprised of two elements: *Aish* (fire) and *Mayim* (water). For example, heavenly spiritual reality — relative to earthly reality — manifests harmony, balance, and peace between the elements of nature. The task of the starseed is to draw down the days or revelations of heaven to earth to reveal harmony, balance, and peace universally.

What are we doing as starseeds with our Biorelativity? We are bringing down fifth-dimensional energy into this third-dimensional world and giving it form. Just like Archangel Michael and Archangel Metatron talk about, we are to be able to bring down the light and make it into form. That is really special.

"He makes peace in his heights," said Archangel Michael. This angel of water and Archangel Gabriel, the angel of fire, do not extinguish one another. The two opposite forces of nature represented by these two archangels reside together in peace, for both nullify their individuality before the Creator. This is the level of consciousness characteristic of heaven.

What are the sages saying? This level of consciousness that's characteristic of heaven is in the beginning of the second chapter of *Bereshit*, when the divine essence, God, created man in his own image and his own likeness.

Now, everyone can talk about images easily. The difference of likeness or similitude is not really touched on that much. The word "similitude" is a better description of the level of consciousness characteristic of heaven. What does that mean? It means that you have peace and that opposites come together and become complements, forming an ionic bond — not covalent bonding, but ionic bonding.

At the level of souls in the category of sight, you basically have the Divine. Just on this level of worlds, the *Tet* symbolizes form as present within matter. So too at the level of souls, *Tet* symbolizes the soul as hidden within the body.

Throughout the nine months of pregnancy, the mother constantly aspires to the moment of birth, the visible manifestation of fulfillment. Now, being that a majority of spiritual students are female and have had motherly experiences and know that situation, what helps or catalyzes and amplifies the actual birth is the mother constantly visualizing the actual summation of the birth of the child.

Similarly, the souls of the *B'nai Yisrael*, the starseeds, aspire mutually to bear a world of truth and good out of the womb, which represents the *Tet* of our present world of deceit and suffering. This peace of unity between souls when striving together for true peace on Earth enables us, even in the present, to receive blessings from the Divine.

Inner and Outer Wombs

The divine essence pays up front. In other words, when you have the intention of doing something good, you get paid for it up front. Thus, there exists simultaneously an outer womb and an inner womb. The outer womb is the reality that contains the present world, which has the characteristics of deceit and suffering. The inner womb is the common aspiration of the souls of Israel for a world of peace, good, and balance.

Within this aspiration of the inner womb, the new world, the new fetus nurtures on that consciousness. As Kabbalists, we know that for the nine months that the fetus is in the world, it is actually learning

Torah from the archangels. The outer womb contains the *Tet* of *Tamei*, or impure. The inner womb is the *Tet* of *Tahor*, or pure. In other words, it's paradoxical. The whole existence is a paradox. The power of good transforms into the word *Echad*, which is defined as "oneness." In sacred geometry, we also seek to unite the new heavens and the New Earth, which is the secret of the *Tet*.

Thus, at the level of divinity, the *Tet* represents the concealment of God's essential name. Now I'm going to give God's essential name. I have to do this now.

By the way, I didn't finish that thought about the twelve permutations of the four letters, which usually makes twenty-four permutations. Because there are two *Heys*, there are only twelve permutations, but the twelve permutations of the word — I have to sing it to you so you'll understand the correlation and the real meaning of the Sacred Triangle. Now, these are the twelve permutations of the name, and you'll be familiar with this. Before I start, I have to say *L'shem Yichud* — the name of oneness. [Tones indescribably.]

Now, does that sound familiar to anybody? That's the unification of the Sacred Triangle, and it's here in the letter *Tet*, which actually impregnates the situation to come out with that unified consciousness.

✳ ✳ ✳

Wisdom as Looking for the Good

David: I want to focus on the second sphere of the Tree of Life, which is geographically represented by the Bodensee (Lake Constance), which is in southwestern Germany on the Swiss and Austrian border. This sphere represents wisdom and has the Native American spirit guide Chief White Eagle.

What is wisdom? We are talking about goodness, so I want to give you this expression from the Kabbalah: *Gamzu L'tova*. It means "that too is for the good" or "that too is good." Now, in talking about goodness, in the Kabbalah everything eventually is for the good. This is a profound statement, and the key to understanding it is to look for the wisdom in everything that happens. You have to realize that in evaluating events, it is your perspective that is important.

When you are at the higher perspective and are looking down, or when you are in the higher spheres of the Tree of Life and are looking down, you can see your past lives, your present lives, and your future lives. You can see what is going to happen to you. For example, maybe you lost your job in the present, and it's really bad. It has made you very depressed that you had to lose the job. *Gamzu L'tova* — this too may have good in it — because another opportunity is going to open up for you, and this wasn't going to be apparent to you until maybe another month or so. If you had been working at that job you lost, you might not have the freedom or wouldn't have been traveling around to be exposed to this new opportunity.

So even in the face of apparent misfortune, there can be hidden goodness that you cannot see. From a higher perspective, misfortune could be an illusion, because everything eventually is for the good. This is also profound, saying that the Creator is good and all events that are happening now on Earth are inherently good. It is wisdom to know this and to be able to use this higher perspective to understand the working of the creation. So *Gamzu L'tova*.

It is hard for us to say this, especially when we look at the cosmic drama that is unfolding now on the planet. When we look at all of these unbelievable catastrophic events, all these wars and all this destruction to the biosphere that is occurring on this planet, it is difficult to say *Gamzu L'tova*. That, too, is for the good, yet we do not have all of the information. We do not all have the higher perspective that is available to us.

Sometimes we have to imagine what Earth would look like from a different perspective, but not everyone is capable of grasping the whole Earth drama from a higher perspective; there are only a few of us who can do that. The goal in using the Tree of Life is to try to move consciousness to that level of wisdom and look at the whole planet from the higher and more beautiful perspective of the second sphere — wisdom.

A Closer Look at Permutations

I want to talk about permutations. This is a concept in the Kabbalah that has to do with using the names of God. We are frequently referring to names, and each sphere in the Tree of Life has a name and a special name of God. The *Tetragrammaton* is *YHWH* or *YHVH*. *YHVH* may be more correct, as I said earlier, because Hebrew does not have a *W* sound, so I'm going to use the *YHVH*.

A permutation is taking one letter — in this case, *Y* — and adding additional letters and vowels to it. We have the vowels *A, E, I, O,* and *U*, so the permutations for *Y* are ya, ye, yi, yo, and yu. Then you go to the letter *H* and add vowels to it: ha, he, hi, ho, hu. For the *V*, it is going to be va, ve, vi, vo, and vu, and then you go back to the *H* again. The idea in permutation is that you are working with the sounds of the name. Ascended Master Chief White Eagle sings, "*Hey ya ho ya hey, hey ya ho ya hey,*" which almost sounds like a permutation of Hebrew letters, and the name *Yahveh* has been chanted before in a beautiful song.

The Kabbalah is focused on sounds and names, and one of the tasks of humanity is to unify the name of God and do so with these permutations. This is considered an extremely high meditation practice.

"In the Beginning" or "with the Beginning"?

The first word in the Torah is *Bereshit*. *Reshit* means "beginning," and *Be* is "with," but the English translation of this word is "in the beginning." It also could be translated as "with the beginning," which has a slightly different meaning from "in the beginning." I think this is interesting because modern particle physicists are now studying what happened "with the beginning" of the universe. One of the main focuses of cosmology is the study of the beginning. Modern astronomers, physicists, and astrophysicists realize that we must understand the beginning.

It sounds like more happens with "with the beginning" because it means there was something before the beginning while "in the beginning" makes it sound like there is a point when everything began and before that point there was nothing. The very first line in the Torah is "with the beginning, God created the heavens and the earth."

There are different names for God, and the one used in the first line of the Torah is *Elohim*. It also can be spelled as *Elokim*, which is the plural form and means "gods" but of course is defined as "God." In the Tree of Life, there are ten to twelve aspects of God, so the plural *Elokim* could mean that the Creator uses all these divine aspects for the creation, including wisdom, undifferentiated energy, and understanding. Think about that.

There are many aspects of the Creator. We have the aspect that is filled with wisdom, which sometimes is depicted as an old wise man. Another aspect of God Almighty, and then we have the aspect that is defined as balance. And if you take the name *YHVH*, which is *Yahveh*, and put the letter *Shin* (sh) between the first *Y* and *H*, you get *Yeshuva* — which is *Yeshua* — which means "he who is saving" or "the savior."

According to the medieval Christian mystics and Christian Kabbalists, the idea of Jesus/Sananda coming to Earth was focused on completing the name of God on Earth. This is purely a Christian mystic idea and is not found anywhere in Jewish thought: One aspect of the name of

God includes being a savior. In this thought, the Hebrew letter *Shin* was added to the name *YHVH* and the *H* sound was added, thus developing the name *Yeshuva*, or *Yeshua*, which means "salvation" in Hebrew. His energy is in the center sphere of the Tree of Life in Montserrat.

* * *

Acher and Rabbi Meir

Mordechai: I want to correct something. In the story about the four rabbis who went into the garden, the one named Acher was not the student of Rabbi Meir Baal HaNes; he was the teacher. Meir Baal HaNes was a man of miracles, and Acher was his teacher. So Acher pulled up on his horse at his student's house on *Shabbat* while the student, Rabbi Meir, was in a lesson with ten or eleven other students. A student came to tell Rabbi Meir that Acher was outside on his horse. Rabbi Meir left his students and went out to walk with his teacher while he was riding the horse, and they had a study — a *Limood*. When he got back about fifteen or twenty minutes later, Rabbi Meir's student asked him, "Why did you go out with him? Why did you even go to meet him? He's breaking *Shabbat*; he's considered an outcast. Why did you go with him?"

Rabbi Meir replied, "I went with him because I look at him completely open and with no judgment, and I take from him the good that he has to teach me. I took it that way." That's a lesson for all of us — to only see the good in people. That is the whole thing.

The Sound of *Tet*

We'll go back to sight, sound, and number. In the category of sound, the letter *Tet* appears in many places. It represents inclination. We're talking about judging correctly, and guessing is not allowed in anything — whether it's for a judge (a *Dayan*) or any of us. We cannot judge with a guess. We should not judge at all, but if we choose to judge, then we certainly cannot guess.

"For there is no guessing in Jacob" is a quote from the Torah. Jacob is the central column that is shared with Lord Sananda. He corresponds to the attribute of truth. We're going to get to that word, "truth." True judgment, as it's said, gives truth to Jacob and his son Joseph, who represents the most essential extension of Jacob's property. Simple truth personifies the power to rectify imagination.

Rectifying imagination could also be considered guessing. Joseph the Righteous said to his brothers, who didn't recognize him, "For a man like me is surely able to guess" — the ultimate rectification of the guessing nature of imagination, the consummate conversion of imagination into the rainbow of manifestations of divine inspiration. What does that mean in Hebrew? *Ruach Hakodesh* is the task of the *Mashiach* (Holy Spirit is the task of the Messiah).

For this reason, we are taught that *Mashiach* — which is spelled *Mem-Shin-Yud-Chet*, equals *Nachash* (snake); they both equal 358 — will kill the evil snake and thereupon be given the princess, the pregnant maiden discussed above. The consciousness of divine inspiration in prayer is taught in the Zohar. So what we're talking about here is having certainty in our imagination so we can produce the rainbow of manifestations of imagery.

In the level of divinity in the category of sound, *Choshen*, or the breastplate worn by the high priest in the Holy Temple, is a permutation of *Nachash*. *Nun-Chet-Shin* spells snake, and *Chet-Shin-Nun* is the breastplate. The names of tribes were affixed to the precious stones — the twelve etheric crystals — affixed to this breastplate. When the king would pose a faithful question to the high priest, such as whether or not Israel should go to war, certain letters of the breastplate would shine.

The high priest, if worthy to receive that *Ruach Hakodesh*, would be able to permute the letters illuminated by virtue of a secret name of God that was written on a parchment and put in a secret place concealed in the breastplate into a meaningful answer. The full name of the breastplate is *Choshen Mishpat*, which means "breastplate of judgment." Our sages teach that its purpose was to rectify the property of judgment in the soul and to atone for false judgment. That breastplate was thus a divine aid to confront the primordial snake in the soul, chill its evil manifestation, and clarify its latent potential. It would not only clarify, but also act as a catalyst and amplifier to level out the playing field.

The letter *Tet* can also be found in the word for bed, *Mita*, which symbolizes the spiritual as well as the physical setting of man and wife uniting for the sake of drawing new souls into this world. This can be understood by the three levels of the soul — the three levels of worlds, souls, and divinity. At the level of divinity, the *Shekhinah*, the divine presence, the third partner in the aspect of conception, is revealed above the bed of man, as the sages say — in reference to the bed of our father Jacob, the divine setting for the birth of the twelve tribes of Israel.

The meaning of the inclination of this level is purely superconscious and is reflected by the musical intonations of speech in the reading of the Torah. This is the secret of traditional Torah — cantillations, *Ta'amim* (literally, "tastes" or "reasons"). There are four levels of the Torah: letters (*Otiot*), crowns (*Tagim*), vowels (*Nekudot*), and cantillations (*Ta'amim*) — the highest level. So reading the Torah can be compared to the singing or chanting of the Indians. The singing or cantillations of the Torah can also be compared to the chanting of the Tibetan monks, the Japanese monks, the Buddhist monks, or any similar group on the North, Central, or South American continents. They are all singing or chanting the names of God; that's what brings it all together. The wisdom concealed in the cantillations leads directly to superconsciousness and to its revelation, which awaits the coming of the redemption and of the light of repair.

The Numbers of *Tet*

Now my favorite category: numbers. *Tet* equals nine. Let us refer again to the *Sephirah* of wisdom. Starting at the bottom sphere, the level of *Malchut*, you can go up nine spheres and be at the level of wisdom. That's what the *Tet* is trying to express when it gives birth, because the *Tet* is responsible for impregnation. What are we impregnating? We are impregnating all of the divine help that we can get to bring down fifth-dimensional light. Now, there are many nines, and there are many wombs, but we have to get to the level of souls in the category of number.

The number nine at the level of souls relates to the nine months of pregnancy. Both the form of the *Tet* and its number allude to the great wonder of new life being nurtured within a mother's womb. In the truest sense, a woman is the vessel where potential becomes actual. Through her, the spiritual blessing of new souls descends into a physical body of this world.

The nine months of pregnancy are necessary to complete the development of the nine general divisions of body and soul. The three levels — the head, the body above the abdomen, and the body below the abdomen — each divide into three. Each of the resulting further nine develops by means of interinclusion. We spoke about that a few lessons ago.

Now, $9 \times 9 = 81$. This is really the secret of 9: Any multiple of 9 adds up to 9.

$3 \times 9 = 27$ and $2 + 7 = 9$

$9 \times 5 = 45$ and $4 + 5 = 9$

$7 \times 9 = 63$ and $6 + 3 = 9$

$8 \times 9 = 72$ and $7 + 2 = 9$

$9 \times 9 = 81$ and $8 + 1 = 9$

Abraham was first named Abram without the *Hey*, which is equal to 243. What is 243?

3 x 9 = 27

27 x 3 = 81

81 x 3 = 243

243 + 5 (extra H) = 248. We'll stop here with the magic number of 248.

❋ ❋ ❋

Harmony and Wisdom

Shalom, Shalom, Shalom. Greetings. This is **Sananda**. I send you blessings from the center of the Tree of Life, from the beauty of Montserrat, which is the holding place for this etheric crystal known as beauty. Let the harmony and beauty that is the core of the goodness of this dimension emerge directly into your lifetime, into this lifetime.

This is the beauty of the Tree of Life. This is the beauty of *Tiferet*. This is the understanding that you can call on beauty and harmony to fill your life *now*. Isn't this a great gift — to have this power? You have the power to speak; you have the power to pray with great prayer, to pray with great intention.

You can call on the center of this Tree of Life and speak these words: "May the beauty, the wisdom, the understanding, the loving kindness, and the divine judgment, which is for the good — may all of these things emerge now into my life and be merged into a unity." This is what the Tree of Life is showing you: that all these spheres can be united and that they are united in *Tiferet*. They are united in Montserrat, Spain. This is the great beauty; this is the great strength — that everything is united.

We also have this beautiful concept of the Holy Spirit. All of you know that the Holy Spirit is also talked about as the Father, Son, and the Holy Ghost. But they are united in the Holy Spirit. The Holy Spirit is the divine light, the divine spirit that comes to this planet, that comes to you from this place of beauty and harmony, where you can call on *Ruach Hakodesh* — the Holy Spirit — to be with you.

I will sing through the channel the words *Ruach Hakodesh*. As you hear the vibrations of these words, speak to yourself and say: "Let the *Ruach Hakodesh* fill my life today."

[Sings: *Ruach Hakodesh*.]

May the Holy Spirit fill you with the harmony and the light of *Tiferet*, the harmony and light that is represented by Montserrat. And may the Holy Spirit also bring you wisdom in this month.

Now, Chief White Eagle will speak to you. Blessings in the Holy Spirit, which is filling each one of you now. This is Sananda. Good day.

* * *

Receive Divine Wisdom

[Chants: *Hey ya ho ya hey. Hey ya ho ya hey. Hey ya ho ya hey. Hey ya ho. Hey ya ho.*] Greetings. I'm **Chief White Eagle**. I bless each of you and let you connect with your inner wisdom. This Tree of Life is showing that you contain all of these aspects within you, for God, our Creator, works in you so that you have the divine wisdom. Let the divine wisdom come to you, and let the cosmic understanding of this planet, of this dimension, and of this universe be downloaded now inside of you.

In a sense, this is a return. The Kabbalah is a galactic map, and really, it is not that you are gaining new wisdom but that you are returning to your nature. You are returning to the wisdom.

I, Chief White Eagle, call on Father/Mother Creator of light, of all, for each of you to be filled now with divine wisdom, represented by Bodensee, the second etheric crystal and represented by this chanting: [Chants: *Hey ya ho ya hey*].

Know that the ancient Israelites were also native peoples. Know that they were like the Native Americans: They were in the desert, they were living close to nature, they were looking at the skies, and they were harvesting the beauty in agriculture. Ultimately, we are all native peoples, and all our roots go back to a time when humans were native. This is the unification of the Holy Spirit that Sananda talked about. I am Chief White Eagle. All my words are sacred. *Ho!*

* * *

Questions from the Class

Alessandra in Washington, DC: I have a question for Modechai: What was the reference you made that had to do with ionic versus covalent bonding?

Mordechai: Basically, it relates to man and woman in the ionic bonding of creation, whether it be in *Olam Haba* ("the world of heaven") or *Olam Hazeh* ("the world of Earth"). There is an ionic bond in all of that. Now, we're down here on the third dimension where there is a covalent bond. The only thing that makes this covalent bond is the fact that we attempted to unify, but in this world, there is mainly separation, and we seek bonding.

Wherever you have some bonding, it is in a covalent manner, but once you connect to the fifth dimension, you connect to *Olam Haba* or *Shama'yim* — heaven. The term "heaven" is a way to express that fifth dimension where you are in the process of ionic bonding. When male and female come together, as I've said, the divine essence — the *Shekhinah* — is above that bed. Many women during conception have actually visualized what was going to come out nine months later. That is ionic bonding.

Remember, we have to practice. We have to practice with our imaginations, with our imaging, because there will be times when we won't be able to connect in the physical, and all we'll have is our connection to the *Ruach Hakodesh* and to the inclination of the divine essence.

Cora: What would you recommend? To go into a meditation?

Mordechai: Use a group of crystals you are close with, send it to the Dome of the Rock, and let the archangels take it from there. From the Dome of the Rock, it's going to shoot up straight to the ring of ascension, and then from there, you can take it and do what you want with it.

Yud **Reveals the Spark**

CLASS 11

Mordechai: Before I start on the birthing of the *Yud*, I would like to finish up on the pregnancy of the *Tet* and the number 248. It's an important number and definitely deserves further clarification. Three to the fifth power is 243, which is also the sacred gematria of Abraham's name before he got the extra *Hey*; the name Avram is 243 (+ 5 [Hey] = 248).

Before we birth this *Yud*, we must understand that the word for truth in Hebrew is *Emmet*, which is 441, and 4 + 4 + 1 = 9, so truth is a 9. By the way, 441 is the square of 21.

Then we have the word *Ohr* (light). The sacred gematria value of *Ohr* is 207, and 2 + 7 = 9. The word *Shabbat*, *Shin-Bet-Tav*, is 702. Is it not amazing that *Ohr* is 207 and *Shabbat* is 702? Each in gematria equals 9. But here we are at 3 to the 5th power (3^5), which equals 243.

There are five *Chasidim* and five *Gevurot* — five kindnesses and five judgments. What we're doing most of the time in prayer is sweetening the judgments. When you add that 5 to 243, you get 248. This is a very important number because of the number of words in the prayer *Sh'ma Yisrael*, the most important prayer in the Jewish liturgy: "Hear, listen, oh Israel, the Lord our God — the Lord is one!" What do you want to hear? You want to hear those silent, quiet voices, the whispers we go into meditation to listen to. That is *Sh'ma Yisrael*. That is 248.

Besides that, the name Avraham (with the extra *Hey*) equals 248. The angels Raziel and Uriel each equal 248. Raziel means *Raz*, the secrets of the Creator. There was a book of Raziel that was given to Adam (the first Adam). It was used, abused, and given to other people — his descendants down the line. Nimrod, the infamous emperor, abused this book; that is where he got all his power from. But finally he was killed by Jacob's brother, Esau.

Anyway, getting back to 248, Uriel is an important angel. He's directly under Archangel Metatron, and his name totals 248. He is also in *B'tzelem Elohim*, or in the image of the Elohim, which is also 248. The most important combination of 248 is the word *Chelkeek*, and we're going to get into that because of the *Yud*. This is how we're going to birth the *Yud* — with *Chelkeek*, which means "fraction of a moment."

When we go into meditation and when we connect with all of our friends and entities, we are in the now — in that moment. With the *Chelkeek*, with the actual fraction of a moment, we will get into the *Tet* as it gives birth to the letter *Yud*. The infinite point, the letter *Yud*, is the only letter that hangs in midair. All the other letters are attached or grounded. The *Yud* is not grounded.

The Interinclusion of the Infinite

The letter *Yud* is a small, suspended point that reveals the spark of essential hidden good within the letter *Tet*. Look at *Tet* again and notice the end of the letter where it dips down. That is the hidden good! What is hidden within the *Tet* is what we're giving birth to right now. The secret of this point is the power of the infinite to contain finite phenomena within itself and express it to apparent external reality.

Finite manifestation begins from a zero-dimensional point. Most of us are familiar with the term "zero point." An aspect of this includes developing a one-dimensional line and a two-dimensional surface. This is alluded to in the full spelling of the letter *Yud*, which is *Yud-Vav-Dalet*. The *Yud* in those three letters is the point, the *Vav* is the line, and the *Dalet* is the surface. Those of us who have read the great book *Flatland* (by Edwin A. Abbot) know it describes how a two-dimensional being cannot understand three-dimensional existence, and a three-dimensional being cannot understand a four- or five-dimensional existence.

Before the contraction of God that allowed the universe to come into existence — in Hebrew, we call it in *Tzimtzum* — the power of limitation was hidden, latent within God's infinite essence. Following this contraction, this power of limitation was revealed.

Let's take a spyglass, the kind you would use if you were at sea, and look at the horizon (so you have to use a really long spyglass). Imagine the spyglass having seventy sections; that's the spyglass of the Tree of Life with which we're working. Now, as you open up the spyglass, you have seventy small sections. The interinclusion occurs when you put the bottom back into the top and everything is hidden. Everything is within everything — within every cell and within every subatomic frequency.

The Sight of *Yud*

We're going to get again to the sight, sound, and number. In the category of sight is a formed point, a crown above, and a pathway below. The *Yud* is the only letter that is suspended in midair. At the level of worlds in sight, the pathway of the *Yud* is the initial point of space and time. Visualize a dark circle with a straight line coming down into it. The line represents energy the Creator sent out. The light came down to create space for the third dimension — actually, for all dimensions. That's because that circle represents all five worlds, but we'll just take the third dimension for now.

The line went all the way down to the center. When the line hit that center, the Creator took it back. That was the *Yud* that expanded all the way into making space, the space for time — time and space. It also represents natural wisdom, the wisdom of Solomon. We're going to get into King Solomon today because he really was a genius. Why? He was known for his decision making and his great judgments. That's because he had a complete connection. That's where his understanding and his wisdom came from.

Also, in the level of worlds, the direction and purpose is the consciousness of the present moment or *Chelkeek*, which equals 248. Once we get into that consciousness, it's easy to make the connection.

At the level of souls of this category of sight, the body of the *Yud* is a wedged point. On the second level of souls is the wisdom of the Creator as manifest in the judgment of Solomon. Herein lies the power of self-nullification. In other words, to self-nullify — to lose your ego — takes power. It takes strength. You can't just say, "I'm going to take my ego away, and I'm just going to go self-nullify myself." It doesn't happen that way. As a matter of fact, that was one of the questions I asked: "How long do you think it'll take you to get rid of your ego?" The answer is, as long as you want it to.

The level of divinity is also in the category of sight. The crown of the *Yud* above and the wedged point of the *Yud* with a little crown on top of it — that's where everything comes from. That's the essence of the *Yud*. Also, the wisdom of the divine essence inspired and directed the genius of Solomon. Solomon created the Holy Temple. When it was built, it was one big connection. All that copper, those two copper towers, created an absolute connection to the fifth dimension. A revealed omnipresence is in the beginning and end of every letter; from the beginning to the end of every letter is the *Yud*. In other words, all the letters come from the *Yud*. And the *Aleph*, the first letter, begins with a *Yud* and ends with a *Yud*.

The Sound of *Yud*

Let's get to the category of sound. In sound, the letter *Yud*, or *Yad*, means "hand." It also means "to thrust" or "to cast." The easiest example is thrusting or casting a fishing rod with a hook, line, and sinker.

At the level of souls in the category of sound, we have intelligence and friendship, acknowledgment, making space for others, and empathy. Empathy is a very important word going into the future. At the level of divinity in sound, the infinite will be able to sustain the creation. That this creation is regenerating and is re-created every moment is the point I was trying to make with the *Chelkeek*. That's the moment that represents each individual's nanomoment in which the world is re-created.

It is not easy to comprehend the re-creation of every moment. That's why all the great sages say that every moment is new. If we really had the *Emuna* — the certainty — to understand that the past is the past and the next moment is a whole new world, we could start fresh right now.

The Numbers of *Yud*

Now we get to the category of numbers. The letter *Yud* is the number ten, and it says in the holy scriptures that the tenth shall be holy. So what does ten represent? What I said in the class about the *Aleph*: Our world exists of ones and zeros, and that is exactly the letter *Yud* and the number ten. This is the essence of the computer age, of all the technology, and of going into the future of science and technology. It all starts with zero and one, and that's the number ten.

Then we have the ten divine utterances through which the world was created. What were these ten divine utterances? They call them the Ten Commandments, the Ten Utterances, but what were they? They

were ten living holograms. When the Creator gave His first two utterances and all the souls went right into the hologram, into the light, they
didn't even want to hang out anymore. They went right into the hologram, and the bodies flew 25–30 kilometers away. It's a whole story
unto itself.

* * *

Looking at Letters and Gematria in the Tree of Life

David: Today we are going to understand the Tree of Life by using
the letters, because the letters are also numbers. This is important to
understand because in Hebrew, *Aleph* (A) is 1, *Bet* (B) is 2, *Gimmel* (G)
or *Kimmel* (K) is 3, and *Dalet* (D) is 4.

Mordechai has been talking a lot about gematria, which is taking
words and their numerical values and adding them up. In modern
physics, they are actually looking at the essence of everything as numbers because there are a certain number of atoms and a certain number
of protons, and the total essence is information. Everything in the universe is vibrating and has a particular numerical value.

If you look at the English letters *A–B*, *B* would be spelled out or
transliterated as B-E-E, and *G* might be G-E-E and *D* would be D-E-E.
Here we have done the same thing with the Hebrew letters, and the
nearest equivalent to the letter *Yud* would be *Y*.

The sacred name of God, which we have explained in earlier classes,
is *Yahweh*. (That is not the correct pronunciation, but we will use it for
the purpose of this lecture). And the first letter of *Yahweh* is *Y* or *Yud*. It
is important to understand that the first letter of the unpronounceable
name of God is *Y*, the *Yud*.

Mordechai also mentioned a famous prayer in Judaism: *Sh'ma Yisrael*. It is the prayer you say first thing in the morning and supposed to
say many times during the day. It also should be the last set of words
you speak before you die — if you are conscious at that moment. The
prayer is simple: "Hear, oh Israel" — or it could be "listen, oh Israel"
(it is like a command) — "the Lord our God, *Yahweh*, the Lord is one."
It is talking about the unification. So the unification of all these spheres
becomes the basis of the understanding.

Mordechai also talked about a concept called *B'tzelem Elohim*. The
orthodox would not say the actual word *Elohim* but replace the *H* with
a *K*, even though it refers to *Elohim*, so: *B'tzelem Elokim*. I define the
B'tzelem as "the aura" — the aura of God — and here we have the

reference to our auras and the image, so we are created in the image of *Elohim*.

The First Act of Creation

I want to talk a little bit about *Tzimtzum*. In the Kabbalah, the first act of creation was not the big bang. If you study modern physics, it would go back to the nanosecond before the big bang. Actually, they go right up to that point and stop, for the laws of physics do not explain how something came out of nothing; there is no way. In the world of modern physics, we have the laws of Newton, which cover the movements of large bodies (such as planets) and gravity and everything that we can see. Then there is the world of subatomic matter, which is quantum physics. In the world of subatomics, particles seem to follow different laws than the large bodies do.

In the Kabbalah, they are saying, "Well, do we go back to this point?" Mordechai called it the "zero point." I find it is also called the point of singularity, where the whole world, the whole universe, all matter, was a dot (but smaller than a dot) — infinitely small, infinitely dense.

When the big bang occurred, there was an explosion. That is what the modern scientists believe was the first act of creation: the big bang. But the Kabbalah says, "No, the first act of creation was the withdrawal of the Creator, leaving a space for the creation." Mordechai beautifully described it as the Creator withdrawing and then there being a finiteness. Then there was one point left, and that became the big bang.

Please understand that in the Tree of Life, above Mount Fuji, above the first sphere, is another energy. That energy is the infinite light, which is also called *Ain Soph Ohr*. Here you have the spheres, but above the sphere is something like a vibrational half-circle representing the infinite light, the light that is without end.

The first manifestation of undifferentiated energy is represented by Mount Fuji and Archangel Metatron in our diagram. There is actually an energy above the infinite light, but that infinite light is incomprehensible and cannot be seen by us; it is the hidden part. But remember, in our new diagram with twelve spheres, our new paradigm, what was hidden is now becoming known. So the hidden knowledge is being revealed.

Jokes to Help Understand Self-Nullification

I also want to talk about the concept of self-nullification. There is a famous joke in the Kabbalah about self-nullification: A rabbi and an assistant rabbi are in a large synagogue. The assistant rabbi goes into the temple and sees the main rabbi praying before the center of the temple, saying,: "I'm nothing. I'm nothing. Please accept me. I'm nothing." This is self-nullification — the death of the ego.

Then the assistant rabbi says, "Oh, this is how to become enlightened." (Remember, the whole idea of the Tree of Life is that on a personal basis, we use it to become enlightened, and on a planetary basis, it is used to bring this planet into the fifth dimension, into the Garden of Eden — the *Gan Eden*). So the assistant rabbi says, "Oh, okay — I'm nothing. I'm nothing."

Both of the rabbis are saying, "I'm nothing." When the janitor walks by, he can't believe his ears. He hears both of these famous rabbis saying, "I'm nothing," so he decides, "Oh, this is the way that I can become enlightened."

So the janitor goes into the temple and says, "I'm nothing. I'm nothing." Then the chief rabbi stands up, looks at his assistant, and says, "Look who thinks he is nothing!"

Anyway, that joke represents the idea of self-nullification, but you have to be something or someone to be nothing. How could a mere janitor be nothing?

There are other ideas about the levels of the soul, and we will get into those with the letters and the levels of the worlds because the Tree of Life is actually divided into four levels. Take a look at all the spheres of the Tree of Life and remember that we are working to unify them, but to do so, we have to separate. At the top, we have undifferentiated energy. We have wisdom in sphere two. Then Lake Moraine is understanding. Next, we have hidden knowledge. After that, we have loving kindness and compassion. Next comes strength, discipline, and judgment. In the center, we have balance, harmony, and Messianic energy. After that, comes the idea of the creation of a new Earth society, and opposite that, we have the creation of sacred places and sites, which is a key concept in planetary healing. Creating sacred space is something we are doing through our planetary cities of light work. Next is shimmering, the vibrational frequency used to accelerate our aura so we can go into other dimensions. Then we have the Earth interaction with the third dimension, and finally, there's manifestation. We are trying to manifest a New Earth that is connected directly with fifth-dimensional energy.

* * *

Mordechai: I appreciate that joke because I have heard it before. I have another cute little joke that gets the point across: There's a rabbi who passes away and goes to heaven. He's waiting in line. He says, "I'm a rabbi — can I step up a little bit?" Instead, the line gets bigger in front of him. He can't understand what's happening. He asks, "What's going on? I've done some wonderful, good deeds all my life, so why the delay?"

He then sees an average guy come in who's ushered to the front of the line. The rabbi is in shock. He's completely blown away. In an excited state of mind, he asks, "Who is that guy that just walked in? They shoved him right to the front of the line, and now he's already through?" The rabbi adds, "And I'm standing in line all this time? What's the story?"

He sees one of the assistant entities and calls him over and asks, "Can you please explain to me what's going on?"

The entity says, "When you get your turn, we'll tell you. You have all the time in the world, so don't worry about it."

So finally after a certain amount of time, the rabbi gets up to the front and says, "I must ask you this question: Why did that gentleman have such a priority to get in?"

"Well, Rabbi," they say, "we'll tell you. You've done very well in your incarnation. You've meant very well, but when you gave your lectures to your congregation, at least 80 percent of the congregation went to sleep. When this bus driver pulled up and the people got on his bus, he drove like a cowboy, and everybody on the bus started praying with all their hearts for God to please save them."

Tens, Twelves, and the *Yud*

Now, in the letter *Yud*, I have to get to the level of divinity in the category of sound. The fact is that the *Yud* is the first letter of the Creator's name, *Yahveh*. It is like Earth going around suspended in nothingness. There is something to be said for that; it's a beautiful thing.

Let's get to the category of numbers. I must say in review that there are many tens. For instance, in the category of number in the level of worlds, they say the tenth shall be holy. You have the ten utterances through which the world was created. Then you have the ten things that were created on the first day and ten things created at dusk at the end of the sixth day. You have the ten generations from Adam to Noah and then another ten generations from Noah to Abraham, and from Abraham to Moses were six generations. So what you have are twenty-six generations, and that is what they say is 26 — the sacred gematria of *Yud-Kay-Vav-Kay*, the four letters of the divine *Tetragrammaton*, the Creator's name.

Then you have the ten pure animals and the ten categories of forbidden magic. (Everybody would like to know what the ten categories of forbidden magic are, but we'll leave that for another time.) There are ten battles of Joshua. The number 248, brought up at the beginning of this lecture, is an important number because there are 248 bones in the body (so says the Torah, the sages). Also, there are 248 organs and 365 sinews, which makes 613 (according to the Bible). The sinews are equal to the number of days in the year. So 248 + 365 = 613, and that is the number of deeds. Also, 248 is the number of the good deeds we should do and 365 is the number of not-good ones that we should watch out for and avoid.

At the level of souls, we have the ten or twelve *Sephirot*. You must understand that ten is the basic number and that twelve is also an important number because it helps make the Tree of Life understandable. Actually, to make it understandable, you'd need a hundred of these spheres, but twelve will have to do because that is the number of etheric crystals that the Arcturians put in place on Earth.

Twelve is also the number of crystals that are in the breastplate of the high priest. By the way, who is the high priest in upper Jerusalem? It's Archangel Michael. He is the high priest of the holy temple in Zion in upper Jerusalem. When he speaks, he's coming from the complete authority of knowing what is what. I love him.

The ten or twelve *Sephirot* in this Tree of Life are actually the Tree of Knowledge, representing the energies of these twelve crystals both in the breastplate and in the ethereal now. We have the ten tribes of Abraham. Abraham went down this Tree of Life because when he got down to the end, his name was Avram, which is 243. That was the 243 (or 3 to the 5th power). But when he passed all his trials, the Creator gave him the letter *Hey*, which equals 5, so he went from Avram to Avraham, or from 243 to 248.

There is a *Minyan* (the number of people needed in Judaism to begin a prayer service) of ten men. I'm going to spend the rest of the time on this *Minyan* concept. There is a rule. This is a cosmic, galactic rule. When ten starseed souls come together in one room, it automatically brings the *Shekhinah*, the divine essence. Now, this is very important because you need unity — the unity we have in the Group of Forty — to be useful and to take the light and make it into a form. Very few places have complete unity.

That's the whole secret: the unity of these ten men. I say ten men, but I'm sure 80 percent of the starseeds are women, and the women ask, "Why does it have to be ten men? Why can't it be ten women? What's wrong with that? We have souls. We count, don't we?" And we bring out the Torah, and the men are right there at the ark and putting their hands on it and kissing it, and the women are stuck behind a curtain. And the curtain opens up, and they put their palms up, and they try to get that energy, and they do get that energy. Why are the women all the way in the back and the men are all the way in the front? Because the men need it.

The men really need it. They are in such need of correction, of balance, of harmony, that they're the ones who need to be there. The women are balanced. They pay the bill through pregnancy. And what do they do? They do all the work. They're covered. All they have to do is hold up their palms, their ten fingers, and they get more light than the guy standing right next to it.

There is a great joke. A woman wants to get an *Aliyah*.[1] She says to the rabbi, "Listen, my husband said he'd give you plenty of money, and he got his *Aliyah*, and now he's passed away, and now I want my *Aliyah*. You want a check? I want an *Aliyah*."

But the rabbi says, "You don't need one; you're already there."

"I don't care. I want an *Aliyah* just like everybody else," she replies.

So the rabbi says, "You mean like every other man? Why do you want to go down and degrade yourself? You already got equal to the whole Torah. What do you need an *Aliyah* for?"

That's the whole point. The female energy knows self-nullification through pregnancy, through birth, through taking care of all the kids — through doing all the work. I compare this to the lion. There are four sacred animals: the lion, the eagle, the ox, and man. Unless man corrects himself and goes through self-nullification and does *Teshuvah*, he's like all the other animals.

Now, I usually use the lion, because what does the male lion do? He sleeps, he eats, and he doesn't do too much. The female hunts the food, gives birth, and pretty much does everything. The male wakes up, and even if there's an attack, he only gets up if the women can't handle it. Then he has to go to work.

* * *

A Meditation on the Name of God

Shalom, Shalom, Shalom. Greetings. I'm **Archangel Metatron**. You are preparing yourselves and opening up your auras, and you are opening up your crown chakras so that you can receive this highest light. The highest light comes from meditation and using the letters and sounds of the name of God. In reality, when you are studying self-nullification, the beautiful wisdom is that self-nullification occurs automatically when you are meditating on the name of God.

It is not, as you say in your language, rocket science. It is not complicated. It does not require thirty years in a cave, but you can self-nullify by focusing on *Yud-Hey-Vav-Hey, YHVH.* I will teach you a special exercise today. We will do it quickly since we are limited, but you can extend this.

Say with me as loud as you can:
　YUD-HEY-VAV-HEY.
　YUD-HEY-VAV-HEY.
　YHVH.

And now say a little bit softer:
　Yud-Hey-Vav-Hey.
　Yud-Hey-Vav-Hey.
　YHVH. YHVH.

Now go one level softer:
　Yud-Hey-Vav-Hey.
　Yud-Hey-Vav-Hey.
　YHVH. YHVH.

Now go inside yourself in silence and say the letters in Hebrew, and then say them in English, just as I have done. We will go into silence now as you do this.
　[Silence.]

Now we will do it softly again:
　Yud-Hey-Vav-Hey.
　Yud-Hey-Vav-Hey.
　YHVH. YHVH.

A little bit louder:
> *Yud-Hey-Vav-Hey.*
> *Yud-Hey-Vav-Hey.*
> *YHVH. YHVH.*

Go one level higher:
> *Yud-Hey-Vav-Hey.*
> *Yud-Hey-Vav-Hey.*
> *Yud-Hey-Vav-Hey.*
> *YHVH. YHVH. YHVH.*
> [Tones: Ooooo.]

Let the letters *Yud-Hey-Vav-Hey* be in your aura. Let these letters be right at the top of your crown chakra so that the energies of the *Yud-Hey-Vav-Hey* fill your whole aura with light. May you become self-nullified. You will experience the self-nullification in the light of *Yud-Hey-Vav-Hey.* You will feel a unity with yourself and a unity of the energy of *Yud-Hey-Vav-Hey* that will give you a balance, remove all fear, remove all anxiety, and vibrate you into the fifth dimension and into a unity. For the universe, this world is appearing as a duality, but that is the major illusion — the illusion of duality that is overcome by the unity of *Yud-Hey-Vav-Hey. Baruch Hashem* — blessed is his name. I'm Archangel Metatron. Good day.

A Review of
Aleph through *Yud*

CLASS 12

MORDECHAI AND DAVID

Mordechai: It's important that we internalize as much of this information as possible. It's not just a matter of understanding; it's a matter of feeling it. What are these twelve spheres in the Arcturian Tree of Life? It's important that we understand the makeup. This Tree of Life is a map — an energy map where the only password to the software is consciousness, quality consciousness, the SLQ, or however you want to express it. It's important that we understand the power of Hebrew letters.

In the tower of Babel, about 4,000 years ago, it is said (and the Zohar quotes it) that the whole Earth was of one language and unity. There was only one language back then during the building of the tower, and that language was based on Hebrew letters. The letters were formed 2,000 years before creation — or before the creation of Adam, or however you want to look it. Two thousand years! You must understand that's not 2,000 of our years, because one day in the fifth dimension is equal to 1,000 years down here.

Let's get some of this minor math out of the way. If one day upstairs is 1,000 years down here, then one year upstairs is 365,000 years down here. Multiply the 365,000 by the 2,000 years, and you get that it was 730 million years ago that these letters were formed. That says a lot because that's before Atlantis, before Lemuria, and even before the entities who came down here to look for the right protoplasmic bodies for souls to house themselves for this experiment or test that we are going through.

That's a very long time, 730 million years ago. It started with the *Aleph-Bet*. What happened? They had unity, but the Creator wanted to destroy the people who were building this tower, because it wasn't just a tower; it was a nuclear fortress.

The *Zohar* quotes that these guys were, believe it or not, at war with heaven. The third dimension went to war with the fifth dimension. There was no even playing field, but these guys had a lot of chutzpah. The divine essence could not really get rid of them because they were unified. That's the big secret. It was like one big mafia.

So what did the Creator and all the councils do? They added seventy more languages to the playing field. That confused everybody. That's why the Torah was translated into seventy languages. That was 4,000 years ago.

Since then we've had offshoots, new dialects, and acute accents, but the Hebrew letters have tenure. They have a lot of tenure, and we really have to give them a lot more respect — or at least attention — if we want to reach the goal of understanding this Tree of Life.

Our goal is to get to *Chochma*, the second sphere, the circle on the top right of the tree — divine wisdom. To use the phrase that Chief White Eagle uses, "This is the time when divine wisdom is necessary." It is needed by all of us starseeds because, as they say in Hebrew, *Lama* (why)? The response is *Cacha* (because). So it is.

It's more than just *Cacha*. It's really an important spiritual expansion. That was the word I was looking for — expansion. We are looking to expand ourselves and our souls all the way up this Tree of Life to the level of *Chochma*. But before we get to *Chochma*, we have to look at where we are: We're on the bottom.

I want to get one important thing straight: Everything I'm saying is truly, absolutely galactic. To think that these Hebrew letters are for the Jews exclusively is a severe corruption. That should be considered a ploy by the other side to prevent this light-force energy from coming down here from the fifth dimension. The letters are absolutely for everyone and for every language, because this Tree of Life is universal and multidimensional, and it represents unity — the unity of this Blue Jewel. That's where we are going.

A More In-Depth Explanation of Interinclusion

To make the summary simple, let's go back to a few classes ago when I was trying to define that most difficult word — "interinclusion" — and

I used the example of a spyglass. Because we went through ten letters, let's imagine we have a spyglass that has ten sections. You'll have to expand it to look at the horizon. This spyglass we're using has ten one-inch sections that come out.

Start with the first section, the first letter: *Aleph*. This is what we have done with these ten Hebrew letters. *Aleph* starts with the two *Yuds* and the *Vav*. It is the first letter in the ten utterances or holograms, so it is number one, which we discussed. Now, we're going to take the letter *Aleph* and enclose it in that one little lever; we're going to push that first section of the spyglass, the one closest to the eye, in one notch. Why? Because the *Aleph* was not a vessel. It was a happening, an active letter that channels.

The next letter is *Bet*, which is a house and is shaped like one. The *Aleph* sort of jumped into the *Bet*, so you couldn't really see it. The *Aleph* included itself in the *Bet*. That's why when you push that first section of the ten into the second section, when you put the *Aleph* into the *Bet*, all you see is the *Bet*.

Now, *Bet* is a letter that represents stability. It has a solid line on the bottom going across. The *Aleph* has two areas that touch the bottom: the bottom of the *Vav* and the bottom of the *Yud*. It's secure, so the *Aleph* felt secure by including itself in the *Bet*. But the *Bet* is so secure that it wants to be mobile. It wants to have a little fun. We all have to accept change — the one thing that is constant and that we have to accept, whether we like it or not. So the *Bet* figured it would jump into the change.

The next letter is the *Gimmel*. The *Bet* jumped inside and included itself in the *Gimmel*, so we push the spyglass up one more notch. Now we have both the *Aleph* and the *Bet* inside the *Gimmel*. What is the *Gimmel*? Enthusiastic energy. It wanted to do nothing but provide enthusiastic service for the Creator, and the best it could do was symbolically create the planet Jupiter so that we could have miracles, so that we could have things above nature, and so that Earth could have a protection shield.

The next thing the *Gimmel* wanted to do is jump and run after the *Dalet*. Remember that poor *Dalet*? It was just standing there humbled. It tried to run away and not look back, but it finally realized it could really use some help. So it slowed down, and the *Gimmel* caught up and ran into it. The *Gimmel* sustained the *Dalet* and gave it sustenance. Push that spyglass up one more notch so that you have the *Aleph*, the *Bet*, and the *Gimmel* inside the *Dalet*.

The *Dalet* now is satisfied. It's not poor anymore, and it could add only one thing — a little *Yud* on the bottom to show its appreciation to the divine essence for its being satiated and completely recharged. So in its thankfulness, it brings on the smallest but most powerful letter — the *Yud*, which we discussed and described as a galactic paradox. This is the most powerful letter; all the letters are made up of this letter, and it volunteers a leg for the *Dalet*. What happened when the *Yud* became a leg for the *Dalet*? The *Dalet* became a *Hey*.

So now you have the *Dalet* including itself inside the *Hey*. Why? Because the rain is cleansing, and the *Hey* is the vessel. There are two of these vessels in the Creator's name.

Now you have the *Aleph*, the *Bet*, the *Gimmel*, and the *Dalet* all inside the *Hey*. The *Hey*, being a vessel like the *Bet*, wanted to move a little bit because it was the letter that fell with Adam. The *Hey* was separated from the other three letters in *Hashem*'s name. It was the last *Hey* that fell.

Once the female energy comes around the mountain — and we'll be here for it — our job will be to bring that *Hey* back up to its position as the last letter of the *Yud-Hey-Vav-Hey*. Since the *Hey* wanted to move a little bit, the best thing it could do was jump inside the *Vav*, the next letter, because the *Vav* is the third letter in the *Yud-Hey-Vav-Hey* name. It included itself in the *Vav*, so push that spyglass up another interinclusive notch. I want you to get used to this word "interinclusion" because you're going to hear a lot about it in the future.

The *Vav* had everything. It had all five other letters, and all it needed was a crown, so it went inside the *Zayin*. You basically know where I'm going with this: into a ten-digit interinclusion. The *Zayin* had everything with it, and it went into the *Chet* — along with the rest of the Hebrew letters. The letter *Chet* went to impregnate the *Tet* because the *Tet* is where pregnancy happens, and the *Tet* gave birth to the *Yud*.

God bless everybody. I hope you all really get to understand these letters.

✳ ✳ ✳

The Names of God in Each Tree of Life Sphere

David: I'm going to summarize the Arcturian Tree of Life, but also I'm going to discuss with you the associated names of God with each sphere because we are talking about a map. [Editor's Note: Refer to the Tree of Life Key.] We are talking about an energy grid, and each energy sphere has a corresponding name of God that you can use to activate the energies for yourself just by meditating and using the name either in prayer or as a mantra.

Now, the original Kabbalistic Tree of Life has ten spheres and one hidden additional sphere that represents hidden knowledge. In some books, it was included as the eleventh sphere, but usually it had a transparent or dotted line around it because it wasn't supposed to be a real sphere. But in our Arcturian Tree of Life for planetary healing, the Arcturians have said that hidden sphere needs to be part of the tree in full consciousness because the hidden knowledge that has been available only to a few people throughout the millennium now is available to everyone.

The twelfth sphere in the Planetary Tree of Life is a totally new sphere. It is the sphere that interacts with the bottom sphere, which means the fifth dimension is now interacting with the third dimension, and we are all experiencing that now.

I'm going to go to the very top, Mount Fuji, which is undifferentiated energy and is known as *Keter*. That is the crown, and the Hebrew God name for this is *Ehyeh Asher Ehyeh*, which is translated as "I Am That I Am." Many of you have seen this concept of the I Am presence. This concept, I believe, comes from this top crown — "I Am That I Am." So with *Ehyeh Asher Ehyeh*, the undifferentiated energy, we compare it to electrical voltage that is so high we can't really download it because it is just a pure light.

Remember that no one is able to see God's face; even Moses was not able to see God's face, because if God's face appeared to Moses, then Moses would die because God is so bright. So Moses was able to see the shadow of this face, and that, apparently, was powerful. We even say in the Kabbalah, "Let the light of God's face shine on you," which is a great compliment and great blessing, even if it's a shadow of the light.

The second sphere is *Chochma* — wisdom. We define this geographically as Bodensee, an ancient lake in the center of Europe, and the spirit guide and teacher is Chief White Eagle, who represents wisdom or divine wisdom. The name of God in this sphere is *Yah*. Some people know *Yah* because it is part of the name *Yahweh*.

The third sphere, which is Lake Moraine, is understanding. "Understanding" in Hebrew is *Binah,* and the divine name of God for this is *Yud-Hey-Vav-Hey*, YHVH. This is like *Yahveh* without the vowels. The guide for this sphere is Archangel Michael.

The fourth sphere is *Chesed*, and we call this loving kindness and compassion for Earth. This is represented by the Ascended Lady Master

Quan Yin, and the divine name is *El*. The location is Mount Shasta, which we are using for planetary healing.

The next sphere, number five, is Volcán Poás, which is strength, discipline, and judgment for Earth. Sanat Kumara is the guide and teacher, and the name of God is *Elohim*. In Hebrew, this sphere is called *Gevurah*.

Right in the middle between Lake Moraine and Bodensee and between Mount Shasta and Volcán Poás is hidden knowledge revealed, or *Da'at*, and the guide is the Arcturian Lady Master Helio-ah. We are in the time when hidden knowledge is being revealed to us. It is amazing that we are even able to discuss hidden knowledge, because this information has been protected for many centuries and only certain people were allowed to be exposed to the information that we are now discussing with you. The name of God for this sphere is *Elohim Tzevaoth*.

The middle sphere, Montserrat, is balance, harmony, and sacred Messianic light. This is called *Tiferet* in Hebrew. This sphere has the divine name of *Yahveh*, or *YHVH*, but it is pronounced *Adonai*. In this sphere, number six, the guide and teacher is Sananda/Jesus because he represents the Messianic light.

Now we go to the seventh sphere, Grose Valley, which is also called victory (in Hebrew, *Netzach*). This one really makes sense if you think about the creation of a New Earth society. The victory of all our work as starseeds is going to be manifested in a new world order, in a new world society of justice, where the environment and everything is going to be in balance. Things now are not balanced. White Buffalo Calf Woman is the spirit guide for this sphere. She is bringing a New Earth society, a new way of being.

The next sphere across, number eight, is *Hod* — or splendor — represented geographically by Lake Taupo in New Zealand. The Arcturians have modified this as "creation of the sacred places and planetary cities of light" because the planetary cities of light and the sacred places are giving off light. The Hebrew name for God in this sphere is *Elohim Tzevaoth*. We hear *Elohim Tzevaoth* often because in Kabbalistic prayers we say, "Holy, holy, holy is the Lord of Hosts." The Lord of Hosts is *Elohim Tzevaoth*. And Mary — or Miriam, the Hebrew name for Mary — is the spirit guide and teacher.

Then we go to Barrancas del Cobre, or Copper Canyon, in Mexico, which is right below Montserrat in the Tree of Life. This sphere has the energy of shimmering. In Hebrew, it is known as the foundation, and some people also refer to it as the astral plane. The Hebrew word for this sphere is *Yesod*. Shimmering is the ability to interact and bring yourself into the higher dimensions through vibrating your aura. *Yesod* is the first stage in recognizing that there are other dimensions, not only this one. We are connecting with those other dimensions through the shimmering. The divine name for this sphere is *El Shaddai Chai* — "the almighty living God."

The next sphere is Serra da Bocaina, which is located in southwestern Brazil between Sao Paulo and Rio de Janeiro. This sphere shows Earth's interaction with the third and fifth dimensions, and Juliano is the spirit guide overseeing that.

The last sphere is on the bottom and is represented geographically by the beautiful lake in Patagonia, Argentina, known as Lago Puelo. This sphere represents manifesting higher energy on Earth. It is also known as the kingdom, which is *Malchut* in Hebrew. The divine name of God here is *Adonai*. Remember, *Adonai* actually means, in direct translation, "my lord." This sphere is also referred to as the manifested world of the third dimension.

❋ ❋ ❋

Working Your Way up through the Tree of Life

Mordechai: We have to really understand this Tree of Life. I'm an Aquarian with Gemini rising; I read fronts and backs of books — just turn to pages, you know, just to feel like the angels are opening a page for me. I'm sure we've all had some of that. But where I like to go in the Tree of Life is straight up the middle, because the shortest distance between any two points is a straight line. That straight line goes from Lago Puelo on the bottom all the way to Mount Fuji on the top. That is the line. The real shortcut is getting up from number ten, Lago Puelo, to Montserrat, the *Sephirah* of beauty — *Tiferet*.

There are many different names for God. Understand that each one of these spheres has ten times ten — one hundred — *Sephirot* inside it. Actually, there's a lot more. It goes on and on like an infinite network similar to those marketing pyramids. It just keeps going and going. It's incomprehensible; it's unbelievable. Once you get to Montserrat, you are at the center of the tree. In the actual Tree of Life, you must understand where we are. Where we are is called the tree of knowledge of good and evil.

Now, we are taking this Tree of Life glyph, and we understand it as representing a beautiful, divine plan. It's a set of step-down transformers that gets you to where you have to go or where you've earned to go. To get through each of these hundred levels (also called grades) in each sphere, you have to have garments. Each garment you receive is for whatever good deed or good thing you've said or done. The more garments you have on you, the more fire you can handle. Imagine these garments as safe sheets of clothing. All of these garments are ethereal material, and you will need a lot of them to get to the heights of where we're going, figuratively speaking.

We're going all the way up through sphere eleven to two and three. But once we pass number six, we have to meet the main qualifications to proceed. Now *Tiferet*, which means beauty (balance plus harmony) and lies right below sphere eleven, is sparked by the ring of ascension. We are also discussing number ten, the bottom *Sephirah*.

All that we're looking at is contained in sphere ten. It's important for us to understand this because we're talking about infinite dimensions. We're putting all these infinite dimensions on one page. It's highly impractical, inconceivable, and incomprehensible, but we're trying to simplify it for everybody. The bottom line is always the connection, and the connection gets you to understanding. The only way you can get to sphere three, Lake Moraine (understanding), is to get from the hidden knowledge from Montserrat (sphere six), to Istanbul (sphere eleven), which is *Da'at*.

Yes, you can go through *Gevurah* (sphere five) or *Chesed* (sphere four), but we're going straight up because that is the shortest way and the most understandable. At the same time, we'll add clarity to simplicity. It may not be possible, but we're trying. As Archangel Metatron said, this Tree of Life is like a crop circle of the supermind. Really, that's what it is.

We don't realize how much we influence that supermind by being unified and learning this Tree of Life. Not only is it a catalyst, but it's also an added thing. This is the purpose for the planetary cities of light. If you put this Tree of Life chart inside a medicine wheel or inside a crop circle, then it is all a big plus. These all are paths to get to divine wisdom. Remember to use the different names of God related to the energy of the spheres.

Read the Zohar to Connect to the Angels
You can scan the Zohar, or you can read it. If you can read it in English, or if you know how to read Aramaic, that is an added plus. I suggest

everybody get a Zohar, and whether you have it in English or Hebrew really doesn't matter. What matters is that you really get a comprehensive perspective on this Tree of Life. The only way to do that is to understand the code book of the Torah, the soul of the Torah, which is in the Zohar.

There are a few good English versions of the Zohar out there, but if you really want to connect, scan the Aramaic letters, because that's almost a commandment for angelic entities to show up around you. How's that for a perk? If you scan or read these Aramaic letters, you can be sure the angels will come up around you. All you have to do is ask, and they will be there. You have a whole congregation of angelic entities who you wish to be hugged by and engulfed by their wings.

* * *

Questions from the Class

Cecelia from New Mexico: I missed the names of God for spheres eight and eleven, Hod and Da'at.

David: We didn't give the name for *Da'at*. For *Hod* it's *Elohim Tzevaoth*.

Mordechai: Actually, for *Da'at* it would be in the *Shin-Dalet-Yud* category, because that is Archangel Metatron's garment, which is *Shaddai* in English.

Tuck: David, this question is more of a simple and practical matter: Describe how we would use this tree to elevate consciousness and access more of the undifferentiated light at the top?

David: To go to the higher light, you have to be in a sacred space such as a planetary city of light. You might want to affirm that you want to live in justice and in a certain way. These are all things that you would do in preparation to go to the higher light. To go to the higher consciousness, you want to experience harmony, and you want to experience the freedom that harmony brings.

You might have imbalances in your life. Maybe you are overly critical; maybe you are creating depression or anxiety because you're so critical. You need to have loving kindness so that you can forgive yourself. This is an example of how you would use it. Then there is certain knowledge about how to go to the undifferentiated light. You might want to study some hidden sacred languages or sacred texts in which people have used certain methods — such as the one the Kabbalah teaches of the repetition of the names of God — to help you get to that state. You might want to meditate, and of course, you also would want to work on having wisdom. And to have wisdom, sometimes you need understanding, and you also need knowledge for that. Then you can go to the top.

Mordechai: How does this help us reach sphere two or three, or possibly the number one spot — is that the question?

Tuck: Yes, essentially. How do we acquire more of the undifferentiated light using this diagram?

Mordechai: The diagram is an energy map — maps, metaphors, and modes, you know? It's a map that goes all the way to millions and millions and billions. How we get to the undifferentiated light goes back to the old basics that the next person is more important than we are and to do all these wonderful works of creation. The only way anybody can receive light-force energy is through desiring to receive it for the sake of imparting. That is the only way you can actually take light-force energy — like we do on our Friday night blessings — bring it down, give it form, and then send it back up to the ring of ascension and out to the ladders of ascension.

The Tree of Life is a graph, a map of how it would be if we spent all our time looking for blessings and people to help, looking to put more spiritual garments on ourselves. The more garments we put on ourselves, the higher we go. Believe me, there is one thing that is absolutely, positively true: The term is *Mida Keneged Mida Bidiyuk*, which in English is "measure for measure exactly." That really is how we get to the undifferentiated light.

We don't even know how we're doing. If we knew how we were doing, we wouldn't be doing this, because the connection to upstairs happens when we don't realize what's happening. To be in that *Chelkeek*, that magic moment, that nanomoment of time when you can actually interact with all of these entities … This is just a map of potential interaction.

Katherine in England: I want to ask Mordechai about the Zohar and about looking at the Aramaic letters. That would be helpful. Is there a particular book that you can order from somewhere, or should I just look on eBay for something in Aramaic?

Mordechai: I want to say that the best version is put out in English by the Kabbalah Centre. It's twenty-three volumes. I don't know how much it costs now. There's a five-volume set put out by the Soncino Press in English that's about $110.

If you're looking for Aramaic letters to scan, I suggest you see whether you can find any of the Kabbalah Centre Zohars on eBay. That would be your best search. Believe me, Katherine, you scan those letters, and you will be busy interacting with everybody. *Bligh Ayin Hara.*

Sandra in Albuquerque: In talking about the interaction as Vywamus and as Mordechai spoke about the interinclusions, I wonder if the golden mean is an aspect of connecting these energies?

Mordechai: What was that term?

David: The golden mean, which is like a balance. In the center of the tree, the idea is that you have to balance it. You can't talk about judgment without talking about loving kindness. There is a balance inherent in the Tree of Life.

Mordechai: I may know what you're talking about in different terms. I want to continue on this answer because this is important. Words are one of the best tools for separation because we are all more familiar with certain terms. If we hear a term we're not familiar with, we think, "What is that? Is it something new?" But it means the exact same thing as the familiar term. Whether it means balance or restriction, the golden mean basically means matching polarities. Is this correct?

Sandra: Yes, that's part of it. It's a continuous unfolding evolvement.

Mordechai: Now, it is a continuous expansion, right? The whole purpose for us is to expand in awareness, to expand our level of soul, so that we can get to this divine wisdom. However you want to say it, harmony plus balance equals beauty. It doesn't matter what words you use or what the words mean.

When I hear "constant unfoldment," I think of my teacher, Archangel Metatron, who is a true unfoldment of the divine will. Now, you're talking about coming up from the bottom. It's just words. The whole thing in the knowing is the feeling. You've got to feel it to know it, right?

Sandra: *I get it, right.*

Mordechai: So when you use this term "the golden mean," it just means a harmonic balance, a harmonic balance of both sides. It is the eternal rebalancing in every nanomoment of the right column and the left column. That's why there's a central column in this creation — because that is our fail-safe for your golden mean.

כך

Kaph: the Potential of Creation

CLASS 13

MORDECHAI, DAVID, AND ARCHANGEL METATRON

Mordechai: Before I start with the *Kaph*, I have to do a lead-in, because I stopped with the interinclusion of the letter *Zayin*, including into the letter *Chet*, which is life. Instead of the fancy word "interinclusion," we will keep it simple and use the word "include," which is the original source of All That Is. "Include" in this context means to integrate something from the inside. There is preclude, include, and conclude. We will include all the letters.

So we have the *Zayin* included in the *Chet*, meaning life. The *Zayin* was completion, and it went into life. Once there was completion, then there was life. From the *Chet*, the eighth letter, once you have life, you have the next desire: procreation. So the letter *Chet* included itself in the letter *Tet* for procreation and impregnated the *Tet*. Then *Tet*, by including itself, gave birth to the letter *Yud*. *Yud* is now the outside of the other nine letters, and that takes us from one to ten.

From here on, we jump ten at a time. In other words, the value of the letter *Kaph* is twenty. If you want to make eleven, twelve, thirteen, fourteen, or fifteen, you just use *Yud-Aleph*, *Yud-Bet*, *Yud-Gimmel*, *Yud-Dalet*, and so on. You do not say *Yud-Hey*; you say *Tet-Vav* (9 + 6), because *Yud-Hey* is that holy combination. So instead of saying 10 + 5, say 9 + 6 — *Tet-Vav*. To keep a distance from such holiness, the number sixteen is actually *Tet-Zayin*, 9 + 7.

Then we have *Yud-Zayin*, which is 10 + 7; then *Yud-Chet*, which is 10 + 8; and *Yud-Tet*, which is 10 + 9 (they call it *Tess-Esrai*). From *Yud-Tet*, which is 19, we then go to the letter *Kaph*, which has a sacred gematria value of 20. The letter *Kaph* is quite powerful because it is the crown. More importantly, it's the power to actualize potential. That is our whole purpose here in the Group of Forty — to actualize the fifth-dimensional light that we bring down as potential and to give it form. First, before you have form, you need potential. There is nothing like having the potential of a crown of the king.

We're going to start with the two letters of the full spelling of the *Kaph*. The *Kaph* and the final *Pey* are the initial letters of the two words for potential: *Koach* and *Priav*, or "actual." Thus the *Kaph* hints at the power latent within the spiritual realm of the potential to fully manifest itself in the physical realm of the actual. The divine essence must create the world continuously; otherwise, creation would instantaneously vanish.

The potential of creation is therefore actualizing at each moment, and when we get to each moment, we always go back to that *Chelkeek*, that fraction of a moment. The world is re-created every moment, every nanomoment. That's why each moment is new. That's the whole thing, to have the *Emuna* of the *Kaph* to know that it's a new world. You could wake up tomorrow morning or you could wake up right now in the middle of this class and say, "This is the first day of the rest of my life," and you would be speaking the truth.

Now, this concept is referred to as "the power to actualize potential ever-present within the actualized." That's a really good Kabbalistic statement; it takes one to create one. In the Kabbalah and *Chassidut*, you are taught that this should be your initial awareness when awakening. Since the literal meaning of the letter *Kaph* is "palm," we're going to go to the palm — the place in the body where potential is actualized.

This awareness is reflected in the custom of placing one palm on the other when awakening before reciting the *Modeh Ani*, which is a prayer we say as soon as we awaken, before we open our eyes: "Thank you, God, for giving my soul back to me one more day so that I can do something constructive with it. I thank you, eternal king, for you have mercifully returned my soul within me. Your faithfulness is great."

Placing one palm on the other is an act and sign of peace and respect, but it also can be a sign of defeat or surrender, similar to the act of bowing before a king. In bowing, you totally nullify your consciousness in the presence of the king. In placing one palm on the other, you enter a state of plea and prayer to the king to reveal new will from his supernal crown to his subjects.

In Eastern religion, it is common to put your palms together and say, "Namasté" when you're Buddhist, Hindu, Taoist, Islamist, or any other religion. When you put those two palms together, you are continuing something started 3,500 years ago at Mount Sinai. It actually started before that, because Abraham knew very well about putting two palms together. We all want to know where it all started, and the *Kaph* is going to reveal some of this beautiful information.

The Potential in God's Palms

Now, this letter *Kaph* is also the root of the word *Kipa*, which is the root of the word "cap" in English, or skullcap. In reference to humankind, it is said, "You (creator) have placed your palm over me." Our sages refer to Adam as "the formation of the palms of the holy one; blessed be he." The awareness of the presence of the palms of God over one's head symbolizes the recognition of his ongoing creation.

The very power to actualize potential is shown in God's palms, and it manifests in our palms also. When we give a blessing to someone here in Jerusalem, we put both of our palms on top of his *Kipa* (if it's a woman, on her head) and mention his name and do the blessing. The person receiving the blessing will feel it because we are required to bless people every day.

There are many ways to bless. You can put your hands on top of the person's head without touching. It doesn't matter how you do it; it's all energy. It is all pure, and it all comes from the *Kaph*. Why? Because the *Kaph* represents the crown, and the crown represents the king. The point is even higher. The very power to actualize potential in God's palms derives ultimately from his crown. The power of will above his head, the superrational will — what we call the superconscious will — is all beyond our awareness. It is there. Ninety-plus percent of what we don't know about our bodies or about Mother Earth is there.

Accepting the Yoke of Heaven

As a verb, *Kaph* means "to subdue or coerce." We are told in the Talmud[1] that at the time of the giving of the Torah at Sinai, they had already agreed they would listen to *Hashem*. They would take on the yoke of the Torah, and the creators put a mountain over their heads to make sure that they said yes to this mission. They already said yes to the written Torah; now they would say yes to the spiritual, oral, galactic Torah! They had a problem accepting that kind of difficult mission. It would be a lot for the people of today to accept such a task. Imagine how it was for the people 3,500 years ago.

They were a little hesitant. They needed a little push and a shove. It's so beautiful. Now, there was so much revealed by the tremendous revelations at Mount Sinai that the people were coerced. Either that or the mountain would get dropped on their heads. So that's the choice, as it were — to respond to acceptance of the yoke of heaven in love.

This was done in love, no matter how I may present it. I try to bring some humor to it, but it is all done in unconditional, divine love from the right hand of the divine essence. The mountain itself appeared to forcefully embrace the people.

The Sight of the *Kaph*

The secret of the *Kaph* is that much is revealed from the little point of the *Yud*. So the *Yud*, when it went, was just a tiny dot — a speck, nothing. It created five worlds, or five dimensions of one world. Yet it goes inside the *Kaph* to show that it is really more — that less is more, as they say on the West Coast.

Now we're going to get into the sight, sound, and number of this letter. In sight, the world exists in the totality of the space surrounding Earth. The Book of Isaiah reads, "It is he that sits above the circle of the earth" [40:20, ESV]. That was written at least 2,500 years ago, so many people believed that Earth was flat, and Christopher Columbus's journey helped to prove it was round. Columbus knew. He knew the world was round — why? Because, you see, he was in Barcelona, Spain, in 1492.

In Spain during the eleventh, twelfth, and thirteenth centuries, I was there. I was incarnated at that time. It was fun because that was the high point of spiritual mysticism for starseeds, only they called them Jews or Hebrews. But Spain was the real mystical capital of the world at that time. And Christopher Columbus knew these Kabbalists because they were all in Barcelona. They all liked to be by the water. You know, Kabbalists — people who study the Kabbalah — like to have a nice ocean breeze. You can find this all over the world; it is true. So he knew the world was round and convinced Queen Isabella of that fact, so she let him go. It's amazing that he took off before the Inquisition intensified with the Jews being expelled from Spain. There are no coincidences, and there are no accidents.

* * *

Undifferentiated Energy Is the Source of Everything

David: Let us talk about this concept of the crown. The letter *Kaph* is compared to the letter *K* in English, so the top sphere — the crown — is *Keter*. The *Kaph* sometimes is also written as a "ch," but it has more of a *K* sound. As the highest energy level, this sphere represents undifferentiated energy, which is energy that cannot be described. It is beyond the Bodensee; it is beyond wisdom. It is beyond understanding, beyond Lake Moraine. So we cannot describe undifferentiated energy, nor can we describe the experience of it.

In a Kabbalah meditation group many years ago, I had the task to see whether I could connect in any way with God. I had the experience of feeling and seeing light, but it was light that could not be described; it wasn't in any form. If light is not in any form, what words can one use to describe it? There are really no words.

Remember the beautiful story of the four rabbis going into higher levels? When they got to the higher levels, each rabbi experienced different energies, and some of them were not able to tolerate the energies. One gave up the faith, one went crazy, one died, and only one — Rabbi Akiva — was able to experience the energy and come back and teach about it. This is a good story to relate when talking about undifferentiated energy because experiencing that energy could be mentally unbalancing. You have to give up your intellect. You have to surrender your wisdom, your ego, and your mind to experience the undifferentiated energy.

Yet the undifferentiated energy is the source of all energy, including those in the Tree of Life. Interestingly, when you look at the Tree of Life, there is energy above the undifferentiated energy, which we call the infinite light — or in Hebrew, the *Ain Soph Ohr*. You probably have heard the words *Ain Soph*, the Infinite Being, which is another aspect not technically on the Tree of Life but shown above *Keter*, the Crown. *Ain Soph Ohr* refers to the infinite light. Sometimes you can even see that above the infinite light is infinite nothing.

When you are talking about the *Keter*, you also need to release your mind and the categories, because the *Keter*, the crown, is beyond duality. It is at a very high level, and at a very high level, everything looks like and is, in fact, in divine order.

Mordechai described the idea that in every moment, the life force is coming into this world and creating each moment. So this energy, this undifferentiated energy from *Keter*, from Mount Fuji, is an active energy. Also, these spheres are not stationary. The energy from the undifferentiated light goes to the second sphere, the Bodensee, wisdom; then to Lake Moraine; then Istanbul; Mount Shasta; and so on.

In other words, there is a flow of energy that comprises the dynamic Tree of Life. It is not static; it is holographic. Each sphere and energy interacts with the others. Even though *Keter* seems to be beyond us, the energy we are receiving from it is going through everything. It is the source of everything. That energy says, "I Am That I Am." Literally, in correct Hebrew grammar, the name should be translated as "I Will Be That I Will Be." I like the adaptation of "I Am That I Am," though, because it refers to the eternalness of this energy.

Some Kabbalists talk about this energy and the Tree of Life in terms of a human face and a human form. They have given different designations, like the head is the *Keter* and then the right side would be the right shoulder. But that concept aside, the energy of *Keter* is continually flowing and creates each moment. If that energy stopped, then the soul world would stop, and we would all disappear.

One Kabbalah teacher wrote that God's eye is open to this universe and that if for one nanosecond the Creator's eye should blink, then the energy of the blinking would end this world. I like that concept because it refers to the source of the divine flow and how important it is to our existence.

Rising to the *Keter*

Now, we also talked about holiness and sacredness. Each name of God is holy and sacred, and each level of the Tree of Life is going up higher energetically. Yet if you look at Montserrat and at Sananda, the energy of Mount Fuji is directly related to Sananda and connects with him. All the spheres touch the center one. All the spheres touch the Messianic energy and light and also touch Sananda.

This is a way of saying that most humans cannot rise above the level of Sananda. Most humans are not able to go to undifferentiated energy. Most humans would even have difficulty going to the higher energy of loving kindness. Certainly, they are not able to go up to the energy of *Keter*; it can be dangerous for us to go up to *Keter* without training because we may not come back — at least not intact.

Sananda says, "You can reach that energy from me, not only though me. It is the way I am offering you." We know that there are spiritual people in other systems, such as Buddhists, Sufis, and whirling dervishes who may be able to experience some aspect of undifferentiated energy, but the message from Sananda is that "I am able to offer you my energies to help you experience the undifferentiated energies and reestablish yourself so you can come back into this Earth." That is a great service.

Remember that the greatest way to rise through the Tree of Life is through service. This service that I believe Sananda offers is a way to go to the top through him. And then you supposedly don't have to deal with the issues of the four rabbis — being threatened with your sanity, losing your faith, or even dying — because you want to come back and be of service. It is a great thought to be at the top and even to talk about the top. And it is a great thought to hear the words *Ehyeh Asher Ehyeh* — I Am That I Am.

* * *

The Three Lines of the *Kaph*

Mordechai: *Asher* is an amazing word. The sacred gematria of *Asher* is 501, and more importantly, when it appears the first time in the Torah, it is the 72nd word. This is a direct connection. The names of the Creator in boxes of nine rows and eight columns connect the seventy-two names, and if you use those seventy-two names, you can actually connect to the two *Ehyehs*.

As long as you have that in your consciousness — that's where we'll go right now, into consciousness. In the category of sight on the level of souls, the three lines of the *Kaph* relate to the three properties of the superconscious. Simple and absolute faith is one, the sublime pleasure in the experience of the unity of the divine is two, and three is the superconscious desire to dedicate one's life to fulfilling the Creator's will. These properties are referred to as "the three heads of the crown," and in turn, they relate to the three actual meanings of the word for crown, *Keter*.

We are talking about the top of the Tree of Life, the crown of the king. The highest of the heads, simple faith, corresponds to *Keter*, meaning "to wait," as in "wait for me a little." This implies that faith entails the practice and confidence that God's ultimate good in his divine intention for each individual soul, together with all creation, will in time be fulfilled.

The number one rule in the Kabbalah is to make restriction. It's like when a father is about to hit his child — God forbid — and the child says, "Daddy, Daddy, before you hit me, please count to ten." There's a reason for this, and it's not that the child is smart, because he knows he's not going to get hit for nothing, or whatever the situation is. It's just that he has some kind of connection to know about restriction, even though he's afraid he's going to get cracked in the face. The fact of the matter is he's trying to give a lesson to his parents on restriction.

So when you get a great idea, when you get a feeling about something, it is not necessarily from your highest good. In other words, you really have to make restriction and then wait and see. It's almost like when you send a pigeon in your possession off, not knowing when it's going to come back, and then you say, "Anything I really love that's really mine will come back to me." If it comes back to you, then you know it's really yours. That's really what we're talking about: to know what is really ours and where we need to be more discerning.

Now, the second head in the crown, the sublime pleasure, relates to the most obvious meaning of *Keter* — the crown. The genuine pleasure of a *B'nai Yisrael* starseed is the intimate experience of standing in the presence of the Creator and king of the universe. Now, how many of us can actually say that we've done that? Some people have, and once you have, there isn't any turning back, because you've been there, you've done that, you've bought back the t-shirt, and you know the difference. You made the connection, and now you have an understanding.

The lowest head of the crown — will — relates to *Keter* in meaning "to surround or encircle." Every *B'nai Yisrael*, or starseed soul, possesses the latent power to decree its will on reality. This potential is actualized by linking one's own power of will to that of the Divine, as taught by Rabban Gamliel: "Make that His will should be your will so that He should make your will as His will. Nullify your will before His will so that He should nullify the will of others before your will."[2] That means "I want what you want." That's what I say to the *B'nai Elohim*: I want what you want. If you want it, I want it. So let's do it.

Now we go to the level of divinity and how the three lines of the *Kaph* correspond to the three levels present in God's infinite light before the beginning of creation. These three levels, when viewed as a whole, hold the ultimate secret of the Divine crown. Above the conscious process of creation, this begins from the initial contraction — or the *Tzimtzum* — of the infinite light. Corresponding to the highest head of *Keter* (simple faith), as reflected in God's very essence, is the absolute bond of God to the origin of souls of the starseeds in the Divine self. The sublime pleasure corresponding to the second head is his delight in each individual as it is linked by him to a specific letter of primordial Torah. Here, the Divine learns Torah for its own sake, not yet utilizing the Torah as the blueprint of creation. It's beautiful.

His will, which is the third head of *Keter*, is the will to create, which appears — or as one would say in the Zohar, "ascends" — into the infinite light. From within this appearance of the will to create, the Torah says you will see that all "comes into the Divine focus" as the blueprint and utensil of creation.

What am I saying here? We have the power to create. God gave us the power to create. He listens to us when we want something. All we need are some garments of good deeds to show that we have good credit in the Bank of *Binah* so that we can take out some loans. The form of the final *Kaph* — and here is a big secret — represents the drawing down of these three levels of divine superconsciousness, the levels of the divine crown, into corresponding levels of the superconsciousness of souls.

The final *Kaph*, as a suffix letter that means "you" or "yours," is frequently used in reference to the Divine, as in the verse "I will exalt you, my God, the King" [Psalm 145:1, World English Bible]. The ability of the soul to relate to the essence of the Creator in second person is its innate power to draw into itself the Divine crown.

* * *

You Can Experience Undifferentiated Light

Shalom, Shalom, Shalom. Greetings, starseeds. Greetings, *B'nai Elohim*, the children of the Creator. This is **Archangel Metatron**.

Each of you has the core of this crown energy — *Keter*, undifferentiated light — within you. Each of you ultimately has the ability to experience the undifferentiated light. This is how you have been made. This is how you have been created. You are the species of Adam. You are the species, and the crown is known as the Adam Kadmon, the original Adam.

The original Adam is the prototype for all of you. Adam Kadmon contains all of the souls and all of the light that has been distributed through the billions of souls that have come to this planet and to other planets. You, the Adam species, are on Earth, but the Adam species is also in the Pleiades and in many other parts of the universe.

I want to describe, in more detail, the crown and what it is like to be

Adam Kadmon, the primordial Adam. "Primordial," in your language, sounds like it is basic or the first, but it is not primitive. It is not the primitive Adam we're talking about; it is primordial in terms of having the ultimate power, because this is the power to experience *Keter*, to experience the undifferentiated light and still maintain the total integration and unity of the self. The paradox is that it gives up the self to be able to experience the undifferentiated light. This is to say that you have the codes within you to be able to experience undifferentiated light just as you have the codes within you to experience the ascension. And we work with you to unlock the codes of ascension.

Now, you have heard this discussion of undifferentiated light, yet you can grasp, sense, or feel it even if it is only at the 1 percent level, or even 0.5 percent. You can experience it. This experience is necessary because we need to have the experience of the Creator's light, the light that the primordial Adam could experience.

The primordial Adam had a vision that is indescribable. He could see to the end of the universe. He could see the original light just like your telescopes can go back to the big bang, to the original beginning, thirteen billion years ago. The original Adam was able to look at that with his eyes and see it.

So this name of God, *Ehyeh Asher Ehyeh*, carries the vibrational energy and tones that help you experience the undifferentiated light. If you to go to Mount Fuji, we will work with you and you will feel enhanced undifferentiated light. Listen to the tones of the sacred name *Ehyeh Asher Ehyeh*, and experience the 1 percent, the 0.5 percent, of undifferentiated light, undifferentiated energy, that is the source of all that is, all that was, and all that will be.

[Tones: *Ehyeh Asher Ehyeh*.]

Experience the light of I Will Be That I Will Be. Experience your connection to the primordial Adam, Adam Kadmon. Experience your ability at the 1 percent or the 0.5 percent level of *Keter*, the divine crown. Just the fact that you intellectually and mentally understand what it is to be at the crown is helping you.

[Tones: *Ehyeh Asher Ehyeh*.]

This Tree of Life is a Planetary Tree of Life also. It is for planetary healing. The key is to understand that the Tree of Life is a dynamic flow and that you must keep the flow of energy going to the planet. This flow of energy has become blocked because humanity has blocked nature and Earth's meridian flow, so the undifferentiated light cannot reach all the sources. And the undifferentiated light is part of the life force that keeps the biosphere in balance.

But remember that the light must be stepped down so that people can integrate it, so that people can tolerate it. You could not tolerate looking at the Sun for a minute; your eyes would go blind. It is similar with the undifferentiated light. Maybe for a nanosecond you can grasp 1 percent of the undifferentiated light, but you would know intellectually that the undifferentiated light is the source of everything. It is the source of all.

Know that there are beings, such as Sananda, who can experience the undifferentiated light and still be intact. Being intact can help you also experience this light.

Blessings to you, *B'nai Elohim, B'nai Yisrael*. You are the cocreators who are able to talk about and experience this higher aspect of the Creator. You are here to protect the flow of this light on this planet so that the flow of light will not be blocked through unnatural interventions on the dynamic flow of this planetary system.

The return of this alignment of Earth with the Central Sun is going to increase the dynamic flow of undifferentiated light coming to the Blue Jewel. I'm Archangel Metatron. Good day.

✳ ✳ ✳

Questions from the Class

Cora: So when we're asking to do the will of the Creator, we start out our day being love: "Allow me to be an instrument of your peace here." And then things happen. You know what I'm talking about — what happened to me recently? It is the biggest lesson of all, understanding the soul's evolution, but here we are. I'm the human being trying to take that in; I'm trying to understand from the human mind. So is there a shortcut there?

Mordechai: That's a good question. You must understand that this is our screenplay. We've written this screenplay. Every challenge that comes at us, we need for some expansion or evolvement of our soul. As my first teacher said, "You know, people talk about free will and free choice, but the only free will we have in this incarnation is how we react to whatever comes at us." In other words, "What's my choice?" Are we going to stay home, order pizza, and watch a movie, or are we going out to see a movie and go out for dinner? That's not a free choice.

Free choice is that in whatever situations we are involved with

— whether they are positive or polarized — the only choice we have is to either be proactive or reactive to that situation. As Edgar Casey said, you either gain in an incarnation or you retard. The whole point for us is to gain in this incarnation. Sometimes when it gets really intense and those intense things come at us, the greatest thing we can do, spiritually, is to just be quiet and let it happen.

Cecilia in New Mexico: *Being in that situation of silence, if you go into silence, you allow, and in that allowing, you then have choice — correct?*

Mordechai: Yes, there is this system. I just added one more word to it, and that is: "you accept, you forgive, you respect, and then you hand it all over to the divine light." That's the only way that we can show that we have complete faith or complete certainty. We have to allow, and the toughest thing to do is remain silent. I mean, sometimes I have to bite my tongue and pinch myself till blood comes out. All of us have our challenges. That's why we're down here. We came down here to be proactive; to understand; and to allow, forgive, and respect all the challenges, polarities, and dualities that come at us.

You know, it's amazing — I didn't get a chance to say a bunch of stuff, but the letter *Kaph* is associated with the creation of the Sun. I talked about how the letter *Bet* is linked to Saturn, *Gimmel* is linked to Jupiter, and *Dalet* is connected with Mars. But the letter *Kaph* created the Sun. That is the crown of this solar system.

David: There's a famous saying from the Kabbalists: "This, too, is for the good" — *Gamzu L'tovah.* That is another way of looking at these events. We have to go to the higher level, *Keter.* Then everything is in unity. Down here is duality. We can see things as good or bad, comfortable or uncomfortable. In the higher level, everything fits together in a great unity.

Mordechai: I want to tell everybody that the letter *Kaph* is equal to the number 20. When you spell the word *Keter* in Hebrew — *Kaph-Tav-Resh* — it comes out to 620. The word for 20 in Hebrew is *Essreem; Esser* is 10. The gematria of *Essreem* is 620, and there are many other numerical connections to perfection.

Lamed: Aspiration

CLASS 14

MORDECHAI, DAVID, AND JULIANO

Mordechai: In this class, we're going to discuss our world, the world of *Malchut*, but we will mostly be visiting sphere eleven, hidden knowledge revealed; sphere three, understanding; and sphere two, wisdom, with the help of sphere one, *Keter*. With the letter *Lamed*, I would just like to introduce it. It is the tallest letter in the Hebrew *Aleph-Bet* and in the Torah. It is the only letter that goes above the line. (There are lines in the Torah so scribes can write evenly.)

This letter *Lamed* is no more or less special than any of the other letters. We will start with the fact that the *Lamed* represents aspiration — the contemplation of the heart. As Rabbi Akiva (the rabbi who made it out of the garden in peace when the three other rabbis could not) says, the full spelling of the letter *Lamed*, which is *Lamed-Mem-Dalet*, is read as short for the three words *Lev Mayvin Da'at* — "the heart that understands knowledge."

We're going to get into some interesting sacred gematria here. The numerical value of this phrase — *Lev Mayvin Da'at* — is 608. The number 608 is equal to the heart, which is *Lev* (32) times *Chava* (19). Now, *Chava* is Eve, Adam's wife. So 32 x 19, or the heart times *Chava*, also equals 608, which stands for "the heart of Eve."

In a great sage's commentary on the story of the Garden of Eden, the original episode of humankind, Rabbi Avraham Ibn Ezra relates that Adam is the secret of the brain, Eve is the secret of the heart, and the snake is the secret of the liver. Basically, the liver represents anger, and the snake has definitely had its share in influencing that.

Adam and Eve, or male and female, are the prototypical spiritual forces of giving and receiving. The marital union and gift of male to female relates to the secret of knowledge. As it is said, "Adam knew his wife Eve." To know this puts it right back into sphere eleven, Istanbul and Helio-ah. For this reason, Adam and Eve are often seen to represent the teacher and pupil. The teacher contracts his or her intellect to a point, which is the *Yud*; the teacher tries to simplify the intellect to make his or her teaching understandable to the student, whereas the student nullifies his or her previous levels of conception to become a fitting vessel for the new, wondrous lessons of the teacher.

What does this mean? We have to unlearn everything we've learned and undo everything we've done. There are many sleeping starseeds who still don't have a clue. They will soon, but the bottom line is we must nullify our previous levels of conception because we are only the results of what we have been taught. We really have to start to use that beautiful word "discernment."

Learning to Teach and to Do

In particular, the form of the *Lamed* represents the aspiration of the truly devoted pupil to learn from the mouth of the teacher. The literal meaning of *Lamed* is "to learn" or "to teach." It means both. The seed of wisdom — which is our goal, alluded to by the letter *Yud* — descends from the brain (Adam) to impregnate the full consciousness of the heart (Eve). In other words, the heart aspires upward to receive this point of insight from the brain. This is the secret of the form of *Lamed* — the heart ascending in aspiration to conceive and comprehend, to understand the knowledge, to get to the point of wisdom. That's the *Yud* situated at the top of the letter *Lamed*.

The *Lamed* is made up of three letters. The bottom is like the letter *Kaph*. Then you have a straight line ascending, which is the *Vav*, and then you have the little curve on the top, which is the *Yud*. We are talking about picking up the hidden knowledge that is revealed, making the connection above the line, and going to understanding. Then once we've turned the connection into understanding, we're on our way to divine wisdom, which is really our goal.

We are told that the *Baal Shem Tov* placed the palm of his hand on the heart of a child and blessed him to be a compassionate, warm human being. The palm, which has the power to actualize potential, becomes manifest at the inner spiritual level. The will of the heart is the crown, *Keter*. To conceive and unite with God, we need to learn the teachings of the galactic Torah. You know, if I say "Torah" without saying "galactic," people start to think I'm talking about religion, that I'm "talking Jewish" or whatever. This Torah may have been given to the Hebrews as a method, but it is a galactic gift, and the Hebrews were supposed to take it to the nations of the world, but there were some blockages there.

Just understand that the secret of the spiritual sequence hinted at the letters of the word *Kli*. Now, *Kli* is the *Kaph*. It means a vessel. This whole Tree of Life is one group of ten, I would say — ten to the twenty-sixth power of vessels. What does ten to the twenty-sixth power look like? Let me show you: 100,000,000,000,000,000,000,000,000. Let's call it one hundred boom-bitty zillion. Ha ha! We must understand the vessel contains the power to actualize the potential, which is actually the palm of the *Baal Shem Tov* (the *Kaph*). To manifest in the aspiration of the heart — that's the *Lamed*. The bottom line is that throughout the Torah, the heart symbolizes the primary concept of the vessel, which is the secret of Eve.

The Sight of *Lamed*

Let's go to sight, sound, and number. In sight, a *Vav*, whose head is the *Yud*, looks downward on a *Kaph*. Those are the three letters that make up the *Lamed*: a downward-looking *Yud*, which forms the head of a *Vav*, which stands, in turn, erect upon the *Kaph*. Then there is a tower soaring in the air. When we do the *Rosh Hashanah* meditation, we have an extra-large *Lamed*. It isn't just a regular *Lamed*; it is two-and-a-half times the size of the regular *Lamed*. It stretches up into the heavens.

Lamed is the secret of the rectification of the power of imagination. So if we wish to add some power to our thought-form processes and thought-form strength, the *Lamed* is a very good letter on which to meditate.

In the category of sight in the level of worlds, the *Lamed* represents a three-stage rocket soaring into outer space. First, the ascending rocket ship — the *Lamed* — semi-circles Earth as a whole with all three pieces, or stages. To get above the atmosphere, is must be shot like a slingshot halfway around the planet. Then, as it goes around, the rocket drops the first stage of itself going up (the *Lamed* drops the *Kaph*). The second piece (the *Vav*) drops off right after the slingshot motion and goes into outer space, and then what's left is the capsule. The rocket breaks through the gravity barrier, leaving only the capsule with the astronauts inside — or in the case of the *Lamed*, souls, which are the *Yud*.

The second representation in worlds is of humankind's aspiration to understand the universe. Both of these things are at the level of worlds, the lowest level of the *Lamed*. At this level, the *Lamed* characterizes humankind's desire and aspiration to understand the nature of the world they live in. This motherly instinct in the heart of humanity strives to know Mother Nature, which is Eve, the mother of all life.

How does Eve relate to the Blue Jewel? Eve is actually the influencing factor of the aura of Earth. The mother of all life, the ever-soaring quest into the heights of understanding the universe, is symbolized by this flying tower of the *Lamed*. Just as the *Yud* is the smallest of the letters, so the *Lamed* is referred to as the biggest of the letters. "Thinking big" can relate to all worldly affairs — especially aspiring to understand and eventually conquer the secrets of nature, or to rise above nature.

At the level of souls, the humble and sincere heart of the wise man continually aspires to ascend higher and higher in his comprehension of the wisdom of the Divine and his Torah. The power to nullify all previous preconceptions together with the tremendous desire for knowledge and truth are the prerequisites necessary to pierce the barriers of humankind's innate physical, emotional, and mental limitations. This power to nullify all previous preconceptions leads to a tremendous desire for knowledge and truth.

* * *

We Are Vessels Created to Hold Light

David: Today we are learning about the nature of the cosmos. We are learning how the Tree of Life is an understanding of our nature and of our Creator. The configuration of these spheres represents duality, polarity, and balance, and hidden knowledge is necessary to bring about a new balance.

Each one of these spheres, as well as each human, is a vessel that was created to hold a certain amount of light. We were created to hold a certain amount of understanding, wisdom, hidden knowledge, kindness, and strength, and we are able to balance everything. We have the ability as vessels to hold and practice shimmering.

This is a new energy, a new light that is given to us, the starseeds. The shimmering requires that we build our vessels so that we are able to hold the light. Holding the light involves using our mental, physical, emotional, and spiritual selves. We need to understand how we can relate to the process of different dimensions. We have to have a mental conception of how to work so we don't lose our sanity. Remember the story of the four rabbis going into the garden? One actually lost his sanity. The one who died did not have the proper mental body or belief system to integrate higher light.

Nullify Separation

We have also been discussing nullification. We are nullifying that which is based on duality and our limited conceptions of how we are educated, and I like to use the cultural education of Aboriginals as an example of this. The Aboriginals are brought up learning about dreams and dreamtime. This is not something with which we in the West are brought up; if a Western child has a prophetic image in a dream, he or she usually is not listened to, and the parents might even discourage the child from working with the dream. But in the Aboriginal world, expression of dreamtime and the dream world is encouraged. Therefore, in many ways, some of the early Aboriginals have a better relationship with the dream world. So some cultural patterns that we have learned really discourage the expansion of consciousness.

Mordechai mentioned Rabbi Akiva, a famous rabbi who lived around the time of Jesus. He was born in AD 50 and died in AD 135. At this time, Israel was occupied by the Romans. He was such a great teacher, and his is an interesting story. The Romans asked him to renounce his religion and his belief in the one God, but he refused, so they burned him at the stake. He was actually joyful in his death, knowing that it was the final test for him. As he was being burned alive, which is a horrible way to die, he was reciting the prayer of unity: "Hear, oh Israel, the lord, our God, the lord is one." That is saying that we are all united. He kept his spiritual unity even in the face of a painful death!

These spheres in the Tree of Life also are united. Even though we separate the spheres, they are all united in one energy. And this is the beauty of it; it is what we are working for.

Speaking to Heal

I want to discuss *Baal Shem Tov*, who is known as the Master of the Good Name. He lived in Poland from 1698 to 1760.[1] *Baal Shem Tov* was the name he was given by his followers, but he had another name,

Yisrael ben Eliezer. They gave him the name Master of the Good Name (*Baal Shem Tov*) because he had special powers, including the ability to speak and heal by using the names of God.

That is part of the Kabbalah — when you can say words and heal with them. Remember there are different levels of healing. There's hands-on healing like in Reiki, massage, and medicine, but the highest level of healing is sending energy and speaking the words. Speaking the words is part of the healing process.

We Are Vessels of Hidden Knowledge

I want to look again at the concept of Adam and Eve because they are the first prototypes of humans. The idea is that Adam and Eve are androgynous. "Androgynous" means that they had male and female within each of them. In the Old Testament, a rib was taken from Adam so that Eve could be created, so there was a separation; we go from androgyny, which is the male and female united, to separation of the male and female. And that, in part, is duality.

In the original creation, Adam was in the fifth dimension. Then came a separation, and the question is, can you live in the fifth dimension with the separation? In many of the readings and channelings I have given, I find that people have been male and female in other lifetimes. We all are androgynous in our true nature.

When the vessels or spheres were first created, they were simple points that could not interact with each other. All they could do was receive from the Infinite Being, *Ain Soph*. For this reason — because they could just receive — they were called vessels. To receive God's light, a vessel must be connected to God, and therefore, humans have the special ability over all other creatures to make this connection with God. But if humanity has received God's light — if we have received light as vessels — then we must resemble God, so we are made in God's image.

As humans, we have free will and choice, and the only reason we can have that is because evil exists. Evil is a complicated and deep concept in the Kabbalah, even in other philosophies. For years people have debated why evil exists. The existence of evil is related to allowing a person the chance to do good.

Now, God's light was given, but the vessels were not able to hold the light. They could not hold all the light of infinite wisdom that was given. They could not hold, for example, the light of infinite understanding. (If we think about that, we are also limited. We can grasp certain things, but we still cannot grasp all there is to know. We will know the true reason for everything on this plane.) Because the vessels could not hold everything, they were overwhelmed by the light and they shattered. This was the famous breaking of the vessels. The broken pieces fell to a lower spiritual level, which became another part of the third-dimensional universe. It is at this level that evil manifests.

In unity, there is no evil, but evil manifested in the third dimension as the result of the breaking of the vessels. Part of our roles as starseeds is to bring these shattered vessels back into unity. The world now needs certain understanding, a certain loving kindness, and certain judgments. Our role as starseeds is to bring back these vessels so that they can be repaired. The word for repair in the Kabbalah, which describes this healing process, is *Tikun*.

So now we are working in the vessel of hidden knowledge. We are working to bring to this planet the hidden knowledge, the hidden secrets of the different dimensions and of the different aspects of shimmering and the fifth dimension. We are going to create a new balance for understanding on this planet to bring a better restoration of all of this light.

✳ ✳ ✳

Learning the Torah

Mordechai: I want to get back to Rabbi Akiva. He was among the greatest. He was among the ten sages who were tortured. He was burned to death — that's a pretty intense way to go. They combed his skin with metal combs, just as you would scale a fish, and then they hung his whole skin from a post in the public marketplace. But the advantage of a *Tzaddik* like Rabbi Akiva is having *Emuna* (faith). You know, I always have to bring up *Emuna*, and then I have to talk about Rabbi Akiva, because he didn't feel one bit of pain during his intense death. Why? Because, as it is said, the second — the nanosecond — that metal comb touched his skin, he left his body. The way judgment works upstairs is exactly measure for measure, so the rabbi was immediately united with his higher soul, and his earth body was cohabited by another less-advanced soul that needed to go through that tortuous death as a major *Tikun* for his evolution. That's a big secret. That's really what you get from learning the Torah.

Learning the Torah for the sake of fulfilling its directive in order to rectify your soul is the most all-inclusive of *Mitzvoth*, or good deeds.

There are 613 deeds, and that is equal to all of them. Learning the Torah serves as a foundation and catalyst in motivating performance of all the other 613 deeds. As our sages teach, "learning the Torah is equal to them all." Learning the Torah not only sharpens the reader's intellect in the sense of logical, analytical reasoning but also rectifies one's initially unrectified power of imagination. The process of rectification follows the three stages of submission, separation, and sweetening taught by the *Baal Shem Tov*.

But here, separation is separating oneself from the common, from the evil — if you want to call it that. David used that. It was a beautiful correlation there — the sweetening of the judgment. That's what we do when we study the Torah and when we do all these wonderful healings and miracles with similitude, with the likeness of our Creator. One who learns in order to teach is granted the ability to learn and teach. One who learns in order to do is granted the ability to learn, teach, guard, and do.

In *Chassidut* — the essence of the *Baal Shem Tov*, Rabbi Nachman of Breslov,[2] and all the others — we are taught that teaching a beginner previously uninitiated to the wonder of the Torah and its *Mitzvoth* is the greatest of all deeds. This is actually teaching the Tree of Life, because the Torah and the Tree of Life are one — like identical twins. Thus, when you learn, intending to become qualified to initiate others into the Torah and *Mitzvoth*, you are simultaneously "learning in order to teach" and "learning in order to do" at the very highest level.

What I just told you was the sound of *Lamed* at the level of souls. In the lunar/galactic/Hebrew calendar, a full month possesses thirty days. In Hebrew, there are two words for month: *Chodesh*, which is literally "a new month," and *Yareiach*, "moon." The Moon and its cycle of birth, apparent death, and spontaneous rebirth symbolize the *Sephirah* of *Malchut*, the kingdom, which is on the bottom of the Tree of Life. The *Sephirah* of *Malchut* is personified by King David. In the service of our blessing of the new moon, we explain King David is alive forever. And *Malchut* is referred to as the lower mother whose heartbeat enlivens all of nature.

David is spelled *Dalet-Vav-Dalet*, which equals fourteen. King David was the fourteenth generation from Avraham. (This is just for people who need some numerical backup.) The only thing that is numerically perfect in the entire third dimension is the Torah. I will say this: It is a privilege to be able to study the Torah and to study it here in Jerusalem. I would be privileged to answer any questions anybody has on anything, anything they ever questioned that nobody could answer. I will take a shot at it.

There are four levels of Torah: the *Pshat*, the basic, which is the literal; the *Remez*, which is like a hint; the *Drash*, the Midrash — the great stories, the metaphysical stories; and the *Sod*, the secrets. When you say the Hebrew word *Pardes*,[3] it can refer to the names of the *Pshat*, the *Remez*, the *Drash*, and the *Sod*. But if you study the *Sod* first, you take the S — which is on the bottom of *Pardes* — and you put it on top before the *P*. That becomes "spard," which is close to the word *Sephardi* in Hebrew and refers to a Jew of Spanish or Portugese descent. Studying Kabbalah first and then the *Pshat*. When you do it that way, everything becomes very clear, very quickly.

* * *

David: I just want to begin my part by discussing the four levels of the Torah. You read the first level, which is the literal part, and some of the stories don't make sense. They are stories, but in a literal sense, they are not really that powerful or meaningful. But then you have what I call the metaphorical level, which depicts the stories as symbols. Then the other level that Mordechai mentioned is the hidden, which refers to the fact there is hidden meaning in the biblical stories. So there are different levels — the basic, the literal, the metaphorical, and the hidden.

* * *

Remove the Physical through Shimmering

Shalom, Shalom, Shalom. Greetings. I'm **Juliano**. We are the Arcturians. In this lecture we want to look at the spheres of Serra da Bocaina and of Barrancas del Cobre, or Copper Canyon, Mexico. We want to look at both of them because these spheres represent the interaction of the third and fifth dimensions, but in particular, Barrancas del Cobre (Copper Canyon) represents the sphere of shimmering.

This is a definite new energy that the Tree of Life is being designed for you to understand. It is a new light, you are a new vessel, and a new place in your vessel is being created for you to shimmer. You have developed the mental, and you have developed the physical — the spiritual light and understanding.

You see, understanding also relates to you personally. It doesn't just relate to the Planetary Tree of Life. Understanding relates to the fact that you need to have some grasp of what we are talking about when we are shimmering. And when we are shimmering, we are saying that your true nature is not this physical body. The physical body you are wearing is like a shirt: It is a beautiful, colorful shirt, and it has many links, but you are going to take your shirt off when you die or when you ascend.

The idea of shimmering is that you can remove the physical. You can remove physical limitations. You can remove the laws of physics on the third dimension when you bring your body into the shimmering energy field. At that point, the real you, which is your aura, the energy field, takes over. The real you is this energy field; your body is in an energy field. When you die, your body dies, but the energy field, the aura around you — which, by the way, has been explained as resembling the nature of God — ascends; that body goes into the other realms.

Now, with shimmering, we are practicing the ability to vibrate the aura at a higher speed, because when the aura, the energy field, the spirit, came down to this third dimension, it had to slow down. It had to adjust. It is as if you are going on the autobahn at 150 miles an hour and then you come into a city. You can't go 150 miles per hour in the city; you have to slow down to the speed limit. There's a speed limit on the third dimension — a vibrational energy-wave speed. But shimmering is teaching you that when you are in alignment — when you have the right mental, physical, emotional, and spiritual alignments and balances — you can begin to increase your vibrational speed.

I'm asking each of you to shimmer now. Feel the vibrational aura. Feel your cosmic egg. Shimmer. Shimmer. [Tones.]

Know that the shimmering light is also a protective light, that when you are shimmering, normal third-dimensional danger will not affect you. You will be protected. Shimmer. [Tones again.] Hold the light. Let your vessel expand so that you can hold the light of shimmering.

Remember that each vessel on the Tree of Life contains all other vessels. In order to shimmer, you have to have the understanding and the wisdom, and you have to want to connect with the infinite light and the hidden knowledge. You must want to connect with the kingdom, with the *Malchut*. All of this becomes centered in the one sphere in which you are working. And now we have the new sphere that we have added — the shimmering sphere that represents an interaction of the third and the fifth dimensions, which is closely related to an etheric shimmering crystal. I'm Juliano. Good day.

✳ ✳ ✳

Mordechai: I just want to add another simple analogy about shim-mering and feeling the higher vibration of the cosmic egg. I've used a massager once in a while on my wife, and when it is vibrating on my hand, it's easy for me to imagine that level of vibration pulsing 100 or 200 times a second. That's what sort of catapults me into realizing the higher vibration of the cosmic egg. You can use a hair cutter or some other vibrating device — any kind of thing that you can put into your consciousness. Shimmering is really the fastest shortcut to self-healing. If you keep that cosmic egg in a healthy shape at a high pulse rate, you cannot help but increase your immune system.

Mem: the Fountain of Divine Wisdom

CLASS 15

MORDECHAI, DAVID, AND ARCHANGEL METATRON

Mordechai: The letter *Mem* is the central column of the whole *Aleph-Bet*. It is truly central. We call it the fountain of wisdom, and you're going to find out why right now.

The *Mem* is the letter of water. It is the first letter of the Hebrew word for water, *Mayim*, which is spelled in Hebrew *Mem-Yud-Mem*, which equals 90. This letter symbolizes the fountain of the divine wisdom of the galactic Torah. The waters of a physical fountain or spring ascend from their unknown subterranean source. The secret of the abyss in the account of creation is revealing itself on Earth. The fountain of wisdom expresses the power of flow from the superconscious source.

In the terminology of Kabbalah, this flow is from *Keter*, the crown, to *Chochma*, which is wisdom. The stream is symbolized in Proverbs as the flowing stream, the source of wisdom. In particular, we are taught that there are thirteen channels of flow from the superconscious source to the beginning of consciousness.

Thirteen is a very powerful number. It is so powerful that the powers that be have always made it a bad-luck thing (Friday the 13th, no thirteenth floor in buildings). Why? That is all completely upside-down and false. In Hebrew, the word that describes this is *Hafuch* — opposite, or upside-down. The real power of thirteen is the power of the central column. In particular, these channels correspond to the thirteen attributes of mercy revealed to Moses at Sinai as well as to the thirteen principles of the Torah, the superrational logic, or the metaphysical secrets and metaphysical essence of the Torah.

The *Mem* is the thirteenth letter of the *Aleph-Bet*. In Kabbalah, we are taught that *Mems* appear in the "primordial air," outer space, into which the letter *Lamed* soars. The letter *Lamed* comes before the *Mem*.

Each attribute of mercy[1] is in fact a contraction of relatively infinite wisdom at the level of the superconscious — in other words, waters that have no end. In order to channel and reveal a flash of wisdom onto the "screen" of consciousness, it's as what was shown at Mount Sinai; these were living holograms, and the *Mem*, or the water, is the essence of those living holograms.

Now, the *Mem*, number thirteen, we've spoken about before. Both the words *Echad* (unity) and *Ahava* (love) equal thirteen, and that is another secret of the letter *Mem*. The closed or final *Mem*, the source of the fountain of wisdom, connected and included within its subterranean, superconscious source, corresponds to the secret of *Echad*, or one — unity.

The open *Mem*, which is sort of like an upside-down *Tet* (remember the *Tet* was like a bundle, a womb to hold the pregnancy) from which emerges the point *Yud*, which is on the top-right corner of the open *Mem*, is conscious insight. It is the manifestation of love, the will to cling to another's soul. We'll explain that as we go on.

Mem is 13 plus 13, which equals the sacred gematria of the union of the 13 of *Echad* (one/unity) combining with the 13 of *Ahava* (love), which equals the name *Havaya*. This sacred name helps one attain the power to draw into consciousness the wisdom of the Torah.

Now I'm going to include one thing here before I go on. The name *Havaya* represents the *Yud-Hey-Vav-Hey*, but if you look at those letters in Hebrew — Y-H-V-H — they do not express *Havaya*; they actually express "yavah." But as things go, this represents a paradox. If you go backward from the Creator's name, *Hey-Vav-Hey-Yud*, you can see the expression *Havaya*. That's a little extra secret for you. This is just another confirmation that everything is a paradox.

The Sight of *Mem*

In the category of sight, we're going to use models, metaphors, and maps. That's beautiful. The open *Mem* is a square with a small opening at its lower-left corner. The closed *Mem*, the final *Mem*, is completely square. Now, in the category of sight at the level of worlds, the open *Mem* is a flowing stream. Remember, it's all about water. As we will see, water is everything in our lives. The closed final *Mem* represents an underground stream. How would you explain an underground stream? It's a stream that *Ima Adama/Gaia/Mother Earth* might use and appreciate. And also at the level of worlds, the *Mem* represents the womb.

At the level of souls, the flowing stream is the source of wisdom, and the open *Mem* is self-consciousness. The closed *Mem* represents the unconscious states of being and the power of reproduction.

At the level of divinity in the category of sight, the closed *Mem* represents the arrival of the ascension, or as they say in Hebrew, the *Mashiach*. It also represents the waters of *Teshuvah* (repentance). *Teshuvah, Te-Shuv-Hey*, remember, is the returning of the *Hey* to the other three letters of the *Yud-Hey-Vav-Hey*.

The Sound of *Mem*

Now at the category of sound, the *Mem* — water — is a blemish. Water and blemish are opposites — another paradox. Now, at the level of worlds, water has the ability to glue substances; in other words, what goes into water dissolves and becomes one with it. Then we have water's descending nature.

I can get into that because water is the essence of sharing. There is nothing that shares more than water. If you throw a glass of water on the floor, you'll find that it keeps spreading out until it evaporates. It's the epitome of self-sacrifice, and that is in its descending nature.

Also in the level of worlds, the plenitude of water is related to life's dependence on it. In other words, this planet, the Blue Jewel, is 70 percent-plus water and we are 86–90 percent water. As far as the blemish is concerned, the concealment of God's light is in the lower worlds, which includes nature. Nature is naturally blemished because we are here.

At the level of souls in sound, the root of the soul is without blemish. The love of God flows forth like water.

At the level of divinity in sound, water is a representation of the Torah. The closed *Mem* is the first saying of creation. The open *Mem* represents the subsequent nine sayings of Creation — those ten utterances. They're called utterances because there isn't a more acceptable name for them, but they were living holograms. The open *Mem* in divinity is the exoteric dimension of the Torah; the closed *Mem* is the esoteric dimension of the Torah.

Now, an open *Mem* and a closed *Mem* with a *Yud* in between —
Mayim — means water, which is our essence. Without water, we could
not have osmosis, which is the essence of our being in the third dimension. Isn't it amazing that 70 percent of the Blue Jewel is made up of
water and sodium chloride, or salt, which is *Melach* in Hebrew? So
you have to really appreciate that the essence of life is saltwater. That's
really the essence. It's the essence of osmosis, and it's exactly how we
exist. It's all because of water — *Mayim*.

Now, those two *Mems* with a *Yud* in between them, *Mayim*, or
water, is 90. When the *Yud* extends itself down, it becomes a *Vav*, and
then you have the word *Moom*, which is blemish. This is not just any
blemish; this is the blemish to be repaired. How do we know? Where is
the proof? Because *Mem-Vav-Mem* has a sacred gematria of 86, and 86
is also the gematria for *Elohim*. *Hateva*, which is the Hebrew word for
nature, is also 86. This is absolutely certifiable confirmation and proof
that the blemish can be fixed.

As good as water is, that's how bad the blemish is for the other
side, but it can be repaired through the light of *Elohim*. Everything, you
know, is so beautiful. As I said before, water shares.

The positive aspects of water include the womb of Mother Nature
at all levels of physical reality as discussed above: the world's dependence on rain and drinking water, the fact that the majority of Earth is
covered by water, and the phenomenon that 90 percent of the human
body actually consists of water. Natural streams of water are referred to
as living waters, and living waters is also a representation of the Torah.
The Torah is considered living waters.

We have to get back to the level of divinity in the category of sound.
The comparison of Torah to water, "There is no water except Torah," is
drawn from the life-giving qualities of water mentioned above. Just as
the material world could not exist without water, so too the very existence and sustenance of all worlds is continuously dependent on the
goodly waters of the Torah. Our sages teach that God looked into the
Torah and created the world and that the world was built by kindness,
the loving kindness of the waters of the Torah. Just as water quenches
bodily thirst, so do the waters of the Torah quench spiritual thirst.
Remember, I am referencing the Torah as a galactic gift. This Torah is
purely multidimensional.

The prophet Isaiah stated strongly, "Oh, all who are thirsty go to
water." The fact that the prophet must exclaim "Oh!" to human souls

indicates that the waters in question are not obvious to the soul but rather belong to a higher level — to the level of divinity.

The Numbers of *Mem*

We move on to my favorite category: number. The letter *Mem* is the number 40. Forty squared is 1,600. At the level of worlds, to show the power of 40, there were 40 days of the flood of Noah, and 40 *Seah*[2] is the minimum quantity of rainwater that is needed for a kosher *Mikveh* — or as we call it, a purifying, sanctifying ritual bath. In the Torah, there are also important 40-year periods in the lives of Moses, Rabbi Hillel, Rabbi Yochanan ben Zakkai, and Rabbi Akiva. Each one of these sages lived for 120 years in Jewish legend, and their lives were divided by three. They each had three 40-year segments. Now, the most important thing to understand about these names is that they were all incarnations of Moses. Reincarnation is a beautiful thing, and that's why it is said that Moses comes into this world in every generation — especially in this generation. Everybody is here for the "really big show."

According to Jewish thought, there are 40 days from conception to the initial formation of the fetus. "And the rain was upon the earth 40 days and 40 nights [Genisis 7:12, KJB]." As it says in the Zohar, the day that the Torah was translated out of Hebraic/Aramaic and into Greek, there were three days of darkness, proving that when you translate something out of Hebrew and into any other language, it loses over 95 percent of its energy. I'm being conservative; it actually loses more than 99 percent of its energy — or a nano less than. So please be aware. And at the level of divinity, we have the 40 days of lower *Teshuvah* for the sin of the golden calf. You know how you hear people say, "You've got to fast for 40 days"? Well, this is really the essence of all of that. There's also the 40 days of the higher *Teshuvah* when Moses received the second set of tablets. Then there are 40 cubits, which is the height of the entrance to the sanctuary of the Holy Temple.

Now, Moses went up to Mount Sinai three times. The Hebrew Bible, says two times, but there was a third time. He went up earlier with his brother Aaron, and they left Aaron's two sons, Nadav and Avihu, at the foot of the mountain. Moses went up three times to meet the starmasters up on top with their leader, *Yud-Hey-Vav-Hey*. *Adonai Tzevaoth* was there. Moses spent 40 days there three times, so that $3 \times 40 = 120$ appears many times. Why is it 3×40? Because it's 40 for the right column, 40 for the left column, and 40 for the central column in the Tree of Life.

In reference to the punishment and rectification of souls, the Torah states their number to be "in the number 40." Our sages explain that number, which is "in" 40 to be 39, or 40 - 1; the number is "in" 40. So what is in 40? Every number from 1 to 39 — sort of like an automatic triangle of 40. And what's 39? Thirty-nine represents *Tal*, the dew that comes down from heaven. And if you multiply 39 x 10, you will get the sacred gematria of the word *Shama'yim*, which is heaven, and what is *Shama'yim*? *Aish* plus *Mayim* — fire plus water. It's so perfect!

Upon the revelation of Mount Sinai, Moses ascended the mountain and remained there for 40 days and nights. During this period, the hearts of the people were filled with great anticipation and longing, whereas for Moses, the experience of this period was surely one of divinity — in particular, "worlds in divinity." The 40 days relate to almost everything; everything that is holy, everything that is sanctified, takes 40 days. Forty also relates to the Groups of Forty as a powerful number to bring group cohesion.

Mem Is a Vibration

The important thing is to understand that the *Mem* is a vibration, a frequency. Just think, how powerful is the *Mem*? Think of all the names and terms we're familiar with that begin with the *Mem*: Archangel Metatron; Archangel Michael; Moses; Mordechai; *Mashiach*; *Melech* (king); *Malach*, or angel; the teacher Moreh; the Kabbalist Mekubal; the word *Magen*, *Mem-Gimmel-Nun*, which means a shield; and *Magen* David, which means the shield of David. In the word *Magen*, *Mem-Gimmel-Mem*, the *Mem* represents Michael, the *Gimmel* represents Gabriel, and the *Nun* represents Archangel Nuriel. That is a beautiful shield, if I do say so myself. Then we have *Mayim*, which of course is water; *Ma'amin* (my people); *Mezuzah*; and *Mearat Machpelah*, the cave where Adam and Eve, Abraham and Sara with their son Yitzchak, and Joseph are buried.

We have a very important word, *Mazal*, which means luck. Now, *Mazal* is actually all the light that you bring down in your blueprint when you're doing your screenplay. It's like you come down with an American Express card. (It used to be platinum, but I hear now it's a black card.) It takes you anywhere you want to go. You want to jump on a shuttle and fly around the Blue Jewel? No problem. With this card, with this light or luck, you can do it.

Using the *Mem*'s Vibration

We're going to get into the repair, and I'm going to try to express it in the frequency of the letter *Mem*. We just discussed the beginnings of words and names of powerful beings that begin with the vibration of "mmmm." Now we're going to concentrate on the ends of the words with the vibration frequency of "ohm," as in *Shalom*.

Why, you ask? Why does David start all of his channels with *Shalom*? It's that frequency of "mmmm." It is a powerful frequency. It is actually a corrective/healing frequency. You're using the frequency of the letter *Mem* at the end of a word.

I will do it in a progression you are familiar with, in a vowel breakdown: *Aimmmm, eemmmm, ahmmmm, ohmmmm, oommmm*. When you extend that sound and vibration, you can visualize your lips vibrating to that frequency. Now, we're going to take the vibration of that frequency and imagine it is the same vibration as your cosmic egg. If you make this "mmmm" sound until you really feel your lips vibrating and you transfer that vibration to the cosmic egg, then you will be on your way to balance and health. Try it. You just might like it. This is the most important thing I've discussed in this class — the frequency of the *Mem*, the vibration of your lips, and matching that vibration with your aura, with your cosmic egg. God bless.

❋ ❋ ❋

Repairing the World

Shalom, Shalom, Shalom. Greetings. This is **Archangel Metatron**. You have been discussing the sacredness of the number 40 and the sacredness of the vibration of *Mem*, which brings a harmony. You know that the expression of this sound brings you into a balance., but how exactly is this balance to be understood? The change that comes to you has to do with opening up to the higher worlds, to the higher energies.

When you are learning about this Tree of Life and about these different energies, you must open your third eye. You must open your crown chakra, and you must open yourself to higher light, higher wisdom, and higher knowledge. You must also be open to higher compassion and higher judgment.

When you hear the vibration of energy from the Tree of Life, those vibrations open you up to the higher energies that will bring you into a greater unity, a greater balance. So you want to be in unity with your higher self, with your soul purpose, with this planet, and with the planetary healers.

When the mission was given to establish forty Groups of Forty, it was with this understanding that the sacredness of the numbers would create a vibrational energy field that would open people up to their higher wisdom and to the higher spheres. This, then, brings us to the point where you are opening up or unlocking your inner codes. You are opening yourselves up to this higher balance. You are here for your divine providence; you are here to participate in this project, to do the work of the repair, the *Tikun*. It is *Tikun ha Olam*. There is the sound again — *Olam*. It is the world, and thus this phrase from Hebrew means "the repair of the world."

[Tones: *Tikun ha Olam*.] It means "the world to come."

The world to come is the fifth-dimensional world that you are going to move into. But your work is not completed here on Earth yet. Why are you here? Why are you here on the third dimension? Why don't you want to just go up to the fifth dimension right now? Why did you have to bother to reincarnate here on Earth? Because it was divine providence that you would be participating here in this gigantic repair of the world. Remember that *Shalom* also contains the word *Olam*. *Shalom* can then mean "to bring perfection, peace, and harmony to the world."

Bringing the Planet into Balance

Someone has to understand that to bring this harmony into this planet there must be a balance. In the reincarnation cycle, there is an interesting phenomenon. If someone is too materialistic and focuses too much on wealth, then in the next lifetime, that person may come back and have to be a monk. Such people may want to deny themselves of any materialism to counterbalance what they did have in the previous lifetime.

I think it is important that you understand that sometimes the imbalance and counterbalance expressed in the Tree of Life may take another lifetime to bring it back into balance. This lifetime you are now in, in many ways, is balancing other lifetimes. This world — *Olam Hazeh* — is out of balance. It is a world you are seeking to repair, to bring a new balance to — a new balance that is contained in the vibration of the *Mem*, in the vibration of *Shalom*. [Tones.]

The vibration of the *Mem* sound relates to the 40 and to finding this balance. This new balance that is to come to Earth was contained in the energy field of the 12/22/12 Central Sun alignment. Think about the Maya: That name that is now associated with prophecy for your future world also starts a *Mem*. This alignment is a manifestation of a new balance, a new harmony. How do we balance — how do we manifest this balance — through the Tree of Life?

The key is to know that all of these energies, the positive and the negative, the male and the female, the hidden knowledge, the undifferentiated energies, the energies having to do with the Messianic light, have to become manifested in the third dimension in some way. That is for you personally and for you as a planetary healer.

Each of you now, in this point, has a rare and special opportunity to connect with the light of the Messiah, the Messianic light — the light that is contained in the central column, in Montserrat. The spirit guide for this sphere is Sananda/Jesus. The energy of the Messiah is a divine intervention transcending the third dimension, bringing in a transcendent light of the Messiah that will bring an awakening of a new balance.

This is the light of the Messiah. This is the light of the central column. This is the light of the central sphere that opens up your consciousness to the essence of the Messiah. When everyone's consciousness is opened up to the energy of the Messiah, they are able to receive the light of the Messiah, and then they are able to receive the knowledge of the Messiah. Remember, the Messianic light, the sphere of Montserrat, is exactly in the center of the Tree of Life. The center touches all the other spheres. It is the only sphere that has its energies touching everything, and that includes the energies touching the *Yud-Hey-Vav-Hey*, the energies of the divinity — the undifferentiated energies.

The Messianic light, the light of Montserrat, serves to step down this divine light in a balanced way so that it can be transmitted to the lower spheres. This is the biggest mission: learning how to transfer the higher light from the divine sources down into the lower sources of manifestation. If you are able to do that, then you are fulfilling your divine service.

Listen, we are talking about *Mem*, which also includes the powerful word *Mitzvah*. *Mitzvah* means a good deed, a deed of divine service. *Mitzvah* is a commandment, but it is also a service. It is a *Mitzvah* to do this divine work of planetary healing. This is a higher service than even meditation, higher than even the chanting. It is the doing of this great service of planetary healing that helps to repair the world. I'm Archangel Metatron. Good day.

Nun: Fish

CLASS 16

Mordechai, David, and Archangel Michael

Mordechai: This is the sixteenth class on the Arcturian Crystal Tree of Life, and this is about the letter *Nun* and the final *Nun*, representing the Messiah — the heir to the throne. I'm very excited about this class, and soon you will see why.

In Aramaic, the letter *Nun* means "fish." The *Mem* that we discussed previously refers to the waters of the sea, which is the natural medium for the fish. The *Nun* swims in the *Mem*, covered by the waters of the hidden world, and creatures of this hidden world lack self-consciousness. Now, I've mentioned two phrases here: "hidden world" and "lack of self-consciousness" — both relating to fish. The hidden world, as we starseeds know, includes the fifth and higher dimensions. The lack of self-consciousness that we discuss almost every chance we get is all about self-nullification. Unlike fish, land animals revealed on the face of Earth possess self-consciousness.

Starseeds' souls divide into two general categories symbolized by fish and land animals. The two prototypes of these categories are the leviathan and the behemoth. The leviathan is a huge fish that existed before creation. What is the largest "fish" you can think of? The humpback whale? Imagine that multiplied by 1,000. That represents a species that the Divine plays with as a pet. The behemoth really is an animal. It relates to an ox because it's among the strongest of the animals, but this is not to exclude the hippopotamus, rhinoceros, or elephant. The ox represents Joseph in the galactic Torah because he broke the world bank 4,000 years ago.

Presently, these are the two categories of souls corresponding to the two innate tendencies and attractions of the soul — either to the concealed and secret or to the revealed. In the future, these two prototypes — the leviathan and the behemoth — will unite in battle, each killing the ego of the other. Thereafter, they are to blend together in true egoless union. Their meat will be served as the feast for the righteous when we go through the stargate. The souls of the righteous will actually consume the very root of consciousness of our present level of soul to integrate or digest into a totally new and higher level of consciousness. Remember, everything is about consciousness.

I'll give you some gematria. The leviathan, which is *Lamed-Vav-Yud-Tav-Nun*, equals 496. Now, the word *Malchut* has the letters *Mem, Lamed, Kuph, Vav,* and *Tav*. In numbers, it comes out to 40, 30, 20, 6, and 400, which also equals 496. Also, *Malchut* — in the Kabbalah and in the world of divine emanation — is represented by the sea whose tides are controlled by the power of the Moon, which is the symbol of King David. When we celebrate the new moon, we are really celebrating the first sliver of light from the dark new moon, so we say, "David, the King of Israel, is alive forever." Here is the whole sentence: When *Malchut* is sent to enliven the lower worlds, it is symbolized by Earth.

The *Nun* with Kingdoms and Rulers

There is an upper *Malchut* and a lower *Malchut*. (This is because one tree of life can be represented as a series of ten spheres above each other.) This gives absolute confirmation and certification of *Sephirah* twelve (Serra da Bocaina, Earth's interaction of the fifth and third dimensions, represented by Juliano), which is just above the bottom sphere (number ten, Lago Puelo, manifesting higher on Earth and guided by Vywamus). It's no accident that Vywamus, the soul psychologist, is here to help us in our lower existence.

In Hebrew, the *Nun* also means "kingdom" and, in particular, "the heir to the throne." Remember, every sphere has a throne on top, a *Keter*. There is a *Keter* on top of each one of these circles. The *Nun* is the fourteenth letter of the *Aleph-Bet*, which equals David, *Dalet-Vav-Dalet* — or 4 + 6 + 4, which equals 14. He is the progenitor of the eternal kingdom of Israel. The heir to David is the *Mashiach*, or the Messiah. Messiah ben David, *Mashiach* ben David, of whom it is said in Hebrew,

"*Lifnai shemesh yanoon sh'mo*": "As long as the duration of the Sun, his name shall rule."

Now, what Sun are we talking about? We can talk about our Sun, but we're also talking about something a little bit more infinite than that: the Central Sun of this galaxy. Our sages teach us that one of the names of *Mashiach* is *Yud-Nun-Vav-Nun* (which means "to rule"), cognate to the actual spelling of the *Nun*, which is *Nun-Vav-Nun*. Also, *Mashiach* is known as "the miscarriage." The *Nun* does not appear in Psalm 145, but it is supported by the Divine's mercy, as expressed by the letter *Samekh*.

The *Nun* and Falling

In general, the letter *Nun* corresponds in the Galactic Torah to the image of falling, but not the way we think of falling. The soul of the Messiah experiences itself as continuously falling and dying, and were it not for the ever-present hand of the Divine catching it, it would crash to the ground and shatter to death. But as we know, there is no death. The consciousness of the fall is the reflection of the egoless state of the fish in its natural medium of water when forced to reveal itself on dry land.

When does this happen? This is similar to the experience of a hidden righteous person being forced from Above to reveal him- or herself for the good of the starseeds and the world. Now, remember what I just said: "a righteous person being forced from Above." "Above" is with a capital *A*; in other words, it refers to all the righteous souls that we talk about — Malchitzedek (whom you know as Malki Tzedek or Melchizedek), Lord Sananda, Moses, Abraham, the *Baal Shem Tov*, the Ari, and all these great ones. We might as well bring in all of the saints.

Now, the meaning of the word "saint" is "one who shares until there's nothing left," which is what water does. Water goes down and spreads out until it evaporates. We find this exemplified in the life and teachings of the *Baal Shem Tov*, and it will be epitomized in the life of the Messiah to come. Ultimately, the destiny of the Messiah and his generation, us, is to assume the level of the sea on Earth — to experience paradoxically selfless self-consciousness. In the verse in Isaiah, with which the Rambam concludes his code of law, the law of kings culminates with a description of the coming of the Messiah: "For the earth shall be full of the knowledge of the Lord, like waters cover the sea" (Isaiah 11:9, KJV).

The Sight and Sound of *Nun*

Let's reference sight, sound, and number. In the category of sight in the level of worlds, the letter *Nun* is a natural vessel. We talked about vessels such as the *Tet*, which holds the pregnancy, but the *Nun* is a vessel all unto itself. The first thirteen letters, *Aleph* to *Mem*, represent the light, the male energy, so there's the light and there's the vessel. The next nine letters represent the vessel, and *Nun* is the first of those nine letters. It represents bending over in humility, subservience, and faithfulness. That's at the level of worlds.

For sight at the level of souls, *Nun* is pure humility. It is the vessel of true insight into *Halachah*, which refers to the Jewish laws. If you are purely humble and you go without ego, then you can realize how the laws are really meant for such a situation or state of mind. In the level of divinity, the final *Nun* is an extension of the infinite.

Here's a beautiful question: How can you extend the infinite? I'll give you a hint: There's an upper and a lower extension of the infinite — the light above and the light below.

In the category of divinity in the level of sight is Moses, the faithful servant. He wasn't the only one, but he's the one who's been given the podium — the lectern — so to speak.

In the category of sound or name, we have fish of the sea, the symbol of reproduction. Everything we've spoken about relates to conception, pregnancy, and birthing.

* * *

The Energy of *Nun*

David: We are talking today about the letter *Nun*, which is equivalent to the letter *N* in English. In Hebrew, letters have a configuration when they are at the beginning of a word, but at the end of a word some letters have what is called a final configuration, like the final *Nun*, and those letters look different at the end of words.

When we talk about letters, we try to think about how each letter carries an energy. For me, the energy of *Nun* is contained in the word *Navi*, the Hebrew word for "prophet." It is also a verb that means "to prophesy." A Hebrew word that has the final *Nun* sound, the end sound, is *Natan*, which means "to give."

We have some great lessons in these two words — the lesson of prophesy and the lesson of giving. Remember, the highest energy is found in doing the service — in giving to others. A prophet gives or shares his or her energy and connection to the upper worlds. The prophet is able to go up into the upper worlds, and we are studying the Tree of Life so we can expand our consciousness into the upper world.

Expanded Consciousness versus Constricted Consciousness

Now I want to talk about the concept of consciousness, because we have expanded consciousness and we have constricted consciousness. Obviously, when you want to be a prophet or you want to prophesy, you use expanded consciousness. In expanded consciousness, you understand that there is an interaction occurring among all of the spheres of the Tree of Life. You also understand what Mordechai explained: that there is a duplicate world expressed by Serra da Bocaina, which is the interaction of the fifth-dimensional world with the third-dimensional world. This is a great expression of how everything is interrelated.

In constricted consciousness, you have a narrower focus and do not see how everything is connected. One great pain in the duality of the third-dimensional world in which we live is that we often have the experience of restricted consciousness. The idea of restricted consciousness means that we don't see the relationship of everything. Not only that, but we do not experience the unity of everything. One great goal of the Tree of Life is to demonstrate unity. One great Kabbalah teaching is to find ways to experience the unity in everything and find ways to help other people and other energies merge into that unity. The ultimate unification, then, is unity with the Creator.

What can we do to experience expanded consciousness? What can we do to experience the energy of the prophet? Remember the great prophet Eliyahu in the Hebrew tradition ascended. It is actually the second recording in the Torah, or in the *Tanakh*, the books of the Old Testament, in which a prophet ascended. The first case is Enoch, who ascended and became known as Archangel Metatron.

The beautiful story of Eliyahu was that his student, Elisha, did not want him to ascend. But Eliyahu had the gift of prophecy, and you know, people want to be around prophets. And it is the same thing with the ascension: Everyone I have talked to does not want to stay on Earth; they want to ascend. Now, some people do want to stay to help things, but most people want to ascend. The beauty of the story of Eliyahu is that when he ascended, his energy as a prophet was transferred to his student, Elisha.

So one great idea of the letter *Nun* and of prophecy itself is that you are energy, and that energy is reaching higher as you head toward the ascension. As you are reaching Serra da Bocaina and the energy of that sphere, you are interacting with higher energy. As you interact with higher energy, you have expanded consciousness. When you have expanded consciousness, you are able to prophesy. You have greater psychic powers. Those psychic powers can include telepathy, visions of the future, thought projection, and of course, doing the work we are doing with shimmering. This is because when we are talking about Serra de Bocaina and the energy of that sphere, we are talking about experiencing the energies of the higher levels through shimmering.

You may be in constricted consciousness, but do not worry, because being in restricted consciousness is not necessarily bad. For example, having restricted consciousness is necessary in certain situations where you are threatened, and it is also necessary for functioning on this plane. I think that we can look at restricted consciousness as a contraction. When you are in restricted consciousness especially, you want to attach yourself to the higher spheres. That means you need to think more about Serra da Bocaina, the higher world, and attach yourself to there. And of course, the highest world is the world of the Creator.

Falling Away from Ego

Mordechai also talked about self-nullification, which is a fancy word that, by my definition, means "becoming egoless." But "egoless" means that you are removing your desires, including the one to dominate. I look at it in the famous expression in the Kabbalah: "Not my will, but thine be done." The idea of nullification is sometimes expressed in this concept of being nothing. But saying "I'm nothing" is really a way of expressing that you empty yourself of your ego.

I want to mention one other energy for *Nun*, because I'm saying that energy is contained in the word. This word is *Nephilim*. You have probably heard it before, and it comes from the Hebrew word *Nephal*, meaning "to fall," so it refers to the fallen ones. These fallen ones are described in Genesis as higher, almost extraterrestrial beings who, for one reason or another, fell. They could have fallen from higher consciousness or from another plane, and they came into this world. They are the fallen ones — a mysterious expression of higher, larger beings who have fallen into the third dimension.

In some channelings, there have been reports of people who were at higher planes and came to visit this plane, and for one reason or another, they could not return back to their motherships. So they "fell." The *Nephilim* could be beings from other dimensions that for one reason or another got stuck in this dimension.

I want to conclude my short presentation on the expanded consciousness by talking about a well-known concept in the Kabbalah: *Ruach Hakodesh*, or as you have in Christian mysticism, the Holy Spirit. To be able to prophesy, to be able to be in the energy of *Navi* and to be connected to Eliyahu and the traditional prophecy, you have to have *Ruach Hakodesh*. People want to have the energy of the Holy Spirit. This is what Jesus had, and this is what is taught about the Holy Spirit in the Christian teachings. It is the energy of *Ruach Hakodesh*, the Holy Spirit.

* * *

The *Nun* as a Vessel

Mordechai: The next word I want to follow up on *Nun* with is the word *Ne'eman* (*Nun-Aleph-Mem*-final *Nun*), meaning "faithful." *Ne'eman* begins and ends with a *Nun*. It is related to the coming of the Messiah. If you take that first *Nun* from *Ne'eman*, you get the actual *Shoresh*, or source, of the word "faithful," which is "amen." "Amen" is a word that is universally understood on this planet. Everybody — one way or another — says amen.

Now, *Nun* is also the first of the vessels of the next nine letters. *Oni* means "poor man," whose secret is the eye — which is the *Ayin*, because the *Ayin* represents the eye — focused solely on his "empty vessel," the *Nun*, longing for even a single point of sustenance from above, not yet drawn down into the physical manifestation, the suspended *Yud*.

A rebellious servant reacts to his inferior, often impoverished position with frustration, or that which we can call a constricted consciousness. In the Kabbalah, we call it a reactive consciousness. There's reaction and there's proaction. We are going to go forward with those two words: "reaction" and "proaction." The whole purpose is to make restriction on the reaction — to count to ten or twenty, or however long it takes, so you can make a proactive choice, a proactive decision. Do not be reactive. In particular, we're going to go with humility because humility and losing the ego, or emptying yourself of the ego, are really quite similar.

Humility is the vessel necessary for receiving true insight into the divine will. We really have to go forward with this "true insight," which David wanted to bring out in *Ruach Hakodesh*. It's really insight from the connection. The only way to get to divine understanding and to divine wisdom is through the connection. This has been stated by Vywamus and others many times.

This is really important, the whole ball of wax: We came down here, and that's one thing all the great sages and all the rabbis, no matter how much they differ with each other, all agree on. They agree that the purpose of creation is for us to go back and return to the Creator's light, for us to go back home through the stargate and to where we came from. That is the whole purpose of our coming down here in the first place.

To understand this, picture two sages disagreeing on a point of law. The decision accepted as law by the prevailing majority then reflects the opinion of the proponent who is most humble rather than intellectually brilliant. *Halachah* — the law — like water, descends from its source on high to the lowest possible basin: the soul and mind of the humble sage.

Intellectual brilliance, like fire, is in a state of continual ascent to conceive and express new insights in understanding; whereas humility, characterized by the sincere desire to simply receive and faithfully convey the teachings of previous authorities, descends like water. For this reason, King David was the master of the law — as were all the great sages.

The Fallen Ones

Now I will talk about the fallen ones because, unfortunately, as it was explained through many of David's channelings, when you are up in the fifth dimension and you look down here into the third dimension, it looks pretty simple, pretty easy down there: "No problem. I can do that! I can get through that!"

Well, these angels (who later became the fallen ones) went to the Divine Father and said, "Look what's happening down there. These guys are falling apart. We can do much better than that." The Divine Father asked, "You think you can? Well, then, so be it!" And *poof!* He sent them down here.

These fallen angels and two master angels thought they were hot stuff and that they could do it. They didn't realize that down here we have what's called "negative inclination" or the *Yetzer Hara*. It comes with the package. When you come down to this planet, you become part of what my first teacher's teacher called "the territory of Darth Vader." When you come down here, you're on the dark side, and that dark side enters as soon as you come out of the womb. *Boom!* It sticks right onto you. The only time you really have a chance to even the playing field is after the age of twelve, thirteen, or whatever the situation is.

I want you to understand what *Nephal* is. It's falling, but from the higher perspective, the coming down from the ego is really the falling.

The *Nun* and Reproduction

Now, here's something interesting: On the fifth day of creation, fish were created from water, just as the letter *Nun* (which is fish) follows or emerges from the previous letter, *Mem* — water. The fish were the first creatures the Creator blessed: "Be fruitful, and multiply, and fill the waters in the seas." That is right out of Genesis (1:22, KJV).

In nature, fish symbolize reproduction. This is hinted at in the fact that the *Nun* is the only letter whose full spelling — *Nun-Vav-Nun* — is a repetition of itself with a *Vav*, as though to say, "Fish and more fish." The previous letter, *Mem*, whose meaning is water, is spelled by repeating itself without the *Vav* in between: *Mem*-final *Mem*. Which is what? *Memmmmm*. In the secret of the original state of the creation of water, "water in water," remember how the waters were divided? They split. Well, that is exactly the *Mem*: *Mem*-final *Mem*, water in water.

The Numbers of *Nun*

There are five final letters in the Hebrew alphabet. We discussed the final *Mem* and the final *Nun*. The actual value of the final *Nun* is 700, which is 14, the original number of it in the *Aleph-Bet*, multiplied by 50, which is the value of the letter *Nun*. So 14 x 50 = 700, the actual normative value of the *Nun*. This unique phenomenon of the letter *Nun* hints at the ratio of reproduction. Fourteen equals 2 x 7, and 7 is the word *Dag* — *Dalet-Gimmel*. *Dalet* is four, and *Gimmel* is three. *Dag* means "fish."

The Kabbalah has fifty gates of understanding. These fifty gates appear in all levels of worlds, souls, and divinity, in all spheres of the Tree of Life. Most important to understand is that the fiftieth gate is the stargate, and it's all about 7 x 7 = 49 + 1, which is the fiftieth gate, the stargate, which is our shortcut straight up, right to the Arcturians and to *Mem*, or Archangel Metatron, who opens the door.

✳ ✳ ✳

Interaction with the Lower Spheres

David: Before I begin the channeling, I want you to take a look at the

Tree of Life again. We are talking about the bottom of the Tree of Life, which is Lago Puelo, and then Serra da Bocaina interacting with it so that there is another dimension we are beginning to understand. Then we are also talking about Lake Taupo, which is the creation of sacred places and planetary cities of light, and Grose Valley, which is the creation of the New Earth society. Because everything that is being manifested comes from above, and because everything is interactive, I'm going to work in my channeling of Archangel Michael from Lake Moraine. This is a higher level of understanding, even though we are talking about the lower spheres. Remember, even though you are at the lower sphere, you are still grasping the energies and the interactions of all the spheres.

* * *

Divinity Has No Constriction

Shalom, Shalom, Shalom. Greetings. I'm **Archangel Michael**. So you are studying this beautiful energy, and today we look at the energy of *Navi* and Eliyahu Ha'navi. Eliyahu is the prophet who was able, through expanded consciousness, to see and experience all of the light above and to understand that this light above has been constricted to come into this dimension. This is a deep concept because the nature of the divinity is expansiveness. The nature of the divinity has no constriction.

This third dimension was created with restriction, but that is the will of the Creator — that this beautiful place known as the third dimension be restricted. But even though this dimension is restricted, there are opportunities for expansion. There are opportunities to open.

One of the great openings comes through prophecy. It is said that all prophecy ended in the falling of Israel, in the historical ancient times. But I want to say that there are many great expanded-conscious people on this planet now. The ability to prophesy is connected directly with your understanding of the Tree of Life and your understanding of how to use this energy.

The fact is that you, through your expanded consciousness, can prophesy, and you can see the future. But in order to prophesy correctly, you must remove your ego. You must remove thoughts such as, "Oh, I'm so cool that I can prophesy" or "I'm going to use my power of prophecy to win the horse race or to win the lottery." That is ego. You must totally empty yourself — self-nullification. But I also speak to you about the greatest way to expand your consciousness, which is through the energy of the Holy Spirit.

The Holy Spirit is filled with the light of the highest force, the highest energy. So listen to these words, because the words bring the energy to you directly, more than even what I'm speaking. First, I will give you the words of the prophets Eliyahu and Elijah.

[Tones in Hebrew: *Eliyahu Ha'navi*, Elijah the Prophet.]

Let the energies of the prophet of Eliyahu activate in your expanded consciousness so that Eliyahu will be with you at the ascension. Eliyahu will be at the gateways of the ladders of ascension to greet you.

[Tones again: *Eliyahu Ha'navi*.]

Let your mind expand, for you have within you the ability to prophesy. You have within you the codes of ascension. You have within you the ability to ascend. But please, first do not seek to prophesy, but rather seek expanded consciousness. Then the ability to prophesy will come with that. It is ego to seek the number to win the lottery or win a horse race. That is not the way toward expanded consciousness. Expanded consciousness comes with unity and unifying, and that is where we speak about the Holy Spirit, the *Ruach Hakodesh*. So listen to the Hebrew words *Ruach Hakodesh*, and feel within you the vibrational energies, because the words will vibrate into your energy field.

[Tones in Hebrew: *Ruach Hakodesh*, Holy Spirit.]

Let the Holy Spirit expand your consciousness. As the final teaching about the letter *Nun*, it is part of the Hebrew word for prophecy: *Navi*.

[Tones: *El Na Refa Na La*, Hebrew for "Please God, heal her now".]

Na is "please." Think about this word "please" as a way of surrender. It is not surrendering as though you are in a battle and you gave up but surrendering the ego; you are surrendering yourself, putting aside the worldly thoughts and connecting with this expanded consciousness. Part of the healing is to experience this word "please." This is also in divine healing because you are saying, "Please God, heal her now."

[Tones: *El Na Refa Na La*.]

Let the healing light — please, God — come to all who are hearing and reading these words. Let the Holy Spirit, the *Ruach Hakodesh*, and the energy of *Navi*, Eliyahu Ha'navi, fill your consciousness. I'm Archangel Michael. Good day.

✳ ✳ ✳

Extending the Infinite and Ritual Immersions

Mordechai: I would like to explain the phrase "extension of the infinite" so that starseeds will be able to understand. On the lower level, it is simply the expansion of the universe. On the upper level, where we have our Father on the throne and all twenty-four elders who sit around him, the expansion is when these elders take off on a project to create new universes and new worlds.

Also, I want to say an important thing about expanded consciousness: In the Keys of Enoch it says we are Project Israel, the Jerusalem Command. As starseeds, we are all Project Israel. As far as the expanded consciousness, just listen to the two words that are repeated most in Hebrew: *Sh'ma Yisrael* – "Hear, oh Israel." Hear what? Hear the still, quiet voice.

I would like to add one other thing: There is a very simple ritual in which all you have to do is find a swimming pool — preferably a heated one if it's cold. Go into the swimming pool with your swimsuit and just dunk yourself once for each of the twelve spheres in the Arcturian Crystal Tree of Life.

It's not about purification or sanctification, even though it is. The most important thing is that we are doing ritual immersions to cleanse our auric energies. This was done way back with the Essenes, in that time and place in Qumran where they had many of these. They are called *Mikvehs* — ritual immersions.

But the most important fact in taking these ritual baths was one word: clarity. Clarity is needed to expand our consciousnesses. I would suggest everyone, if you can, find a swimming pool and dunk yourselves as many times as you can — depending on how warm the water is ten or twelve times will be sufficient — and then it will be a whole different world. Amen.

Appendix A:
Hebrew Glossary

Notes on Hebrew Pronunciation

This is not intended to be a comprehensive pronunciation guide to Hebrew: modern or ancient, classical or rabbinical. Like most languages, Hebrew has undergone many regional temporal changes in its structure and pronunciation.

The primary purpose of this guide is to assist readers in producing verbal sounds that resonate with their respective energies. A full survey of all possible sounds expressible in the Hebrew language is beyond the scope of this book.

Most of the consonantal sounds are very close to how they have been rendered in this text. There are a few sounds that will be unfamiliar to those who do not speak Hebrew. These sounds are listed below.

q: used instead of "k" to indicate a similar sound, but further back on the palate, with the lips more rounded

z: a sound quite close to "ts," as in English "its," with the "t" sound perhaps less stressed

ch: guttural, as in German "Bach," or "Chanoch" and "Enoch"

sh: as in English "she"

r: not quite equivalent to the English "r." Instead it is more like the "r" in French: further back on the palate and rolled forward.

kk, dd, bb, and other doubled consonants: These must be pronounced fully, but smoothly. So *Tzaddik* is "zad-diq," with no noticeable pause between the doubled consonants, but each is pronounced.

For vowels, the following is given as a guide. There are few more disputed topics in the study of ancient languages than the pronunciation of the vowels, especially in a living ancient language such as Hebrew, which has historically been written with no vowels.

A: as in "father"
E: approximately between "eh" and "ay"
I: as in "ink"
O: as in "over"
U: approximately between "boo" and "super"

AI: like "eye"
AU: approximately between "auger" and "aura"
AH: usually at the end of the word, it has a sound similar to the "a" by itself, such the "a" as in "father," but it's lengthened and slightly aspirated: like the English "ah"

Hebrew Letters

The Hebrew letters are not just letters; they are living energy intelligences. When put into word combinations, they represent a mathematical organization that no other language can match. Sometimes they are also words.

These letters can express different things through permutations. In the Kabbalah, this concept has to do with the letters of the names of God and the number of combinations of letters that can be made.

Aleph (A)

The first letter of the Hebrew alphabet, or *Aleph-Bet*, spelled *Aleph-Lamed-Pey*, *Aleph* is composed of the letter *Yud* on top and a *Vav* slanted down in between another *Yud* on the bottom. The *Yuds* represent water, as in "the *Elohim* flew over the waters." There are the upper waters, which connect with the upper atmosphere and the electromagnetic waves, and the lower waters, which represent the oceans and subterranean waters. *Aleph* has many meanings. It is female energy, and it means "action." It also changes a value from 1 to 1,000. For sight, we are not connected to the fifth dimension, yet we are. We have three levels of sound: The action represents physical reality or the lower animal soul of the *Nefesh* that is in the blood and the one that is in divinity — master of the universe. The Divine said to the letter *Aleph*, "My unity shall not be expressed except through you. All calculations and operations of the world are based in you. We are unity, and unity is everything."

Bet (B)

The second letter of the *Aleph-Bet*, *Bet* is a very important letter; more than 1,500 books have been written about it. Within the word *Bereshit*, it means "in the beginning." *Bet* relates to the *Ana B'Koach* because that meditation starts with *Aleph-Bet*. The letters of the *Aleph-Bet* are like stones. The *Bet* represents the house, and a word is built of letters like a house is built of stones. Each whole word is like a house, and *Bet* represents the house of the galaxy.

Gimmel (G)

The third letter of the *Aleph-Bet*. *Gimmel* was birthed out of *Bet*. It basically means "stability," and it represents one with sustenance, one who shares. Its whole desire is to impart. *Gimmel* represents water by sharing until it evaporates. It corresponds to the fifth sphere, Volcán Poás, which is where Sanat Kumara has been placed. *Gimmel* is the hub of everything circular. It is associated with the creation of the planet Jupiter and the energy of greatness and miracles.

Dalet (D)

The fourth letter of the *Aleph-Bet*, *Dalet* represents us in a world with no light except what we can produce. *Dalet* represents the poor, selflessness, or the complete loss of the ego. It shows how to pray in Hebrew — like a poor man prostrated. *Dalet* is the door and the entrance to the truth. It is also the road and the path to the ethereal. When we talk about *Dalet*, we are also talking about the kingdom, which is where we are manifesting all of this energy.

Hey (H)

The fifth letter of the *Aleph-Bet*, *Hey* an assemblage point. It is the act of giving oneself to another. The expression of the *Hey* is thought, speech, and action. Actually, the *Hey* is made up of a *Dalet* and a foot. The foot is really an upside-down *Yud*. The two lower garments of speech and action express oneself to others, so this is really like a one-stop shop. Certainty and understanding are what the *Hey* is all about. The *Hey* is considered *the* fire letter among fire letters.

Vav (V)

The sixth letter in the *Aleph-Bet*, the *Vav* is a straight line, and it actually represents the word "connection." Nonetheless, it possesses two dimensions: an external as well as an internal force. The first *Vav* in the Torah is in the first line, *Bereshit bara Elohim et hashamayim ve'et ha'aretz*, which means "in the beginning, God created the heavens and the earth" It serves to join spirit and matter — heaven and earth — throughout all of creation. It has a value of six, it's Sacred Triangle number is 21, it has the sacred gematria of *Ek-yeh*, a higher divine combination — which is spelled *Aleph*-K-*Yud*-K — and it is the twenty-second letter of the verse.

Zayin (Z)

The seventh letter of the *Aleph-Bet*, *Zayin* symbolizes completion and rulership manifested in the world. This is completely about female energy. The *Zayin* is the Woman of Valor, because that's where completion and rulership manifest in this world — in the feminine energy.

Chet (Ch)

The eighth letter of the *Aleph-Bet*, *Chet* represents infinity. The number eight is the only other number besides zero that has no beginning and no end. *Chet* also represents the female energy. This is why the letter *Chet* represents manifestation and power.

Tet (T)

The ninth letter of the *Aleph-Bet*, the form of the letter *Tet* symbolizes the union of a groom and bride, consummating with conception. The secret of the *Tet* is that it is numerically equivalent to nine. The nine months of pregnancy hold the power of the mother to carry her inner concealed good, the fetus, throughout the period of pregnancy. Pregnancy is very big with this letter because pregnancy is the power to bring potential into actualization. The form of the letter represents concealed good.

Yud (Y)

The tenth letter of the *Aleph-Bet*, *Yud* is the only letter that is suspended in mid-air. At the level of worlds in sight, the pathway of the *Yud* is the initial point of space and time. Check out the eleventh Tree of Life class for more insight on this letter.

Kaph (K)

The eleventh letter of the *Aleph-Bet*, *Kaph* is the first Hebrew letter in the word *Keter*, or "crown." Also, it's the first letter in the word *Chochma* (wisdom). It's a letter of power and sacredness.

Lamed (L)

The twelfth and tallest letter in the *Aleph-Bet*, *Lamed*, is the only letter that goes above the line. It is also a power letter of the month of Libra and *Rosh Hashanah*. With the letter *Lamed*, value of 30, we have some really great connections to the ring of ascension and the ladder of ascension.

Mem (M)

The thirteenth letter in the *Aleph-Bet*, *Mem's* sound — "mmmm" — is one of the most important sounds, and it ranks among the highest vibrations in the third dimension as well as in Hebrew. It connects us with fifth-dimensional energy. The numerical value of the letter *Mem* is 40, a sacred number.

Nun (N)

The fourteenth letter of the *Aleph-Bet*, *Nun* represents an energy of falling (*Nephal*) to lower, perhaps to *Nefesh* (the lowest level of soul), where we all are now, and sometimes even lower (animal).

Hebrew Words and Phrases

Aba: the Father

Acher: "the Other." He was one of four rabbis who went to the garden, and he was not successful. When he returned, he became a heretic.

Adamah: earth/ground

Adon: Lord

Adonai: the female energy and the galactic/cosmic name that rules the third and fifth dimensions. It means "my Lord."

Adonai Eloheynu; Adonai Echad: "Adonai is our God; Adonai is one."

Adonai Tzevaoth: Lord of hosts

Adon Olam: Lord of the universe

Ahava: love. It has a gematria of 13.

Ain Soph: The point above the crown that contains the infinite light. It means "that with no end," so we are talking about infinity.

Aish: fire

Aliyah: a rising or ascending. It means to go up, as in being called to the Torah, or "elevating up," as in moving to Israel. *Aliyah* can also refer to a process of being called up in front of a congregation to read the Torah at a synagogue service.

Amidah: a Hebrew prayer recited silently during daily prayers with the feet together, standing in place

Ana B'Koach: represents the forty-two-letter name of the Divine. It is a powerful meditation containing seven lines with six words on each line. When said with the right intentions, it will instantly bring angels into our presence.

Ari Hakadosh: a powerful Kabbalist of the early sixteenth century. He fostered a charted technology of the divine names to be used during prayer. Most rabbis cannot fathom or barely understand this technology. It takes Kabbalistic tenure to understand half of it.

Aseret HaDibrot: the Ten Utterances (not the Ten Commandments). Their purpose is for us to do good deeds for no reason other than to treat the next human being with human dignity.

Asiyah: the "world of manifestation" or the "world of doing"

Atah: you. It is used in prayer to refer to the Creator.

Atah Gibur: "you are great"

Atah Gibur Adonai: "You are great, Adonai!"

Atik Yomin: refers to the Ancient One or the Ancient of Days

Atika Kadisha: refers to the entity below *Atik Yomin.* All entities are hermaphrodites on those grades of light.

Atzilut: the world of emanation, nearness to the Creator

Aur Hakadosh: holy light

Avahat Chinam: unconditional love

Avra Kedabra: "as it is created, so it will be"

Ayin: represents the eye

Baal Shem Tov: a great *Tzaddik* who fostered the Chassidic movement in the eighteenth century. He focused on the poor working man. He was and is revered as a mystic.

Ba'al Teshuvah: "master of repentance"; one who returns to the divine essence, to the one living God, with love. Where this person stands, the greatest *Tzaddikim* of the generation cannot.

Baruch: bless

Baruch Hu: "blessed are You," referring to the Creator

Baruch Ata: "blessed are you"; putting the Creator's energy into everything that exists.

Balagan: a general term used for chaos, confusion, and argument.

Beinoni: "he who masters his servants." It is a word that, for the sake of simplicity, refers to the average guy, the middle guy.

Bereshit: "in the beginning"

Bereshit bara Elohim et hashamayim ve'et ha'aretz: "In the beginning, God created the heaven and the earth."

Beriah: the world of creation

Beshalach: "and he sent." God sent the Israelites into the Reed Sea (or the Red

Sea) with his right hand. The right hand is what the Creator used to split that sea. [Note from Mordechai: I know this energy. This is my *Bar Mitzvah*, and it is one of the most action-packed, cosmically warring portions of the entire Torah!]

Bet HaMikdash: the First Holy Temple, which was a galactic/Hebraic temple that stood on the Temple Mount in Jerusalem during the First Temple period, between 1006 BC and 586 BC, when the Jewish nation was exiled to Babylon and the temple was destroyed. It was replaced with the Second Temple seventy years later. The Second Temple, like the second set of tablets, did not have the same celestial/galactic connections. It is now the current site of the Dome of the Rock.

Binah: the *Sephirah* of understanding.

Binah Hagadol: great understanding

Birkat Hamazon: the most important blessing of all, which is given after satisfaction of every meal.

Bitul: self-nullification; dropping the ego as best we can

Bli Ayin Hara: "without the jealous eye." This is serious. Nearly everyone in this world leaves it *Ayin Hara* — the jealous eye. It might manifest as cancer, a heart attack, some other sickness, a car accident, a tsunami, a hurricane, or anything else. Saying this phrase often cancels out the other side's negative influence on a particular situation instantaneously.

B'nai: children, as in *B'nai Yisrael*, the children of Israel

B'nai Elohim: the children of the Creator

B'nai Yisrael: the children of Israel, what we call the galactic starseeds

B'tzelem Elohim: "in the image of *Elohim*"

Chai: life. It's spelled *Chet-Yud* and has a gematria of 18. *Chaim* is the plural form. The popular toast *L'Chaim* means "to life!"

Chai B'etzem: "life in the bone"; bone marrow, which creates red blood cells

Chai L'hachayot: the second level of essential life, which is "to enliven"

Chait: sin

Chanukah: an eight-day Jewish holiday commemorating the miracle of a one-day vial of oil lasting eight days. The re-dedication of the Temple in Jerusalem in 165 BC.

Chassidim: people who show kindness, righteousness, and piety. The singular form is *Chassid.*

Chassidut: a sect of spiritual Hebrews who follow the writings of the *Baal Shem Tov.*

Chatoteret: considered to be a "humpback" adjoining *Zayin* and *Vav* to create the Hebrew letter *Chet.*

Chava: Eve

Chaya: the highest soul level and root of the word for "life," *Chai.*

Chayot: living creatures

Chayot Hakodesh: a position that is considered higher than the archangels

Chayut: life force

Chelkeek: a fraction of a moment, a nanosecond

Chesed: the *Sephirah* of loving kindness (and compassion for Earth). It is an energy we can use for many different purposes, such as treating the next human being with "human dignity." It is also the energy of restriction, the energy we use for things like judgments and different ways of containing things so they don't get out of balance.

Chevelai Messiah: pang, or birth pang; almost dying from birth work and bringing forth life. In other words, sacrificing one's life to do the soul's work for our Creator and ourselves.

Chillul: desecration

Chochma: the *Sephirah* of wisdom

Choshen: the breastplate worn by the high priest in the Holy Temple.

Choshen Mishpat: the full name of the high priest's breastplate. It means "the breastplate of judgment."

Chupa: a shelter that people get married under, protecting the seeding of another generation

Churban: devastation

Da'aga: caring for the next human being

Da'at: the hidden *Sephirah* of knowledge

Dagim: the plural form of *Dag*, which means "fish"

Dayan: a judge

Echad: one, oneness, unity

Ehyeh Asher Ehyeh: "I Am That I Am" is a misinterpretation that is frequently used. There is no present tense of the verb "to be" in Hebrew because the present only lasts a nanosecond. You can't always put Hebrew into English. "I Will (Shall) Be That I Will (Shall) Be" is the only correct interpretation.

El Na Refa Na La: "Please God, heal her now"; a special healing chant used to bring healing to another

Elohim: the level of divinity that manifested creation, which has a sense of plurality and oneness

El Shaddai: God Almighty; the garment of Lord Archangel Metatron. This is the energy that protects the doorposts that contain a *Mezuzah*, which is *Shaddai*, which is 314, which is the sacred gematria of Metatron. See *Mezuzah* below.

Emmet: the truth

Emuna: to have certainty, to be sure; blind faith

Et-Aleph-Tav: generally taken to represent all the letters of the alphabet from *Aleph* to *Tav* in one unity. The word *Et* in the Torah means "the presence of the *Shekhinah*, the presence of the divine essence.

Et Hashamayim V'et Ha'aretz: reveals a very hidden name of the Creator. It takes you where you need to be at the beginning of the *Shabbat*.

Etz Chaim: the Tree of Life

Etzem: bone

Even (or *Eh'ven*) *Shetiyah:* the foundation stone, or rock; the rock at the heart of the Dome of the Rock in Jerusalem. It is also known as the weaving stone because it channels the light-force energy that originates in the Central Sun and takes that energy and sends it through the electromagnetic grids of the Blue Jewel to assist in balancing the feedback loop system. Then there is this small hole alongside the stone, on the southeastern corner, that enters a cavern along the edge of the stone known as the Well of Souls. It is the holiest site in creation, and Jewish tradition views it as the spiritual junction of heaven and earth. It is the Ark of the Covenant. Jews traditionally face it while praying, knowing that it was the location of the Holy of Holies in the Temple.

Gadol: big or great; often used to describe God

Ga'ava: ego, pride

Gamzu L'tovah: "this too is for the good." It means that whatever we have to go through is for the highest good, even if we don't believe it or don't like it.

Gan Eden: the Garden of Eden

Ganiv **or** *Ganif:* In Yiddish, it means thief.

gematria: the ancient Jewish practice of interpreting words by determining the numerical values of the letters in each word

Geula: redemption, the light of repair, the female energy that's coming

Gevurah: the *Sephirah* representing strength, discipline, greatness, and justice

Gevurot: judgments and strengths (plural of *Gevurah*)

Gibor: great or greatness, a hero, strong

Gilgul: a circle or a roll. It also means a rotation of souls (reincarnation).

Hafuch: opposite, upside-down

Halachah: laws, pathways

HaMakom: a sacred space, a place that is necessary for the existence of finite worlds, the third dimension

Hashem: "the name"; refers to the many sacred four-letter names of God known as the Tetragrammaton (*YHVH*) and many others. Because the letters are sacred, we are not supposed to pronounce them, so instead we say "the name," or *Hashem.*

Hateva: nature

Havaya: the name of God represented as a cube. It is taken from the four letters *Yud, Hey, Vav,* and *Hey* pronounced backward: yah-vah or wah-hah. Sometimes it is pronounced "Yaweh," but there is no *W* in Hebrew, so *Vav (V)* is used.

Hevel: vanity, what we will have to go through before ascension. This is connected to *Chevelai Messiah,* the pain of almost dying from bringing forth life. The more vanity or ego one has, the greater the "pangs" that must be experienced before ascension.

Hod: the *Sephirah* of brilliant light and splendor. This sphere also represents the creation of sacred places like planetary cities of light. It is the last bit of left-column energy in the Tree of Life before the funnel of *Yesod*.

Hu: he. In prayers, it can refer to the Creator.

Ima: the energy of the Cosmic Mother

Ima Adama: Mother Earth

Kabbalah: the cosmic coded studies of creation and the formation of creation. Kabbalah means "to receive." Combined with the Zohar, the Kabbalah can teach you how to receive, but you can't receive life force energy unless you share what you've got. If the ego is full of itself inside, there is no room for light.

Kadosh: holy

K'dusha: a Hebrew prayer translated as "holiness"

Keter: the *Sephirah* of the crown. Its energy, like ten quintillion volts, is called undifferentiated light.

Kidmutainu: likeness

Kipa: a circular head covering worn by people of many religions

Kislev: the month of Sagittarius, the third month from *Rosh Hashanah,* and the ninth month of the lunar/cosmic/Jewish calendar, usually coinciding with parts of November and December

Kli: vessel

Koach: potential, power

Kosher/Kasher: ready for a connection. It also means "fit" or "proper," and modern usage refers to food that is properly prepared according to Jewish law.

Ko V'cho: Moses saw there was nothing in the Egyptians that could become positive energy at all in future lives or anything he would produce in this lifetime. There was nothing left.

K'ra: tearing

Laivi: the seed level of the priesthood, which is from Moses and his brother Aaron. Both of them were from the tribe of *Laivi.* The Torah spells it *Lamed-Vav-Yud. Levi* (a frequently used but incorrect pronunciation) would be *Lamed-Yud-Vav-Yud.*

Limud: a study

L'shem Yichud: a statement made before a prayer, meditation, or intention that says, "For the sake of the unification of the Holy One, blessed be he and his divine presence, with reverence and love, and love and reverence, to unify the holy name in perfect unity."

Ma'aseh: the making of

Ma'aseh Bereshit: the making of creation

Magen: shield

Magen David: the shield of David, the star of David

Maggid: one who speaks, hears, and interacts with angels; a preacher or guide

Malach: angel

Malchut: the *Sephirah* that represents being on Earth in the tenth sphere — the kingdom. It refers to the burning off of karma through service (with good deeds), sharing, and correcting ourselves.

Malvusheem: In the Kabbalah, these are called garments. The higher garment is thought. This is the expression of one's inner intellect and emotions to oneself.

Man-Se-Pach: the five final letters of the Hebrew alphabet after the first twenty-two letters

Marchefet [Merachefet in text]: hovering, as in the spirit of God, *Elohim,* hovering over the water. It is believed that hovering created reality in the third dimension.

Mashiah, Mashiach: "anointed one," or the Messiah. It describes priests and kings who were traditionally anointed with holy oil as described in Exodus.

Mayim: represents the spelling and the energy of water

Melech: king, used often in prayer to refer to God

Menorah: a combination of seven lamps that represents a mathematical cosmic emblem, the "miracle of lights"

Merkabah: chariot, or "wheels within wheels." In modern Hebrew, it means "a tank." In modern spirituality, it refers to a chariot in etheric form that is used to take spiritual seekers to higher dimensions. In the Kabbalah, it means "God's throne-chariot," referring to the chariot of Ezekiel's vision. It is also used in describing a branch in the Kabbalah called "*Merkabah* mysticism."

Mezuzah: A *Mezuzah* is a small piece of holy parchment written with a higher consciousness that contains the name *Shaddai* (or *Shin-Dalet-Yud*). This is the holy garment that Archangel Metatron wears. A *Mezuzah* acts as a protection shield for each home that has one in its doorway. Beings from the "other side" are always standing at a doorway waiting to attach themselves to an unsuspecting, unprotected soul. So when we look and touch the *Shin-Dalet-Yud* on the front of the *Mezuzah* that's on the doorpost, we are protected. Those in the know have *Mezuzahs* on every doorpost in the house (except for bathrooms).

Michael: The gematria of the Angel Michael is 101. Now, 100 shows completion, but 101 shows a willingness to go the extra mile. Lago Puelo, for example, is self-sustaining; it doesn't get weak. But if we give it energy, it gives away that energy to the other eleven etheric crystals. It is all about giving and receiving.

Midrash: rabbidic literature

Mikveh: ritual immersion

Minyan: a gathering of ten souls for prayer. This completes an invitation to bring the *Shekhina* into the room where these ten souls are praying. It is a cosmic rule.

Minyan **of** *Tzaddikim:* ten righteous men in meditative prayer who can bring miracles, wonders, and change to our world — the Blue Jewel.

Mita: symbolizes the spiritual as well as the physical setting of husband and wife uniting for the sake of drawing new souls into this world; simply: a bed

Mitzvah: commandments

Mitzvoth: good deeds. It comes from the Hebrew word for "commandments," which is *Mitzvah*. So *Bar Mitzvah* is a commandment and a good deed. There are 248 positive *Mitzvoth*. The highest level is doing a good deed anonymously through a third person with no anticipation of receiving benefit.

Mizbayach: altar

Modeh Ani: the first thing a Hebrew person says in prayer after awakening. When we sleep, 90 percent of our souls go to another dimension. How we sanctify the name of the Creator depends on the deeds we do and the way we treat people on any particular day. It measures to the grade in which our souls dwell in the dimension while we sleep. There is just enough souls energy within us to get us through the night. When we wake, it is because we got permission from higher evolution to return to our bodies. So when we say the *Modeh Ani*, it means, "I gratefully thank you, oh living and eternal king, for you have returned my soul within me with compassion. Abundant is your faithfulness. Amen!"

Na: please

Natan: to give

Navi: prophet, prophesy, prophecy

Ne'eman: faithful

Nefesh: the first level of the soul that we experience. It is that which is "down here in the blood" — the animal self. This is also the Hebrew word for "breath."

Neged: against

Nekudot: vowels

Nephal: to fall

Nephilim: the fallen ones

Neshamah: the third level of soul or spirit, the higher self. It is the intuitive power that connects humankind with the Creator, the highest of the three parts of a soul that transcends third-dimensional reality and the Earth ego to link directly to the divine light.

Netzach: the *Sephirah* under *Chesed* representing eternal victory/glory. This sphere also represents Moses and his attempt — with divine help — to spread the light to a New Earth society.

Ohr: light. The fifth time the word *Ohr* is written in the Torah is the forty-second word.

Ohr Ain Soph: the light of the endless/infinite

Ohr Chozer: the returning light, the light that we send back up to heaven that keeps heaven going and represents how we perceive the upper world and the consummation of the creative process

Ohr Ha Kodesh: the holy light

Ohr Ha Mashiach: the light of the Messiah

Ohr Yashar: straight light, the light as a straight line down that descends from God into the worlds

Olam Haba: the world of heaven

Olam Hazeh: this world of Earth

Oni: a poor man

Otiot: letters

Pardes: orchard or garden. The word is commonly used as an acronym for the four approaches to interpreting the Torah: *Pshat, Remez, Drash,* and *Sod.*

Parnassah: sustenance. It is not what we want but what we need.

Pshat: the most basic, literal level of interpreting the Torah

Ratz: run

Ratzon: will or desire

Remez: hint, the second level of interpreting the Torah

Rosh Hashanah: defined as "the Head of the Year." It is the sixth day of creation, known as "Judgment Day." It is the original Adam's birthday and the day he sinned — which is why we're here!

Ruach: the middle soul level, which can be one's self, which is more than the self of humanity. It may be the self that has equal values. *Ruach* also means "wind" and "breath" in Hebrew.

Ruach Hakodesh: Holy Spirit

Sabbath: Saturday, the seventh day of the week. In Jewish tradition and some Christian sects, this day is observed as the day of rest and worship.

Segol: a vowel with three dots in the form of a triangle, representing the corners of the Redemption. Those three columns are the three columns of the Tree of Life.

Sephirah: a circle in the Tree of Life — a sphere — that holds an energy. *Sephirot* is the plural form.

Shabbat: the seventh day of creation; an absolutely, positively galactic and cosmic sacred time. *Shabbat* is the Jewish (Hebraic, cosmic) *Sabbath*, from sundown on Friday until Saturday's sunset. The Seventh-day Adventists observe this. They wear white on *Shabbat* and eat kosher foods. The Jewish people, *B'nai Yisrael* (starseeds) believe that the *Shekhinah* comes on *Shabbat* to be with man and to help make that day holy. *Shabbat* is one day out of the seven that were given to us at Mount Sinai, and what a gift it was, along with the Torah. It is a direct connection to the fifth dimension, but most people don't really know it and don't care to. They don't want to be bothered with it. But it is a sacred and holy time when arcan energy is squared, so take advantage of it and go into the fifth dimension for twenty-four hours on *Shabbat*.

Shabbat **Queen:** *Adonai,* the name of God

Sha'ar Katan: small gates. We close all the small gates that we have created through our reactive modes, as in the telling of a little white lie. We put them in a basket and send them down the river to give back to the divine essence.

Shamayim: heaven, the lower heaven (the fifth dimension)

Shekhinah: the Feminine/Divine Presence or the presence of the Creator

Shechem: the biblical city in the Yehuda/Shomron area where Yosef haTzaddik, Joseph the Righteous, is buried on a piece of land that his father, Jacob, bought.

Shevirah: the breaking of the vessels

Slichah: "excuse me"

Sh'ma Yisrael: "Hear, oh Israel; a prayer said twice daily

Shmita: the sabbatical seventh year

Sod: secrets, the fourth level of interpreting the Torah

Succoth: the Feast of Tabernacles

Ta'amim: literally, tastes or reasons. It also refers to songs or cantillations.

Tagin: crowns

Tahor: pure

Talmud: part of the oral law given at Mount Sinai consisting of *Mishnah* and

Gemara. It was put in written form in the first four centuries.

Tamei: impure

Tanach: represents all twenty-four books of the Torah. The Torah itself represents the first five books of Moses.

Tanna: a very high, wise, and righteous man with very strong psychic powers and a high understanding of the Tree of Life. This person can heal people with sound and the Hebrew letters. To be considered a *Tanna,* one had to make a river run upstream, make it rain from a cloudless sky, and bring someone back from the dead.

Tesha-Esrai: nineteen

Teshuvah or Te-shuv-hey: repentance, atonement, to return the letter *Hey* to its original position with the other three letters of the divine name

Tiferet: a *Sephirah* in the central column that represents balance, harmony, and beauty

Tikun: repair, correction. In Kabbalah, this refers to the concept that the 288 sparks fell from the broken vessels holding the light from the Creator and that it is the task for each of us — to do our own corrective work for our own soul. We are here to do our soul's work with our physical third-dimensional garment called a body.

Tishkach: to forget. We must forget two things: doubt and limitation.

Torah: the first five books of Moses, a precious scripture on holy parchment that is set in cosmic, mathematical perfection. It is not a religious object. The Torah is a whole code with lots of letters, words, and sentences, but the most important of these are the letters. The Torah is a sacred living entity. It is directly connected with the Tree of Life. It is a cosmic womb and a galactic gift from the Central Sun that represents the I Am.

Tov: good, inner beauty

Tovat Meiram Meod: very beautiful and goodly in appearance

Tzaddik: one who lives by the rules of the "Living One"; a spiritual leader; a righteous man; one who lives to do his soul's work, which is his purpose here on the planet

Tzaddikim: many righteous men or women

Tzelem: a shadow of our third-dimensional body that is our connection to our cosmic egg. It is also another word for "Holy Spirit."

Tzelem Elokim: when the Holy Spirit has a direct connection to the fifth dimension and the Elokim.

Tzimtzum: the first contraction or big bang of creation. The power of limitation was hidden, latent within God's infinite essence.

Vav Hahipukh: the *Vav's* function of inverting the apparent tense of a verb to its opposite, from past to future or from future to past

Vav Hakhibur: the *Vav* of connection

Va'yomer Elohim Yehi Ohr, V'yehi Ohr: "And God said, 'Let there be light,' and there was light."

Yad: hand

Yashar: straight, upright

Yechida: the fifth level of the soul, where one really is when elevating in multidimensions from the fifth dimension upward

Yesod: a *Sephirah* of the central column of the Tree of Life that funnels all the energy from above it into the world, *Malchut.* It also represents the bonding of shimmering.

YHVH, YHWH: the unpronounceable name of God (in English, one will sometimes see it incorrectly written as Yahweh)

Yihudim: unifications. Kabbalists believe that humans help to unify the two aspects of the Godhead through prayer. It is important to enunciate a simple statement prior to reciting a prayer to the effect that one's intention is to bring about the unification of God and the *Shekinah.*

Yirah: awe and fear, but awe is more accurate and acceptable. In fact, awe is the key to love.

Yisrael: Israel

Yitzirah: the world of formation

Yom Kippur: Day of Atonement; considered to be one of the holiest days of the year

Yud-Kay-Vav-Kay: Kay is not a Hebrew letter. It is used as a substitute for the letter *Hey.*

Zohar: splendor, brilliant light. It is the basis of much of the teachings about the Tree of Life and Kabbalah.

Appendix B:
Group of Forty Glossary

Adamic *Adonai*
A term used to describe *Homo sapiens,* or Earth humans. Man (Adam) is formed from the earth.

Adam Kadmon
The Hebrew term for the primordial, or first, man. It is the prototype for the first being to emerge after the beginning of creation.

altered (higher or expanded) states of consciousness
A term in modern psychology used to describe different states of consciousness. This includes the dream state, trances, meditative states of consciousness, and also heightened states of consciousness in which one has higher perceptions of reality. This state usually is described as a condition where one can see ultimate truth and is able to experience the present more fully. In the 1960s, this term was used to also describe drug-induced changes in consciousness such as what one could experience with mind-altering drugs.

Andromeda
A large spiral galaxy 2.2 million light-years from the Milky Way. Andromeda is the largest member of our local galactic cluster. It is commonly referred to as our "sister" galaxy.

Andromedans
An advanced, higher-dimensional race of beings from Andromeda. A specific group of Andromedans are currently working with the Arcturians in their effort to facilitate the planetary ascension process of Earth.

arcan
Thought-form energy described as traveling in an arc wave. In Biorelativity, we use etheric crystals implanted within and our own arcan energy to increase the power of our prayers and intentions.

archangel
Generally applies to all angels above the grade of angels. It also designates the highest rank of angels in the angelic hierarchy. The Kabbalah designates ten archangels who correspond to the Tree of Life. They are considered messengers bearing divine decrees.

Arcturian stargate
A multidimensional portal into other higher realms. It is very close to the Arcturus star system and is overseen by the Arcturians. This powerful passage point requires that earthlings who wish to pass through it complete all lessons and Earth incarnations associated with the third-dimensional experience. It serves as a gateway to the fifth dimension. New soul assignments are given there, and souls can then be sent to many different higher realms throughout the galaxy and universe. Archangel Metatron and many other higher beings are present at the stargate.

Arcturus
The brightest star in the constellation Boötes, also known as the Herdsman. This is one of the oldest recorded constellations. Arcturus is also the brightest star seen from Earth. It is a giant star, about 25 times the diameter of the Sun and 100 times as luminous. It is a relatively close neighbor of ours, approximately 40 light-years from Earth. High up in the sky in the late Spring and early Summer, Arcturus is the first star you see after sunset. You can find Arcturus easily if you follow the Big Dipper's handle away from the bowl.

ascension
A point of transformation reached through the integration of the physical, emotional, mental, and spiritual selves. The unification of these bodies allows one to transcend the limits of the third dimension and move into a higher realm. It has been compared to what is called the "Rapture" in Christian theology. It has also been defined as a spiritual acceleration of consciousness that allows the soul to return to the higher realms and thus be freed from the cycle of karma and rebirth.

ascended masters
Teachers who have graduated from Earth or who already are on higher dimensions. An ascended master can be from any Earth religion, including the Native American traditions. They have graduated from Earth's incarnational cycle and have ascended into the fifth dimension. Ascended masters can include archangels, higher beings from the galactic world, teachers, and prophets.

Ashtar
The commander of a group of spiritual beings who are dedicated to helping Earth ascend. The Ashtar beings exist primarily in the fifth dimension and come from many different extraterrestrial civilizations.

assemblage point
1. A concept that appears in the shamanistic world. The assemblage point is a point in the aura. Some people think it is in the back, below the neck. The point is like a valve. When it is opened, you have an input of higher perception. That means you can see the dimensional worlds; you can see the spirits that are around us all the time.
2. The place where things come together, through their resonance of frequencies, as a whole become greater than the parts. The amazing thing is that there are many assemblage points (of frequency) within the Hebrew letters that relate to the Sephirot in the Tree of Life. Once you come to an assemblage point and you know that frequency, you resonate with it and internalize it until the unity in resonance leads to entrainment. Also, the assemblage point can spread and expand on this entrainment. Assemblage points are necessary for interdimensional interaction.

astral plane
The nonphysical level of reality considered to be where most humans go when they die. On the Tree of Life, it corresponds to the sphere known as Yesod.

Biorelativity
Biorelativity focuses on group thought and working together telepathically to send healing energy to our planet. The practice is similar to the concept of group prayer in which people send positive thoughts to change the outcome of an event. In Biorelativity exercises, groups of starseeds around the planet send healing thoughts to specific areas in the world. Storms, hurricanes, and even earthquakes can potentially be averted, deterred, or lessened in strength so that minimal damage is inflicted.

The Arcturians point out that on higher planetary systems, groups continually interact telepathically with their planet to ensure maximum harmony between planetary inhabitants and planetary forces. An example of Biorelativity on Earth is Native Americans praying to the planet as a group, often asking for rain. In Biorelativity exercises, we have the powerful advantage of connecting globally with many different starseeds, uniting telepathically for the healing of Earth.

bilocation
The ability to be in two places at the same time. You can be physically in your body and mentally or spiritually in another dimension simultaneously.

biosphere
A term used to describe the whole environment of Earth, including the oceans, atmosphere, and other necessary ingredients that keep and support all life.

Central Sun
The center of any astronomical star system. All star clusters, nebulae, and galaxies contain a nucleus at their center. Even the grand universe itself has a Great Central Sun at the centers of its structure. In most cases, a giant star exists at the center of all star systems. The Great Central Sun of the Milky Way galaxy provides life-giving energy to the entire galaxy.

chakras
Energy centers of the human body system. These centers provide the integration and transfer of energy between the spiritual, mental, emotional, and biological systems of the human body.

channeling
The process of entering a meditative trance to call forth other entities to speak through you. See also trance channeling.

Chasmal
A mysterious Hebrew term mentioned in Ezekiel's vision. It refers to the mental state through which one passes when ascending from the level of speaking to one of pure mental silence and sensitivity.

Chief Buffalo Heart
An ascended fifth-dimensional Native American guide who focuses on using heart energy to help people ascend.

Chief White Eagle
An ascended fifth-dimensional Native American guide who is very connected to Jesus and other higher fifth-dimensional beings.

corridor
A pathway or etheric tunnel on Earth that leads to a higher dimension. Corridors can be found in high-energy places such as sacred sites on Earth. The Arcturians believe that we can establish corridors within our meditation areas on Earth.

cosmic egg
The optimal shape of the human aura for maximum healing. The egg is a universal shape of wholeness and thus is also referred to as the cosmic egg. Using this shape is part of a dimensional method of healing based on helping people form their auras into this egg shape.

crystal temple
An etheric temple on the fifth dimension that has been made available for our use by the Arcturians. The crystal temple contains a lake more than one mile in diameter, which houses a huge crystal half the size of the lake itself. The entire lake and surrounding area are encompassed by a huge glass dome, allowing visitors to view the stars.

Er'ra
A planet in the constellation of the Pleiades that very strongly relates to Earth regarding its creation (pronounced like "yirah-awe").

etheric
A term used to designate the higher bodies in the human system. In India, "etheric" is used to describe the unseen energy and thoughts of humans.

etheric crystals
Invisible crystals that contain fifth-dimensional energy that have been sent to Earth by the Arcturians. The purpose of these etheric crystals is to provide healing energies to Earth's meridians.

fifth dimension

A higher dimension of existence that is above the first and third dimensions. We currently live on the third dimension, where we are bound by the laws of cause and effect and reincarnation. The fourth dimension is the astral realm and the realm of dreams. The fifth dimension transcends this as the realm of infinite energy and love, and it can be compared to the Garden of Eden. In the fifth dimension, one transcends the incarnational cycle, "graduating" from Earth and going to the fifth dimension. The ascension focuses on going to the fifth dimension. The ascended masters residing there now include Jesus/ Sananda.

Galactic Kachina

In Navajo folklore, a kachina is an intermediary between the higher spirit world and this world. The Galactic Kachina is the intermediary between the Central Sun and this planet. The Native Americans were the first to accept a spiritual philosophy or theory that includes other higher beings throughout our galaxy. They take the perspective of the broader galactic view, which says that we are all part of a galactic family.

galactic spirituality

A spiritual philosophy or theory that accepts the existence of other higher beings throughout our galaxy and therefore takes the perspective of the galactic view in understanding our planetary evolution as part of a galactic family of civilizations.

grid lines

Another name for energy lines that run through the planet. In Chinese medicine, the energy lines that run through the body are called "meridians."

Group of Forty (GOF)

This is a concept of group consciousness suggested by the Arcturians for our use in the ascension process. According to the Arcturians, forty is a spiritually powerful number. The Arcturians emphasize the value and power of joining together in groups. A Group of Forty consists of forty different members who focus on meditating together at a given time each month. The Arcturians have asked us to organize forty of these groups to assist in the healing of Earth and provide a foundation for individual members' ascension. Group interactions and yearly physical meetings are recommended. Members agree to assist each other in their spiritual development.

David Miller has been working with the energies of the ascension for more than fifteen years, and the Arcturians asked him to set up these meditation groups, which have been meeting for more than fifteen years now and have drawn members from all over the United States and Canada, as well as Australia and Germany. At a specific hour during the meditation time, David channels messages from the Arcturians for all group members, and a monthly newsletter is sent out with a transcription of that month's channeled lecture. A group coordinator arranges other group activities, such as healings and group meditations. Additionally, members are encouraged to meet other members — either by phone, letter, or in person.

Meditations also include group healing through which all members of the group focus healing energy on one designated person in the group. Members who are the focus of this healing energy have reported profound healing experiences. All work is directed toward our transformation to higher consciousness through Earth healings and personal healings.

harmonic light
Fifth-dimensional light often appearing as gold balls of etheric energy. This light can be transmitted through the noosphere and can spread energy of balance and harmony wherever it is directed. It can be directed by the thoughts and prayers of starseeds around the planet.

Hebrew words and phrases used often in GOF work
Kadosh, Kadosh, Kadosh, Adonai Tzevaoth (repeated three times): "Holy, Holy, Holy, is the Lord of Hosts." Your *Merkabah* vehicle, the light of the *Merkabah*, is recharged in your system. This is like a battery that needs to be recharged periodically. Your *Merkabah* energy field and your ability to access and unlock the higher codes so that you can travel spiritually through the corridors have been recharged during this time.

- I am one with *Tzevaoth*, I am one with *Tzevaoth*, I am one with *Tzevaoth*. The galactic word "hosts" or angelic forces is based on an understanding of planetary masters and forces. The ring of ascension is a demonstration and manifestation of the planetary core, its "hosts," and the awareness that you have engendered of the planetary systems.

- *Yechudim* is the Kabbalistic name for this unification. We ask Hashem, the Creator, to give us the power to raise our sparks from our lower selves, from ourselves from other lifetimes, and from ourselves from other dimensions. Help us, Hashem, to raise all our sparks so that we can bring them into unity with our greater higher selves. One of the secrets of the unity is to be in service to the light, personal ascension, and planetary ascension. By doing that, we are given special grace and powerful energy to raise all parts of the self.

Helio-ah

A female Arcturian ascended master and Juliano's twin flame.

hermaphrodite

A being with both male and female sex organs.

higher self

The transcendent part of the human self that is to be distinguished from the lower or middle self. In Kabbalah, the higher self is connected to spirit and stays with us when we leave Earth.

holography

In fifth-dimensional work, holography is the ability to access all universal energy from any spot in the universe. Holographic healing is based on the assumption that we can access our greater self through holographic energy.

human aura

A field of energy that surrounds a human being. It is magnetic and appears in different colors depending on the moods, thoughts, and spiritual development of the person.

Juliano

The main Arcturian guide and ascended master working to help activate Earth and Arcturian starseeds toward the ascension.

Kabbalah

The major branch of Jewish mysticism. The Hebrew word Kabbalah is translated as "to receive."

Kuthumi

One of the ascended masters who serves Sananda. In a previous life, Kuthumi incarnated as St. Francis of Assisi. He is generally recognized as holding the position of World Teacher in the planetary White Brotherhood/Sisterhood. An extensive record of his teachings can be found in the works of Alice Bailey.

lightbody
The higher etheric spirit body that is connected to the highest soul energy.

Merkabah
In Hebrew, this term means "chariot," and in modern spirituality, it refers to a chariot in etheric form that is used to take spiritual seekers to higher dimensions. In the Kabbalah, it is the term that means God's throne-chariot, referring to the chariot of Ezekiel's vision. It is also used in describing a branch of Kabbalah called "Merkabah mysticism."

Metatron
Tradition associates Metatron with Enoch, who "walked with God" (Genesis 5:22) and who ascended to heaven and was changed from a human being into an angel. His name has been defined as "the angel of the presence," or "the one who occupies the throne next to the divine throne." In the world of the Jewish mystic, Metatron holds the rank of the highest of angels — that of an archangel. According to the Arcturians, Metatron is the gatekeeper of the Arcturian stargate and assists souls in their ascension to higher worlds.

Metrona-Shekhinah
These are two names for the divine presence. It is that aspect of the Goddess energy that is present on Earth.

Michael
His name is actually a question: "Who is like God?" He is perhaps the best known of the archangels and is acknowledged by all three Western sacred traditions. He has been called the Prince of Light, fighting a war against the Sons of Darkness. In this role, he is depicted most often as winged with an unsheathed sword, the warrior of God and slayer of the dragon. His role in the ascension is focused on helping us cut the cords of attachment to the Earth plane, which will allow us to move up to higher consciousness. In the Kabbalah, he is regarded as the forerunner of the Shekhinah, the Divine Mother, and most of all, he is the high priest of the Holy Temple in Zion of the Central Sun.

monad
The original, elemental creative force. Each one of us contains a portion of that force at the center of our true essence.

multidimensional presence
We can become aware that we exist on several different dimensions. The Arcturians are trying to help us become aware that we exist not only on the third dimension but also on the fifth dimension.

Nabur
A Kabbalistic rabbi and teacher of David in a former lifetime.

noosphere
The thought energy field contained in the aura of Earth. It can be compared to the planetary subconscious, but it is more than that. The noosphere was described by the twentieth-century philosopher Teilhard de Chardin, who linked humanity's evolution to it. The noosphere contains the accumulated collective thought energy of all beings on Earth, both past and present. It is composed of an energy field of subatomic thought particles or thought waves. These subatomic thought particles have not been discovered yet, but they exist around planetary bodies in the universe and allow thought energy around a planet to be stored and transmitted instantaneously across the universe — at speeds faster than the speed of light (186,000 miles per second). The noosphere affects the overall planetary energy field.

null zone
A zone outside of the third dimension but not necessarily in any other dimension. It is an area outside of our known time-space universe structure where time is nonexistent. Some have speculated that the photon belt contains null zone regions and that Earth was temporarily in the null zone until the year 2011.

omega light
A fifth-dimensional light that has high healing properties. This light can help transcend the world of cause and effect; thus it can help produce miraculous healings. The effects of this healing light can be increased by toning the sounds "omega light."

Orion
A superb constellation that dominates the southern winter sky. The most striking part of the constellation is the belt, which consists of three bright stars. No other constellation contains so many bright stars. Rigel, which is outside the belt, for example, is a giant star more than 500 light-years away. Betelgeuse, another star outside the belt in Orion, is about 300 light-years away.

Orions
An extraterrestrial culture that descended from another ancient civilization near the constellation Orion. The Orions have been extremely influential in the genetic makeup of the current human being. Human beings possess a portion of Orion DNA and reflect Orion traits in our current physical, emotional, and mental composition.

photon belt/photon energy
An energy emanating from the center of the galaxy that is about to intersect with our solar system and Earth. Some have predicted that the photon belt contains energy particles that could affect Earth's magnetic field, causing all electronic equipment to stop working.

Planetary Event Scale
It is a concept that is given to us by the Arcturians as a means of measuring planetary events that have harmful consequences of a global nature. An event of a 10 value on the scale would be considered an asteroid hitting Earth, because that major event would cause a mass extinction. Planetary events can be either human-made, such as the Gulf oil spill, or caused by nature, such as Hurricane Katrina. Our biosphere is fragile and now hangs on a thread. Human-made planetary events, such as the Gulf oil spill and the Fukushima nuclear power accident, are causing major planetary effects. Using Biorelativity, we can alleviate some of the harmful effects of such planetary events.

Pleiades
A small cluster of stars known as the Seven Sisters in some mythologies. Some Native Americans believe that they are descended from the Pleiades. It is near the constellation Taurus, about 450 light-years from Earth, and is the home of a race called the Pleiadians, who have frequently interacted with Earth and her cultures. It is said that the Pleiadians have a common ancestry with us.

portal
An opening at the end of a corridor that allows one to go into interdimensional space. This could allow one to go into the fifth dimension.

Quan Yin
A female member of the spiritual hierarchy. In her previous incarnation, she performed many acts of kindness and compassion and is known as the Goddess of Mercy.

Rabbi Hayyim Vital
A Kabbalistic rabbi who lived from 1543 to 1620 in Safed, Palestine.

Rafael
Archangel Rafael is perhaps the most endearing of all the angels — and the one most often depicted in Western art. His name means "God has healed." His career seems to focus on medical missions, as he helps people heal human maladies. He was the angel sent by God to cure Jacob of the injury on his thigh when Jacob wrestled with his dark adversary. He is also considered to be the guardian of the Tree of Life in the Garden of Eden.

ring of ascension
An etheric halo of energy around Earth containing fifth-dimensional light from the ascended masters. This halo is supposed to aid Earth in her ability to ascend as a planet to the fifth dimension. Starseeds are meant to interact with this light through visualizations and meditations.

sacred geometry
Geometric shapes that represent multidimensional energy. When we see these sacred shapes, such as pyramids, it activates higher codes in our unconscious.

Sananda
Known to us as the Master Jesus. Lord Sananda is a galactic entity who works directly with our Creator to bring higher consciousness to not only planet Earth and us, but to over 100 other planets in this Milky Way galaxy. He also likes to be known to everyone as Sananda and as a rabbi in the holy temple.

Sacred Triangle
A term used by the Arcturians to denote a triangular symbol representing the unification of three powerful spiritual forces on Earth: the White Brotherhood / Sisterhood ascended masters (including Sananda / Jesus), the extraterrestrial higher-dimensional masters (such as the Arcturians and the Pleiadians), and the Native American ascended masters (such as Chief White Eagle and Chief Buffalo Heart). The unification of these spiritual forces will create the Sacred Triangle that will aid in the healing and ascension of Earth.

self-nullification
Nullifying or removing the ego, removing the desire. One way to receive all the energies in Kabbalah is to empty oneself. If you can nullify the ego, then you can receive.

shimmering
A methodology and a force in which third-dimensional objects, people, and even weather are upgraded into a fifth-dimensional modality. On a personal level, shimmering allows your auric field to vibrate at a frequency that enables the aura to shift the electrons. The atomic structure of your cells transmutes into a vibratory energy field that elliptically shifts the cellular structures into the fifth dimension, causing a back-and-forth or "shimmering" modality. This back-and-forth shimmering modality actually affects the atomic and quantum levels of your cellular structures.

This shimmering energy is the precursor to the ascension, an accelerated and enhanced shimmering energy in which we elevate ourselves into the fifth dimension permanently. The shimmering energy is also enabling powerful Biorelativity streams of energy to be distributed throughout the planet. In terms of group ascension of the planet, we are working on the scale of a global network.

The evolution of humankind is represented by new abilities and new energies. These new abilities and new energies are related to shimmering energy. The shimmering light is representative of an energy field of telepathic interactions between the third-dimensional starseeds and lightworkers and fifth-dimensional energy, a telepathic etheric force field that is accelerated through etheric crystal work. It can be described as a circular energy field that is distributed around the planet.

spiritual light quotient
The measurement of a person's ability to work with and understand spirituality. This concept is related to the intelligence quotient (IQ); however, in reality, spiritual ability is not related to intelligence. Interestingly, unlike the IQ, one's spiritual light quotient can increase with age and experiences.

stargate
A multidimensional portal into higher realms. Many people are now using the term "stargate" to refer to openings on Earth to higher dimensions when in fact they are describing corridors. The stargate is a magnificent, temple-like, etheric structure that can process and transform many souls.

starseeds
People who have or are born with the awareness of galactic consciousness.
Starseeds may also have memories of past lifetimes on other planets and feel
connected to civilizations of other planets, such as the Pleiades or Arcturus.
Some starseeds have come to Earth at this time to assist her in this evolution-
ary transformation.

tachyon
A small particle that travels faster than the speed of light. A tachyon stone is
an object that contains tachyon particles and is used for healings in much the
same way one uses crystals.

thought projection
A technique described by the Arcturians involving projecting thoughts
through a corridor to reach the fifth dimension and beyond.

Tomar
An Arcturian ascended master, who is the high priest of the Arcturian crystal temple, whose specialty is meditation and working with Arcturian crystal
temple energy.

tones/sacred sounds
Sounds producing a vibratory resonance that helps activate and align the
chakras.

trance channeling
Putting yourself into a light trance for automatic speaking. A trance is a type of
self-hypnosis in which you put yourself into an altered state of consciousness.
There are light trances and deep trances. A deep trance is when you go out
and are almost in a somnambular, or sleep, state. This is the way Edgar Cayce
used to channel. In light trance channeling, you are still awake while bringing
through messages.

Tree of Life
A pattern of energy shown as a galactic diagram composed of ten to twelve
spheres that represent different aspects of the divine mind. The spheres are
shaped in three triads, or triangles, and are arranged in three columns. The
Tree of Life also represents energy forces within each of us.
     The idea of the Tree of Life is to use it and live it. It is not just a static mental

game. The Tree of Life is a healing planetary force directly connected with the Torah, which is a whole code. It is you. The Torah has a lot of letters, words, and sentences, but the important thing is the letters. The letters are living energy intelligences; they are alive. The Arcturians' goal with their students is to begin to activate the energy of planetary healing, but you cannot work with higher energy unless you have a solid foundation. That foundation is a basic teaching of the Tree of Life, which will help bring down fifth-dimensional light. The bottom sphere on the Tree of Life is the kingdom, which is our Earth.

unification

There are unifications within your personal system, your life, that need to be completed. A unification is an alignment and bringing together of energies so that they are harmonious. The same is true for Earth. With unification of your consciousness, you will be uplifted in your personal healings, in your daily planetary work, and in your effectiveness on this realm. A new unification is an activation of that which is in you already and simply needs to be awakened. Kabbalists believe that humans help to unify the two aspects of the Godhead through prayer. It is important to enunciate a simple statement prior to reciting a prayer to the effect that your intention is to bring about the unification of God and the Shekhinah.

From Sananda: You are receiving a golden-orange light from the Father/Mother and from Adonai. They are descending into every cell of your being, your past and future selves. They are descending into Mother Earth and her future self. Many people are being activated to do their work as part of this intervention. This blessing is filled with grace and compassion — two powerful attributes that will bring greater unification with Earth and the galactic self. The I Am presence is going upward through the earth like a rocket. Unify your individual self with Earth and the galactic self. Unify your individual and galactic selves. Let the Sacred Triangle become a sacred pyramid as well.

Vywamus

A fifth-dimensional soul psychologist known for his insight into the psychology of Earth problems and resolution of issues related to starseeds incarnated on Earth.

walk-ins

Humans who have received other spiritual entities into their bodies. This term is also used in reference to the new spirit that has entered the body. In some cases, the original spirit of the person may have left (for example, after an auto accident or some other form of severe trauma) and the new spirit "walks in" to the old body. This is always by agreement of the person vacating the body, before incarnating, to allow the body to continue in service after that particular incarnation is complete. It also allows the "walk-in" being to skip the process of childhood and adolescence to get straight to his or her mission on Earth. The walk-in does agree to honor the commitments of the previous occupant's life. It is agreed and contracted on all sides — not just for the walk-in, but for everything both parties do.

White Brotherhood/Sisterhood
A spiritual hierarchy of ascended masters residing in the fifth dimension. "White" is not used here as a racial term; it refers to the white light or higher frequency that these masters have attained. The masters include Sananda, Kuthumi, Mother Mary, Quan Yin, Sanat Kumara, Archangel Michael, Saint Germain, and many other ascended beings.

White Buffalo Calf Woman
In Lakota Native American folklore, she is the fifth-dimensional spirit being who appeared to bring forth special information about holy ceremonies and accessing higher spirit. She taught the necessity of being in harmony with Earth. Her focus is on the unity of all beings and that all are relations. She is representative of the dawning of a new age.

Zohar
The *Book of Splendor* — written in the second century by Rabbi Shimon bar Yochai. The major book of the Kabbalah. Zohar is the Hebrew word for "brilliance" or "splendor."

Zohar light
Light from the Creator Source.

Bibliography

Rabbi Yitzchak Ginsburgh, *The Alef-Bet: Jewish Thought Revealed through the Hebrew Letters*. (Jersualem: Gal Einei Institute, 1995). (First class: xi, 2–12, second class: 24–36, third class: 38–49, fourth class: 52–63, fifth class: 66–77, sixth class: 80–91, seventh class: 94–105, eight class: 108–119, ninth class: 122–136, tenth class: 138–151, eleventh class: 154–165, thirteenth class: 168–178, fourteenth class: 180–191, fifteenth class: 194–206, sixteenth class: 201–220.)

Ginsburgh, *Awakening the Spark Within*. (Jerusalem: Gal Einei Institute, 2001).*

———. *Consciousness and Choice*. (Jerusalem: Gal Einei Institute, 2004).

Rabbi Aryeh Kaplan, *Inner Space*. (Brooklyn: Moznaim, 1990).

Kaplan, Sefer Yetzirah, *The Book of Creation in Theory and Practice*. (San Francisco: RedWheel / Weiser Books, 1997).

Rav Phillip Berg, *A Gift of the Bible*. (Los Angeles: Kabbalah Centre Books, 1984).

Rabbi Yehuda Ashlag, *The Zohar*. (Thornhill, Canada: Laitman Kabbalah Publishers, 2005).

---

* All of Rabbi Ginsburgh's books and writings are available at www.inner.org.

Endnotes

Class 1

1. http://www.youtube.com/watch?v=mKqgx52Xaus
2. Gershom Scholem, *Major Trends in Jewish Mysticism* (Schocken Books: 1971) 270: "Where the flowing potencies of pure mercy and divine love which are contained in the supreme Sefirah are gathered together in a personal figure, there, according to the Zohar, arises the configuration *Arikh Anpin*, occasionally translated as 'The Long Face,' but actually signifying 'The Long Suffering,' i.e., God, the long suffering and merciful. In the Zohar, *Arikh* is also called *Attika Kaddisha*, i.e., 'the Holy Ancient One.'"
3. The original Hebrew Kabbalah offers different patriarchs for each sphere. For example, Abraham, Isaac, Jacob, and Joseph often are assigned different roles in the different spheres. It is not our intent to present that system here, as it is available in other scholarly texts, such as *Major Trends in Jewish Mysticism* by Gershom G. Scholem, p. 214 (Schocken Books, 1974) and *Kabbalah: An Introduction and Illumination for the World Today* by Charles Poncé (Quest Books, 1973).
4. The ring of ascension is a fifth-dimensional halo around Earth placed there by the ascended masters to assist us in connecting to the ethereal and our higher selves for our ascension and planetary healing work.

Class 3

1. The Schottenstein Edition *Siddur: Sabbath and Festivals Prayers with an Interlinear Translation*. (Brooklyn, New York: Mesorah Publications, Limited, 2000).
2. The Dome of the Rock is a shrine located on the Temple Mount in Jerusalem and is an extremely holy site. The "Rock," also known as the Foundation Stone, is the site of the first and second Jewish holy temple. Muslims built a mosque on this same site because they believe Mohammed ascended to heaven there. Actually, Mohammed never entered Israel physically.

Class 4

1. Jacobsen, Annie. *Area 51: Uncensored History of America's Top Secret Military Base* (Little, Brown & Co.: 2011).

Class 5

1. "Upstairs" refers to God speaking from the highest realm, the highest energy.

2. The Hopi rock is a beautiful, sacred rock on the Hopi reservation in Arizona that describes the life path of our world. It represents a prophecy about a possible "end times" scenario for the resolution of the current Earth crisis. The Hopi believe that humanity is almost at the end of the great purification, which will mark the end of the fourth world and enter into the fifth.

3. Dr. Donald Liu saved two boys before drowning in Lake Michigan on August 5, 2012: http://www.suntimes.com/14266404-761/pediatric-surgeon-drowns-trying-to-save-2-children.html.

Class 6

1. In the Kabbalistic story of creation, the Creator brought down sacred light to create this world. The containers to hold in this light are referred to in the Kabbalah as vessels. The vessels were not strong enough to hold this powerful light in bulk. The breaking of the vessels resulted in the creation of 288 sparks, and these sparks resulted in the plurality of this creation, including the existence of evil.

2. *YHWH* or *YHVH* is the unpronounceable name of God, which literally translates to "eternal being." Because of the holiness of the name, the Kabbalists were not allowed to pronounce *YHWH*. Instead, they would say "the name," *Hashem*, or *Adonai* (my Lord).

Class 7

1. Mordechai used *K*'s instead of *H*'s to avoid saying the sacred name of God, as David explained in Class 1, "Behind the Hebrew Terms."

Class 8

1. The founder of modern Kabbalah who lived in Poland during the eighteenth century. His name in Hebrew means "master of the good name" because of his great spiritual powers.

2. A Jewish holiday occurring after Passover that has deep significance for Kabbalists.
3. The candleholder for the holiday *Chanukah*.
4. The crown represents the crown of the Tree of Life, and it is the energy that connects directly to the Godhead energy, or the Infinite Source.

Class 11

1. A process of being called up in front of the congregation to read the Torah at a synagogue service.

Class 13

1. The Talumd is a summary of Judaic oral law compiled in writing by sages in Palestine and Babylonia that was completed about AD 500.
2. As found in the Mishna Pirkey Avoth records, which translates to English as "Book of Principles" or "Chapters of the Fathers," and is a compilation of the ethical, theological, and judicial teachings and maxims of the Rabbis of the Mishnaic period (http://en.wikipedia.org/wiki/Pirkey_Avoth).

Class 14

1. Schachter, Zalman M. and Edward Hoffman. *Sparks of Light: Counseling in the Hasidic Tradition*, p. 179. (Shamballa Press: 1983).
2. Rabbi Nachman is a famous Kabbalah or Hassidic rabbi who lived approximately 1772 to 1810 in the Ukraine.
3. *Pardes* is the Hebrew word for "orchard" or "garden," but it is often used as an acronym for the four approaches to interpreting text in Torah study: *Pshat*, *Remez*, *Drash*, and *Sod*.

Class 15

1. Each attribute of mercy is in part a contraction of infinite wisdom at the higher level of superconsciousness. These are contained in the sphere of mercy, loving kindness, and compassion.
2. A *Seah* is an ancient Jewish unit used to measure volume. It is equal to about one-third of an *Ephah*, which is about a bushel (dry) or a bath (liquid).

About the Authors

David K. Miller is the director and founder of an international meditation group called the Group of Forty that is focused on personal and planetary healing. He works to direct powerful healing group energy to help heal areas of Earth that need balance, restoration, and harmony. He has been developing groundbreaking global healing techniques using group consciousness. One of these techniques David uses with his group work is called Biorelativity, which uses group consciousness  work to restore Earth's feedback loop system, a complex planetary system that maintains the correct balance of our planet's atmosphere, ocean currents, and weather patterns.

David's mediation group has more than 1,200 members worldwide. In addition to his lectures and workshops, he is also a prolific author, writing nine books and numerous articles on Earth healing techniques. His recent books include *Teachings of the Sacred Triangle* (volumes 1–3), *New Spiritual Technology for the Fifth-Dimensional Earth*, *Raising the Spiritual Light Quotient*, *Biorelativity: Planetary Healing Techniques*, and *Arcturians: How to Heal, Ascend, and Help Planet Earth*. All of these books are available through Light Technology Publishing. Several of David's books have also been published in German and in Spanish. You can learn about David and his work at GroupofForty.com.

Mordechai David ben Avraham Yashin is one of those people you meet and will never forget. His knowledge, directness, and intensity are a unique combination. He is a cosmic Kabbalist who never limits himself to this planet and who sees himself as a galactic being.

Mordechai was born in Queens, New York, in the Hebrew year 5708, the same year that the State of Israel was born. The Hebrew date is *Yud B'shvat*, the tenth day of Aquarius. He attended two New York universities.

After researching several pathways to reach the divine essence, he found that the Hebrew letters had a unique relation to mathematical perfection and that mathematics would be an interesting pathway to the Creator. He began researching that pathway seventeen years ago while living in Del Mar, California. He studied the Zohar and the writings of Rabbi Yehuda Ashlag; Rabbi Shimon bar Yochai; Rabbi Isaac Luria, the Ari Hakadosh; Rabbi Moshe Chaim Luzzatto, the Ramchal; the *Baal Shem Tov*; Rabbi Shneur Zalman of Liadi, the Alter Rebbe of Chabad; and presently he is enthusiastically studying the writings of the Gaon of Vilna.

In the summer of 2002, Mordechai made his first trip to Israel, and after five weeks of extensive travel across the country, he realized that Israel was where he was going to end up, though he didn't know how or when. In 2003 he began lecturing in Phoenix, Arizona, on Kabbalistic astrology as a *Rosh Hodesh* (first day of the new month) lecture. He felt it was important for young people who wanted to get married to be a bit more aware of the potential attributes of the people they would consider marrying. He found there were many people who were getting married as a gamble, astrologically speaking — gambling on their choices. His students enthusiastically appreciated his perspective on Kabbalistic astrology. Later, Mordechai did weekly *Parsha* (portion) classes as well, until he came back to Jerusalem, Israel, permanently in 2006.

He is now finalizing his research in elucidating and simplifying the blending of Kabbalah with the astrophysics of planet Earth and the galaxy and doing the same with the book of knowledge, *The Keys of Enoch*. As he has said many times, "We don't know what we don't know, and it's about time we gave ourselves an honest perspective to make a freewill choice." Mordechai presently lives in Jerusalem, *Bli Ayin Hara*, with his wife and family.

ϟ *Light Technology* PUBLISHING *Presents*

BOOKS BY DAVID K. MILLER

Arcturians: How to Heal, Ascend, and Help Planet Earth

Go on a mind-expanding journey to explore new spiritual tools for dealing with our planetary crisis. Included in this book are new and updated interpretations of the Kaballistic Tree of Life, which has now been expanded to embrace fifth-dimensional planetary healing methods. Learn new and expanded Arcturian spiritual technologies.

$16⁹⁵

352 PP. • SOFTCOVER
ISBN 978-1-62233-002-7

Connecting with the Arcturians

Who is really out there? Where are we going? What are our choices? What has to be done to prepare for this event?

This book explains all of these questions in a way that we can easily understand. It explains what our relationships are to known extraterrestrial groups and what they are doing to help Earth and her people in this crucial galactic moment in time.

$17⁰⁰

256 PP. • SOFTCOVER
ISBN 978-1891824-94-4

Teachings from the Sacred Triangle

David's second book explains how the Arcturian energy melds with that of the White Brother-/Sisterhood and the ascended Native American masters to bring about planetary healing.

Topics Include:
- The Sacred Triangle energy and the sacred codes of ascension
- How to create a bridge to the fifth dimension
- What role you can play in the Sacred Triangle

$22⁰⁰

288 PP. • SOFTCOVER
ISBN 978-0-9715894-3-8

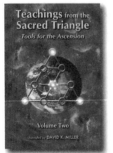

Teachings from the Sacred Triangle, Vol. 2

$16⁹⁵

288 PP. • SOFTCOVER
ISBN 978-1-891824-19-7

Teachings from the Sacred Triangle, Vol. 3

$16⁹⁵

288 PP. • SOFTCOVER
ISBN 978-1891824-23-4

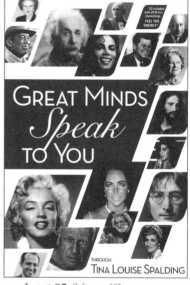

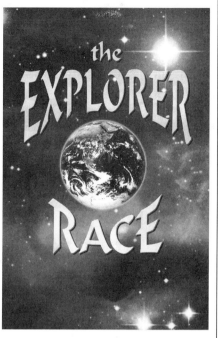

⚜ *Light Technology* PUBLISHING *Presents*

BOOKS BY TOM T. MOORE

THE GENTLE WAY

A SELF-HELP GUIDE FOR THOSE WHO BELIEVE IN ANGELS

"This book is for people of all faiths and beliefs with the only requirement being a basic belief in angels. It will put you back in touch with your guardian angel or strengthen and expand the connection that you may already have. How can I promise these benefits? Because I have been using these concepts for over ten years and I can report these successes from direct knowledge and experience. But this is a self-help guide, so that means it requires your active participation." — Tom T. Moore

$14.⁹⁵ • 160 pp., Softcover • ISBN 978-1-891824-60-9

THE GENTLE WAY II

BENEVOLENT OUTCOMES: THE STORY CONTINUES

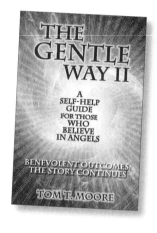

You'll be amazed at how easy it is to be in touch with guardian angels and how much assistance you can receive simply by asking. This inspirational self-help book, written for all faiths and beliefs, will explain how there is a more benevolent world that we can access, and how we can achieve this.

These very unique and incredibly simple techniques assist you in manifesting your goals easily and effortlessly for the first time. It works quickly, sometimes with immediate results, and no affirmations, written intentions, or changes in behavior are needed. You don't even have to believe in it for it to work!

$16.⁹⁵ • 320 pp., Softcover • ISBN 978-1-891824-80-7

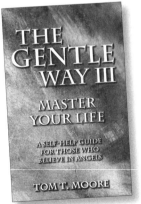

THE GENTLE WAY III

MASTER YOUR LIFE

"Almost three years have passed since *The Gentle Way II* was published. Yet as many success stories as that book contained, I have continued to receive truly unique stories from people all over the world requesting most benevolent outcomes and asking for benevolent prayers for their families, friends, other people, and other beings. It just proves that there are no limits to this modality, which is becoming a gentle movement as people discover how much better their lives are with these simple yet powerful requests." — Tom T. Moore

$16.⁹⁵ • 352 pp., Softcover • ISBN 978-1-62233-005-8

♃ *Light Technology* PUBLISHING *Presents*

THE ANCIENT SECRET
OF THE FLOWER OF LIFE,
VOLUME 2

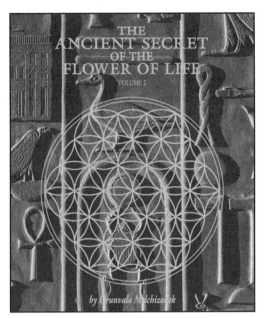

The sacred Flower of Life pattern, the primary geometric generator of all physical form, is explored in even more depth in this volume, the second half of the famed Flower of Life workshop. The proportions of the human body; the nuances of human consciousness; the sizes and distances of the stars, planets, and moons; and even the creations of humankind are all shown to reflect their origins in this beautiful and divine image. Through an intricate and detailed geometrical mapping, Drunvalo Melchizedek shows how the seemingly simple design of the Flower of Life contains the genesis of our entire third-dimensional existence.

From the pyramids and mysteries of Egypt to the new race of Indigo children, Drunvalo presents the sacred geometries of the reality and the subtle energies that shape our world. We are led through a divinely inspired labyrinth of science and stories, logic and coincidence, on a path of remembering where we come from and the wonder and magic of who we are.

Finally, for the first time in print, Drunvalo shares the instructions for the Mer-Ka-Ba meditation, step-by-step techniques for the re-creation of the energy field of the evolved human, which is the key to ascension and the next dimensional world. If done from love, this ancient process of breathing prana opens up for us a world of tantalizing possibility in this dimension, from protective powers to the healing of oneself, of others, and even of the planet.

Topics Include:
- The Unfolding of the Third Informational System
- Whispers from Our Ancient Heritage
- Unveiling the Mer-Ka-Ba Meditation
- Using Your Mer-Ka-Ba
- Connecting to the Levels of Self
- Two Cosmic Experiments
- What We May Expect in the Forthcoming Dimensional Shift

$25⁰⁰ Softcover, 272 pp.
ISBN 978-1-891824-21-0

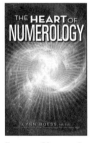

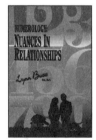

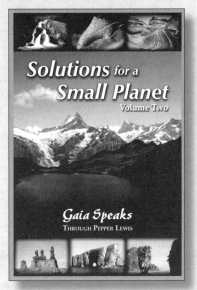

ℨ Light Technology PUBLISHING *Presents*

DIMENSIONAL JOURNEY
– ENCOUNTERS AND TEACHINGS –
BY LINDA BALL BRADSHAW

Linda talks about her experiences on Bradshaw Ranch and even shares the spiritual guidance she received from her messengers during that time. In the years that have passed since her extraordinary experiences amid the red rocks around Sedona, Linda has come to realize that, "Yes, there are high energy spots on this Earth that provide the setting for what many call phenomena."

But there is also another energy spot that creates this setting, and that is ourselves. We as human beings continually evolve, creating higher energy within ourselves. This works as a conduit for those who wish to observe another aspect of life within the cosmos. This path we call life is filled with many wonderful experiences if we only realize how capable we really are. In other words, we all are capable of embarking on our very own dimensional journeys.

THIRTY-TWO FULL-COLOR PAGES
SHOWING OTHER-DIMENSIONAL AND OFF-PLANET PHENOMENA

$19.95
Softcover, 208 pp.
ISBN: 978-1-891824-34-0

TOPICS INCLUDE:
- Lights
- The Invisibles
- More Visitors
- Fear

FULL-COLOR PAGES INCLUDE:
- Magnificent Orbs of Light
- Grays Portals
- Frightening Energies
- Beautiful Beings

Merging Dimensions
The Opening Portals of Sedona
by Tom Dongo and Linda Bradshaw

"In a secluded valley near Sedona, Arizona, strange events mysteriously began in 1992. What does it portend for us all?

"There is a wondrous place I wish to share with you. The encounters I have been privileged to experience there have taken me on a journey like none other. As in all life, some of these experiences have been a bit traumatic and others have taken me to glorious heights of which I've never known.

"There have been myriad occurrences over the past two years, but I have chosen the most vivid of each type to share with you. These are not all that have occurred nor have the experiences stopped. Within this time frame, I compiled the following data, and it is only now that I feel free to release it to the world.

"This information is not intended to achieve any hidden agenda. It is only to inform those who wish to know. Perhaps it may appear a bit far-fetched to some, and for this, I will not apologize. This is merely truth, and I cannot change the flavor or color of an experience to suit another's belief parameters. What is, is. To the best of my human ability, I will share in exact detail all types of incidents that I have, to this point, experienced in relation to this fascinating area. These, I believe, are indicative of many things to come.

"Join me on my journey. I share this with the fervent desire that each reader is inspired in a positive way." — Linda Bradshaw

$14.95
Softcover, 224 pp.
ISBN 978-0-9622748-4-8

TOPICS INCLUDE:
- Galactic Park
- Invisibles
- The Portals in Sedona
- Nineteen Points
- Mysterious Lights
... and much more!

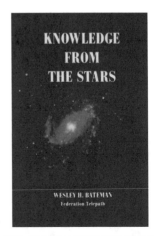